bipolar disorder

bipolar disorder

A COGNITIVE THERAPY APPROACH

Cory F. Newman
Robert L. Leahy
Aaron T. Beck
Noreen A. Reilly-Harrington
Laszlo Gyulai

American Psychological Association
Washington, DC

Published by
American Psychological Association
750 First Street, NE
Washington, DC 20002-4242
www.apa.org

To order   Tel: (800) 374-2721, Direct: (202) 336-5510
APA Order Department   Fax: (202) 336-5502, TDD/TTY: (202) 336-6123
P.O. Box 92984   Online: www.apa.org/books
Washington, DC 20090-2984   Email: order@apa.org

In the U.K., Europe, Africa, and the Middle East, copies may be ordered from
American Psychological Association
3 Henrietta Street
Covent Garden, London
WC2E 8LU England

Typeset in Goudy by EPS Group, Inc., Easton, MD
Printer: Edwards Brothers, Inc., Ann Arbor, MI
Cover Designer: Watermark Design Office, Alexandria, VA
Technical/Production Editor: Casey Ann Reever

The opinions and statements published are the responsibility of the authors, and such
opinions and statements do not necessarily represent the policies of the American Psychological Association.

Library of Congress Cataloging-in-Publication Data

Bipolar disorder : a cognitive therapy approach / Cory F. Newman . . . [et al.].—1st ed.
   p. ; cm.
   Includes bibliographical references and index.
   ISBN 1-55798-789-0 (hardcover: acid-free paper)
   1. Manic-depressive illness—Treatment. 2. Cognitive therapy. 3. Combined
modality therapy. I. Newman, Cory Frank. II. American Psychological
Association.
   [DNLM: 1. Bipolar Disorder—therapy. 2. Bipolar Disorder—drug
therapy. 3. Cognitive Therapy—methods. 4. Combined Modality Therapy.
WM 207 B6158 2001]
RC516 B525 2001
616.89′5—dc21   2001022922

British Library Cataloguing-in-Publication Data
A CIP record is available from the British Library.

Printed in the United States of America

To my precious daughter Lindsey
Cory F. Newman

To Helen
Robert L. Leahy

To Phyllis
Aaron T. Beck

To Joe, Joseph Timothy, Anne, and Gene
Noreen A. Reilly-Harrington

To Peggy and Gregory
Laszlo Gyulai

CONTENTS

PREFACE

In the 1980s, case reports appeared in the literature suggesting that cognitive therapy (A. T. Beck, Rush, Shaw, & Emery, 1979) could be used to help bipolar patients by arming them with an array of self-help skills to moderate their subjective reactions to life stress and to build a stronger sense of efficacy in dealing with a wide range of life demands (Chor, Mercier, & Halper, 1988; Jacobs, 1982). This made intuitive sense. Cognitive therapy takes square aim at the "stress" part of the diathesis–stress of bipolar disorder. This entails comprehensively modifying patients' personal approach to life—what they believe about themselves and their illness, how they construe situations, how they define and solve their problems, how they mobilize their support systems, how they recognize and use their personal strengths, and how they view their future. All of these variables affect the subjective experience of stress, such that the patient who is well-schooled in cognitive–behavioral self-help strategies may have a significant advantage in dealing with incidents that may trigger mood lability and behavioral dysregulation over the patient who is not similarly prepared. It is also reasonable to presume that patients who possess good psychosocial skills lead their lives in such a way as to reduce the probability of incurring avoidable problems compared with the patient who has less well-developed psychological skills. This in turn leads to fewer stressful events and a further reduction in the likelihood of stress-triggered recurrences of the biological diathesis in patients with bipolar disorder.

In addition to the stress reduction hypothesis above, there is evidence suggesting that cognitive therapy can be used to help patients become more willing to engage in much-needed pharmacotherapy (Cochran, 1984; Rush, 1988). In part, the rationale for this approach is that patients have misconceptions about their illness, their prescribed medications, and their "relationship" with their medications. Cognitive therapy can be used to test such beliefs, reduce unwarranted fears, and modify countertherapeutic assumptions about treatment. Cochran's study (1984) in particular was groundbreaking work; she designed a randomized controlled trial to demonstrate that cognitive therapy was more effective than treatment as usual in improving bipolar patients' appropriate use of lithium during therapy as well as at follow-up.

These findings sparked interest in further developing cognitive–behavioral treatment models for bipolar disorder. In the early 1990s, we initiated a pilot study at the University of Pennsylvania in which we treated bipolar patients with up to 1 year of weekly cognitive therapy sessions that were coordinated with the pharmacological interventions provided at the same site. Therapists who administered the cognitive therapy were guided by the treatment manual that was developed for the project (Newman & Beck, 1992). By and large, patients were pleased to include cognitive therapy with their medication regimens. Verbal and written feedback from some of the participants indicated that they felt a sense of empowerment from the model, in which an atmosphere of collaboration between therapist and patient reigned and self-help skills were taught in a manageable, stepwise fashion.

This book represents the development and expansion of the original treatment manual. It touches on most of the major strategies and techniques associated with standard cognitive therapy, borrowing freely from the empirically supported methods used in the treatment of unipolar depression and anxiety disorders. However, to adapt cognitive therapy for the treatment of patients with bipolar disorder, we have taken into account the strong biological component of hypomania and mania; incorporated the literature on stress, its subjective perception, and its role in triggering depressive or manic episodes; and given serious attention to the longitudinal nature of the disorder, with its high risk for suicide.

Cognitive therapy, by definition, posits that meaningful, durable clinical change entails changes in thinking style. In other words, from a cognitive perspective, it is desirable but not sufficient that bipolar patients show a moderation of their moods and a change in their behaviors so they are neither vegetative nor impulsive. Patients must also demonstrate that they view themselves, their life situations, and their futures in more constructive, benign ways. It is hypothesized that such cognitive changes result in bipolar patients becoming less vulnerable to such problems as (a) overresponding to situational stressors, (b) catastrophizing over the meaning of setbacks and disappointments, (c) drawing faulty conclusions about their medications on the basis of early effects, (d) experiencing huge swings in their self-esteem, and (e) assuming that the way they feel at a given moment is the way they will always feel, thus heightening hopelessness and exacerbating the risk of suicide.

We believe that cognitive therapy provides the foundation for an effective clinical technology to assist in the fight against a serious, life-threatening psychiatric illness that has heretofore defied attempts at a straightforward pharmacological approach. We also hypothesize that the use of cognitive therapy, especially if conducted early in the course of the disorder, makes it less necessary for patients to go through unsuccessful, repeated, increasingly complicated regimens of medication. Rather, we anticipate that early interventions with cognitive therapy lead to better continuity of care in pharmacotherapy, with fewer interruptions, changes, and adverse reactions.

During the years in which we have been developing this volume, we have been very pleased to witness the work of esteemed colleagues who are independently applying cognitive therapy in the treatment of patients with bipolar disorder, including the clinical research from the United Kingdom (e.g., Lam, Jones, Hayward, & Bright, 1999; Palmer, Williams, & Adams, 1995; Scott, 1996a), as well as the work of our colleagues in the United States (e.g., Basco & Rush, 1996; Hirshfeld et al., 1998; Otto, Reilly-Harrington, Kogan, Henin, & Knauz, 1999). We believe that we are witnessing the beginning of a promising new era in the treatment of bipolar disorder and that the concurrent validity represented by the work emanating from the above venues will be borne out by the data.

This is not to minimize the difficulties posed by the illness we are studying and treating, nor to ignore either the complex biological processes involved or alternative psychosocial approaches that are currently being studied. Rather, we are enthused that cognitive therapy—a highly empirically supported model of psychotherapy—is being tailored for the rigors of the bipolar spectrum and for collaboration with pharmacotherapy. This represents hope for an improvement in the state of knowledge in helping a population of patients who can use all the assistance we can muster for them.

We should add a short note here about our choice of nomenclature. Over the course of this volume, we use the modern term *bipolar disorder* predominantly, as indicated by the title of the text. However, there are times when we use the term *manic depression*, not to confuse matters but rather to draw a link to the past and to make reference to the colloquial view of the illness. It is also our respectful response to Jamison (1995), who argued that the professional avoidance of saying *manic depression* serves to skirt the issue of how chaotic and painful it is to experience the disorder firsthand.

We offer our thanks to Susan Reynolds and Kristine Enderle of APA Books (along with their editorial team, including Casey Reever, Chris Davis, and Linda McCarter) for shepherding this project with enthusiasm, confidence, and wise advice. Their practical and moral support for this volume was invaluable in helping us transform our early, informal manual into a full-fledged text. We also thank Claudia Baldassano for her expert advice on matters of pharmacotherapy and how it was discussed in our volume. Our gratitude also goes to Jennifer Strauss for her prompt, thorough feedback on the entire manuscript as it unfolded. Her insightful comments and thought-provoking questions were extremely helpful in adding conciseness and clarity to the text. Similarly, the text was improved by Randy Fingerhut's valuable, comprehensive comments on the chapters that provided the overview of bipolar disorder and the cognitive model. Likewise, we are indebted to Julie Jacobs for her review of the finished product just before it was sent to the publisher. Her keen skills as both a journalist and a psychologist made her the best choice to serve as our final "gatekeeper," and we are most grateful for her expertise and diligence in this task. Special kudos also go to Tina Inforzato and Elizabeth Gable at the University of Pennsylvania for their loyal, efficient, and always competent administrative assistance with this project.

We also express our appreciation to all of our colleagues, whose interest in our early manual gave us the impetus to further our work on bipolar disorder. Now that our task is complete, we can all share a hearty laugh about the dozens of times over the years when we had to agree (with embarrassment) when our colleagues would say to us, "It's really about time that you expanded your manual into a book, don't you think?"

Finally, and most important, we acknowledge the central contributions of our patients. They did not choose to have bipolar disorder, and if they had their druthers they certainly would have preferred to do something other than make a painfully personal contribution to the development of a cognitive therapy approach to the treatment of their illness. However, the simple fact is that our patients deserve not only our compassion, but our respect and gratitude, for it has been their participation in cognitive therapy and their struggle with their disorder that have made it possible for us to advance the state of our field.

bipolar disorder

1

BIPOLAR DISORDER: DIAGNOSTIC, EPIDEMIOLOGIC, ETIOLOGIC, AND PROGNOSTIC ISSUES

The term *bipolar disorder*, previously and more commonly known as *manic–depression*, is not a homogeneous disorder. It actually comprises a spectrum of affective disorders, possibly related to unipolar depression, but involving varying degrees of agitation, euphoria, impulsivity, irritability, and psychotic ideation. These symptoms, collectively known as *hypomania and mania*, are what distinguish bipolar disorder from unipolar depression in clinical presentation. The affective, cognitive, and behavioral problems associated with bipolar disorder often appear in cycles of symptomatology, thus causing multiple, problematic interruptions in the sufferer's life and health. As such, bipolar disorder requires treatment over the life span.

The natural course of bipolar disorder is episodic and frequently entails relapses. Without treatment, preferably aggressive in scope and begun early in the course of the illness, patients risk experiencing a progressive worsening of the disorder over the course of time (Cutler & Post, 1982; Goldberg & Harrow, 1999a, 1999b). This may involve shorter interepisode normality, greater duration of symptom episodes, and a concomitant sense of hopelessness. Good premorbid functioning can mitigate against this negative outcome to some degree. Over the years, however, a "kindling effect" may occur (Post & Weiss, 1989), in which symptom relapses occur with less and less apparent provocation over time from stress, changes in routine, or physiological insult. At least half of those treated for bipolar disorder either do not respond or quickly relapse after an early response (Gitlin, Swendsen, Heller, & Hammen, 1995; Goldberg, Harrow, & Grossman, 1995). Thus, the field of mental health is challenged to develop and deliver more robust forms of pharmacotherapy and psychotherapy to improve the degree to which bipolar disorder can be managed successfully.

This pernicious emotional disorder is associated with marked employment difficulties, alcohol and substance abuse, family and relationship discord, and general hopelessness (Goldberg & Harrow, 1999a; Lam et al., 1999). In one study, for example, 57% of patients were found to be unable to maintain employment 6 months after they experienced an acute depressive or manic episode (Dion, Tohen, Anthony, & Waternaux, 1988). Approximately a third of bipolar patients were assessed to exhibit severe occupational impairment fully 2 years following a hospitalization (Coryell, Andreasen, Endicott, & Keller, 1987). Even more dramatic, Gillberg, Hellgren, and Gillberg (1993) found that 89% of patients who had been treated for early-onset bipolar disorder (in adolescence) were on vocational disability by age 30. Epidemiological research puts rates of comorbid mania and substance abuse in the 30% to 60% range (Brady & Sonne, 1995), a condition that represents an additional risk factor for poor treatment outcome. Social dysfunction, including high rates of marital conflict, separation, and divorce, are disturbingly common in this population (Coryell, Scheftner, Keller, et al., 1993). Not surprisingly, the occurrence of suicidal ideation and gestures and the incidence of completed suicide are substantial in this population (Goodwin & Jamison, 1990), thus qualifying bipolar disorder as a major public health problem.

DIAGNOSTIC CONSIDERATIONS

The *Diagnostic and Statistical Manual of Mental Disorders, Fourth Edition* (*DSM-IV*; American Psychiatric Association, 1994) serves as the basis for our description of bipolar disorder and its spectrum of subcategories. The following is a nonexhaustive overview of diagnostic criteria for the various subtypes of bipolar disorder. Later in the chapter we discuss comorbidity, the typical course of the disorder, and prospects for response to treatment and recovery. Throughout this volume, we hope to show the importance of an ongoing process of case conceptualization, so that therapy may be used to address the unique needs of the individual patient, above and beyond his or her diagnostic designation per se.

Bipolar disorder may be construed descriptively as a *melange* of affective disorders, which may include the following: (a) major depressive episode, (b) manic episode, (c) mixed episode, and (d) hypomanic episode. As we demonstrate, the particular combination of these four sets of affective symptoms has direct implications for the specific diagnosis as well as the prognosis. First, we give a brief overview of each of these categories, along with additional diagnostic designations.

Major Depressive Episode

The necessary feature for a *major depressive episode* (MDE) is either (a) low mood, most of the day, every day for at least a 2-week period, or (b) a lack of ability to enjoy things (anhedonia), most of the day, every day for at least 2 weeks. If these symptoms are of sufficient severity to cause significant subjective distress or to adversely affect important aspects of life functioning, then the following problems are assessed as well: (a) low energy; (b) guilt, self-reproach, and feelings of worthlessness; (c) poor concentration and difficulty with decisions; (d) sleep disturbances, including hypersomnia, or all three major subtypes of insomnia (difficulties in falling asleep; fitful, disturbed, interrupted sleep; and early morning awakening); (e) significant changes in appetite and weight, without volition; (f) extremes in psychomotor activity (either retardation or agitation); (g) marked reduction in libido; and (h) suicidal ideation, intentions, or actions.

Patients need not have all of these symptoms to meet criteria for MDE; however, an MDE diagnosis requires at least one of the two overarching symptoms and three or four of the others, for a total of at least five symptoms. The symptoms must not be the direct result of a psychoactive substance, psychotropic medication, normal bereavement, or a general medical condition.

Manic Episode

For a patient to qualify as having a *manic episode*, he or she must have exhibited an abnormally euphoric or irritable mood for at least 1 week, in which many of the following problems have occurred: (a) displays of grandiosity; (b) subjective reports of needing very little sleep for days at a time; (c) pressured speech; (d) flights of ideas and racing thoughts; (e) high disorganization or distractibility; (f) excessive goal-directed activity; and (g) pursuit of high stimulation, including hedonistic and addictive behaviors that put the patient at risk for severe life consequences, although the patients may deny or downplay such risk.

Patients in the throes of a manic episode sometimes exhibit psychotic ideation. At such times, the differential diagnosis between bipolar disorder and schizophrenic disorders may be tricky, especially when the patients' life situations deteriorate markedly (Hackman, Ram, & Dixon, 1999). However, an assessment of the patients' premorbid and interepisode functioning, along with an evaluation of the range of moods that is exhibited by the bipolar patients, can often clear up this diagnostic confusion.

A full-blown manic episode must have occurred at some point in the patient's history for the diagnosis of *bipolar I* disorder to be appropriate. This diagnosis often is made in the context or immediate aftermath of a manic episode. The proper diagnosis of bipolar I disorder becomes more difficult when the patient presents with symptoms immediately suggestive of MDE. The diagnostic situation is made even more treacherous when a patient who has had an actual past manic episode lacks official medical record of such or when the patient minimizes or conceals a history of manic episodes. In such cases, many bipolar patients have in fact been mistakenly diagnosed with a unipolar depressive disorder, thus hindering treatment and mitigating against prevention of future manic episodes. More important, such patients may be put on antidepressant medications which, in the absence of concurrent lithium or other mood stabilizers, may trigger a manic episode (Goldberg & Kocsis, 1999). Arguably, the most distressing clinical situation in which the diagnosis of bipolar I disorder is made follows the discovery of inadvertent iatrogenic effects of antidepressants.

Mixed Episode

As the designation suggests, *mixed episodes* refer to symptoms that would meet criteria for both MDE and manic episode, that last at least a week, and that cause a clinically significant disruption in interpersonal–social and academic–vocational functioning. Individuals who suffer from mixed episodes demonstrate rapidly alternating moods within the context of an overarching manic presentation. Stated alternatively, a mixed episode is a severe manic state that involves a mixture of excessive depressive features (Dunner, 1999). Symptoms such as agitation, insomnia, psychotic thinking, and suicidality are common. Nevertheless, as the designation suggests, mixed states have been difficult to characterize precisely.

Mixed episodes represent a more serious form of bipolar disorder, and they are accordingly more difficult to treat from a pharmacological standpoint (Boland & Keller, 1999). Therefore, they may be a particularly amenable target of additional psychosocial treatment such as cognitive therapy. Mixed states are frequently complicated by substance abuse and general medical illnesses, particularly those involving neurological dysfunction (Himmelhoch, 1986). Such dysfunction is also apparently one of the most lethal forms of the disorder. In their review of the literature on suicide and bipolar disorder, Simpson and Jamison (1999) have concluded that the profile of bipolar patients who are at highest risk for suicide are young men in a mixed state who also abuse alcohol and have had a history of suicidality.

Hypomanic Episode

A *hypomanic episode* consists of mood disturbances similar to full-blown manic syndrome but with lesser duration (at least 4 days), intensity, and disruption of life activities. Patients present with an unusually expansive mood, decreased need for sleep, distractibility, increased goal-directed activity, and sometimes impulsivity regarding hedonistic behaviors. Nevertheless, psychotic symptoms are not present, and patients' moods, although clearly different from the norm, are not extreme or bizarre enough to cause obvious functional impairment. When patients experience at least one such episode to go along with at least one MDE (but without a history of mania), the correct diagnosis is *bipolar II* disorder. These are the "ambulatory bipolar" patients who may never require hospitalization and whose symptoms may be somewhat inconspicuous to naive observers.

Rapid-Cycling Bipolar Disorder

It should also be noted that some bipolar patients (either Type I or II) display four or more cycles within a year and are therefore categorized as "rapid cyclers." Rapid cycling is more common among women, perhaps pointing to the importance of reproductive and other gender-relevant hormonal processes on mood stability.

According to the *DSM-IV* (American Psychiatric Association, 1994), at least 4 days of hypomania or mania and 2 weeks of depression are required to qualify as a *cycle*. By definition, this limits the number of annual cycles to approximately 20. Dunner (1999) noted that the literature has described an apparent subset of this class of bipolar disorder—called *ultra-rapid cycling*—that involves shorter and more frequent episodes than those described above. However, this disorder, too, is fraught with diagnostic uncertainty, because it may represent everything from subsyndromal symptoms that are more consistent with cyclothymia (see below), or may be the result of comorbid substance abuse.

Cyclothymia

One diagnostic category seems to represent a cross between a subsyndromal form of rapid-cycling bipolar disorder and dysthymia. This is the diagnosis of *cyclothymia*, which involves numerous affective cycles, none of which are severe, pervasive, or lengthy enough to meet the full criteria for bipolar disorder. Like dysthymia, the symptoms of cyclothymia must occur continuously over at least a 2-year period, with no symptom-free intervals extending 2 months or more. Differential diagnosis involving cyclothymia can be difficult, especially when trying to distinguish among cyclothymia, bipolar I disorder, and personality disorders that involve labile mood, such as borderline personality disorder (Coryell, 1999).

That cyclothymia, like hypomania, can be considered a subsyndromal form of the more virulent bipolar I disorder should not disguise the fact that it can lead to significant disruptions in functioning. Cyclothymia has a chronic course, and patients with this disorder are at moderate risk for developing bipolar I or II disorder (American Psychiatric Association, 1994). Thus, cyclothymia can lead to impairment and serious life consequences.

"Atypical" Bipolar Disorder

As with many other gross diagnostic areas, bipolar disorder has a "not otherwise specified" (NOS) subcategory, which represents clinical findings that suggest a bipolar disorder that does not fit neatly into the previously described designations. For example, patients may demonstrate manic symptoms without the requisite duration, or they may exhibit periods of hypomania but no history of MDE. Yet another situation in which a diagnosis of NOS may be appropriate is when the clinician is uncertain whether the apparent bipolar I symptoms are the result of a genuine underlying disorder or chemical intoxication alone.

COMORBIDITY IN DIAGNOSIS

This section provides a sampling of some of the general classes of diagnosable disorders that often appear in conjunction with bipolar disorder. It is not meant to cover all possible areas of comorbidity, but rather to highlight the sort of complex problems that clinicians who treat bipolar disorder will face in practice.

Substance Abuse

No other Axis I disorder has as high a prevalence of concurrent alcohol and other substance abuse as bipolar disorder (Tohen & Zarate, 1999), with estimates ranging from 21% to as high as 61% (Brady & Lydiard, 1992; Regier et al., 1990). This compares with an alcohol and substance abuse rate of 3–13% in the general population (Regier et al., 1990). Among all psychiatric diagnoses, bipolar disorder is second only to antisocial personality disorder in terms of concurrent abuse of alcohol and other drugs.

Interestingly, rather than trying to sedate themselves out of their manic episodes, some bipolar patients frequently use stimulants such as cocaine instead (Weiss & Mirin, 1987). This is not counterintuitive when one remembers that manic symptoms include the quest for greater stimulation. In other words, patients in a manic phase may be more apt to use drugs to enhance their high rather than as a method of self-medication (Tohen & Zarate, 1999). Furthermore, there is evidence that the course of the bipolar illness is exacerbated by the abuse of psychoactive chemicals, above and beyond the deleterious effects of the drugs in their own right. For example, drug and alcohol abuse may adversely affect response to lithium (Albanese, Bartel, & Bruno, 1994), exacerbate neuronal kindling (Tohen & Zarate, 1999), produce earlier onset of the bipolar symptoms, and lead to increased psychiatric hospitalizations (Sonne, Brady, & Morton, 1994). It is easy to see how bipolar patients who abuse drugs—especially stimulants in the context of a manic episode—create a vicious cycle of biochemical dysregulation, undercontrolled behavior, increased life problems, magnified negative consequences and stressors, and further susceptibility to biochemical abnormalities.

Anxiety Disorders

Anxiety disorders often occur in the context of bipolar disorder (Chen & Dilsaver, 1995). As Himmelhoch (1999) noted, "The comorbidity of panic disorder with bipolar disorder . . . has a lifetime prevalence of 20.8% in bipolar patients, 26 times that found in comparison control subjects and, surprisingly, 2.1 times that found in patients with unipolar major depressive illness" (p. 237). Himmelhoch called these findings "paradoxical," because bipolar depressions are typified by anergia and apathy rather than agitation and anxiety, and patients in pure manic states often seem devoid of worry altogether. However, anxiety symptoms are common in mixed episodes and in concert with psychotic symptoms, especially those that lean toward paranoia.

Personality Disorders

Recent data suggest that approximately half of all patients with bipolar disorder also meet the criteria for personality disorder (Peselow, Sanfilipo, & Fieve, 1995). These can be exceedingly difficult to assess during hypomanic and manic episodes, when the affective extremes and behavioral undercontrol of bipolar disorder cannot easily be distinguished from Axis II psychopathology. However, during euthymic phases, personality disorders may become more transparent and therefore more amenable to formal assessment and diagnosis. Peselow et al. (1995) stated that Cluster B disorders (the "erratic and dramatic" categories, e.g.; borderline personality disorder) and Cluster C disorders (the "anxious and fearful" areas; e.g., avoidant personality disorder) are equivalent in prevalence, each being twice as common as the Cluster A disorders (the "odd and eccentric" designations; e.g., schizoid personality disorder) among bipolar patients.

We have sometimes found it difficult to perform a differential diagnosis when patients demonstrate symptoms that look like both bipolar disorder and borderline personality disorder. Especially when patients present mixed states and in the context of rapid cycling, it can be problematic to determine whether the patients' mood lability, anger problems, impulsivity, relationship turmoil, and suicidality more appropriately represent symptoms of borderline personality disorder. Again, assessments that are done during euthymic periods, as well as retrospective evaluations regarding time frames that predate the bipolar disorder, can shed some light on this issue. Obviously, patients who meet the criteria for both bipolar disorder and borderline personality disorder will need rigorous treatment to help them learn methods of affect modulation as a way of life, and therapists must be aware of the danger of suicidal behavior at all times.

EPIDEMIOLOGY AND COURSE OF BIPOLAR ILLNESS

Although bipolar disorder is much less prevalent than unipolar depression, it still strikes .8–1.6% of the adult population (Kessler et al., 1994; Robins et al., 1984). Another distinction between unipolar depression and bipolar disorder is that whereas unipolar depression has an adult female:adult male ratio of approximately 2:1, bipolar disorder is fairly evenly distributed among men and women (Goodwin & Jamison, 1990; Lam et al., 1999). In fact, bipolar disorder appears to be an equal-opportunity illness; the data show no appreciable differences in the prevalence of bipolar disorder across genders, age groups, or cultures (Bauer & McBride, 1996).

However, there has been an apparent increase in the incidence of bipolar disorder in the decades since the 1940s and 1950s (Gershon, Hamovit, Guroff, & Nurnberger, 1987), as well as a shift toward earlier onset. This disconcerting trend is not well understood at present. Goodwin (1999) put forth hypotheses such as the following: (a) the increased use of drugs and alcohol in society has led to an increase in lithium resistance; (b) the marked increases in both the social mobility and the divorce rates have brought about more stress and fewer buffering social supports in the lives of potential bipolar patients; and (c) a genetic mechanism involving unstable DNA may have contributed to the development of a more malignant form of bipolar disorder, analogous to what has been found to have occurred in Huntington's disease.

The onset of bipolar disorder typically occurs in late adolescence or early adulthood. A first episode can occur later in adulthood, although this is less common. Some evidence suggests that the illness can be detected in children—typically those who exhibit behavioral dyscontrol or clinical depression or are given preliminary diagnoses of attention deficit hyperactivity disorder (Bowden & Rhodes, 1996; Geller & Luby, 1997; West, McElroy, Strakowski, Keck, & McConville, 1995). One of the most troublesome aspects of the course of the disorder is the extremely high likelihood of repeated episodes of the mood problems, ranging from 80% to 90% probability of recurrence within a few years (Tohen, Waternaux, & Tsuang, 1990; Winokur, Clayton, & Reich, 1969). Even when there is no clear, full-blown relapse, many patients continue to suffer from subsyndromal symptoms between episodes (Gitlin et al., 1995; Keller et al., 1992), which further add to the patients' sense of misery and hopelessness about ever being free of the effects of the illness. Admittedly, it is difficult to study the natural course of manic depression, owing to the widespread application of medications such as lithium that have prophylactic effects (Goodwin, 1999).

Suicide and bipolar disorder have a frequent, tragic relationship. There are two ways to look at this relationship: One can study enlightening and instructive statistics, and one can read compelling, heart-rending clinical and historical anecdotes of lives cut short. Kay Jamison is at the forefront in presenting both of these approaches, with devastating impact. In a landmark work, she and Frederick Goodwin (Goodwin & Jamison, 1990) reviewed 30 studies regarding the co-occurrence of bipolar disorder and suicide and found a mean rate of approximately 19%; in a more recent study, researchers have revised this finding downward to 15% or less (Simpson & Jamison, 1999). Nevertheless, these are strikingly high numbers, and when one also factors in causes of premature death such as accidents and cardiovascular disease, the mortality figure for patients with bipolar disorder climbs higher still (Bowden, 1999). Similarly, Goodwin and Jamison (1990) reported that their review of 15 studies indicated that the prevalence of suicide attempts in bipolar patient populations ranged from 20% to 56%. Again, these figures are extraordinarily high, far surpassing the base rates of suicide attempts and completions for most other psychiatric populations, including unipolar depression (Lam et al., 1999).

These are the dry statistics, and they are scary enough. Jamison (1993; 1999) goes a major step further by putting faces on the victims of bipolar sufferers who ended their own lives. In *Touched With Fire: Manic-Depressive Illness and the Artistic Temperament* (1993), Jamison vividly describes the symptomatic trials and tribulations suffered by some of the most creative, talented, sensitive, and accomplished people in the Western world in recent centuries. Jamison's accounts of the course of bipolar disorder before the advent of viable treatments also drives home the point that the illness is progressive and merciless and can conquer even the most strong-willed and zestful of our culture.

Jamison's volume on suicide (*Night Falls Fast: Understanding Suicide,*

1999) draws a tear-streaked portrait of an accomplished, deeply loved young man who succumbed to his bipolar disorder by shooting himself to death. Again, the message is clear for all who are listening (especially clinicians who work with bipolar patients): even people who seem to "have it all"—who are popular, gifted, physically strong, and provided with competent treatment—can and do still die by their own hand in the face of the ravages of manic-depressive illness. Therefore, any mental health practitioner who works with this population will need to be ready to place the issue of suicide risk front and center on the therapeutic agenda.

ETIOLOGIC FACTORS

The hypothesized causes of bipolar disorder are manifold. Among the most widely cited include a genetic predisposition leading to biochemical vulnerabilities, a critical level of life stress (including family discord), and a cognitive style that has adverse effects on emotionality, thus exacerbating and even triggering the aforementioned biological problems that produce the symptoms. The dichotomous thinking involved in traditional "nature–nurture" debates thankfully is more and more rare, as the appreciation for the complexity of the disorder has grown. A more integrative, collaborative approach is needed between scientists and practitioners from different schools of thought to combat bipolar disorder more effectively (Bauer & McBride, 1996).

Hereditary Factors

Bipolar disorder runs in families. Relatives of those with bipolar disorder have higher rates of bipolar disorder than do relatives of those with unipolar depression or no disorder at all (DePaolo, Simpson, Folstein, & Folstein, 1989; Miklowitz & Goldstein, 1997). People with two parents who have bipolar disorder face markedly higher risk of acquiring the disorder than those who have only one parent with the illness. Although this may reflect environmental influence as well as genetic loading, twin studies (e.g., Bertelsen, 1979; Bertelsen, Harvald, & Hauge, 1977; Vehmanen, Kaprio, & Loennqvist, 1995) and at least one adoption study (Mendelwicz & Rainer, 1977) indicate that a proportion of the transmission of the vulnerability to manic depression is indeed caused by heredity.

Biochemical Hypotheses

Several neurochemical hypotheses have been studied extensively (reviewed in Bauer & McBride, 1996), although no single view has been supported that is incontrovertibly superior to the others. For example, a deficiency in norepinephrine, already hypothesized to be responsible for unipolar depression, was proposed to account for the depressive phase of bipolar disorder as well. Dopamine has been implicated in the study of mania, especially its occasional psychotic features and heightened activity level (Goodwin & Sack, 1974).

More recently, as the evidence for the efficacy of selective serotonin reuptake inhibitors has grown, more attention has been paid to the role of serotonin in manic depression. Goodwin and Jamison (1990) have proposed that fluctuations in serotonin levels may be responsible for instability in catecholamines such as norepinephrine and dopamine, thus accounting for the abnormally wide range of mood and activity states of manic–depressive illness. This view awaits further development and investigation.

Research on neuroendocrine functioning—particularly the operations of the thyroid system (e.g., Amsterdam et al., 1983)—has also shed light on the mechanisms involved in the production and maintenance of symptoms in bipolar disorder. Particularly with regard to the rapid-cycling variant of the disorder, thyroxin supplements may be indicated for patients whose response to more standard pharmacological approaches has been suboptimal (Bauer & Whybrow, 1990).

Another biological conceptualization of bipolar disorder comes from the work of Gray (1990, 1991), as well as Depue and colleagues (Depue & Collins, 1998; Depue, Collins, & Luciana, 1996; Depue, Luciana, Arbisi, Collins, & Leon, 1994), in which they posit that mania is the result of dysregulation in the behavioral activation system. This refers to a hypothesized neurobiological motivational system that modulates approach behavior in the face of cues for reinforcement (Lozano & Johnson, 1999). Among the behaviors and traits that the behavioral activation system purportedly regulates are positive affect (e.g., enthusiasm), energy level, and attention. The dysregulation of this system allows for more intense and sustained reactivity to cues of reward, thus leading to an excessive involvement in goal-directed activity (Johnson, Sandrow, et al., 1999), perhaps at the expense of sleep and proper judgment.

An interesting development in the research on the somatic factors of manic depression involves some findings about the role that biological rhythms play in the development of symptomatic episodes. For example, seasonal peaks have been observed in mania, depression, and mixed states alike, typically in the spring and fall (Goodwin & Jamison, 1990; Jamison, 1999; for an exception to this pattern, see Wehr, Sack, & Rosenthal, 1987). Coincidentally, Jamison (1999) noted that this same pattern seems to occur with regard to suicide. It is not clear at this time how this phenomenon relates to the *DSM-IV* designation of seasonal affective disorder (SAD), which involves depressive episodes that accompany winter months when diurnal light–dark cycles are most heavily weighted toward darkness. However, there is some evidence that bright light can induce manic symptoms

(Bauer, Gyulai, Yeh, Gonnel, & Whybrow, 1994). Likewise, sleep patterns are germane to the onset of manic–depressive disorders, such as when excessive wakefulness triggers a wider range of hypomanic and manic behaviors and when prescribed bed rest dampens manic cycling (Wehr, Sack, Rosenthal, & Cowdry, 1988; Wehr et al., 1998).

Related to the above findings is the social rhythm stability hypothesis of bipolar disorder (Ehlers, Frank, & Kupfer, 1988; Ehlers, Kupfer, Frank, & Monk, 1993), which holds that the symptoms manic–depressive patients display stem in part from a tendency toward instability in daily activity and related social stimulation, with resultant adverse effects on their circadian rhythms. Frank et al. (1994) have integrated this theory into the more standard form of interpersonal psychotherapy (IPT) to create interpersonal and social rhythm therapy (IP/SRT). The goals of this approach are to teach patients how to regulate and stabilize their sleep–wake cycles, to understand and manage their personal lives to conform with a well-functioning circadian rhythm, to appreciate how their manic–depressive symptoms affect their personal lives, and to prevent and solve problems that arise in their social relationships.

As noted earlier, the course of bipolar disorder may involve a biological "kindling" effect, such that succeeding episodes of symptoms become more and more autonomous, taking on a life of their own (Post, Rubinow, & Ballenger, 1985, 1986). Analogous to models of seizure disorders, in which repeated exposures to convulsant stimuli can lead eventually to a decreased threshold for future seizures, the kindling theory of bipolar disorder holds that fewer and fewer external stressors may be needed to trigger manic episodes over the course of the illness. If further support is found for this hypothesis, the implications for the importance of early, effective intervention become even more obvious. For example, patients who are treated with and maintained on pharmacotherapy at the first episode and who are taught (e.g., through cognitive therapy) to deal effectively and confidently with major life events can prevent the sort of frequent relapses that may lead to unprovoked, kindled episodes in the future.

Stressful Life Events as Triggers

It is important for bipolar patients to construe more benignly the inevitable, stressful changes that are part of the life cycle, as well as some stressors that are unusual and extraordinary. By doing so, they can succeed in reducing the subjective, negative interpretations that may exacerbate dysphoria, hopelessness, and poor problem-solving. This assertion stems from the growing body of research indicating the linkage between significant life events and affective abnormalities (Ellicott, Hammen, Gitlin, Brown, & Jamison, 1990; Hammen, Ellicott, & Gitlin, 1992; Hunt, Bruce-

Jones, & Silverstone, 1992; Johnson & Miller, 1997; Johnson & Roberts, 1995; Kennedy, Thompson, Stancer, Roy, & Persad, 1983).

An interesting question arises: What type of life events, under what conditions, differentially result in bipolar depression versus mania? Johnson and colleagues (Johnson, Meyer, Winett, & Small, 2000; Johnson, Sandrow, et al., 1999; Johnson, Winett, Meyer, Greenhouse, & Miller, 1999) have begun to address this complex, fascinating issue. Their data suggest that negative life events (intuitively) predict bipolar depression but that in combination with a high behavioral activation system they can trigger mania. Additionally, low social support and low self-esteem are more apt to trigger bipolar depression than mania, but excessive focus on goal attainment can stimulate the onset of a manic episode. Johnson, Sandrow, et al. (1999) were quick to point out that clinicians should not discourage their bipolar patients from striving toward goals. Rather, therapists should alert their patients to the possibility that by excessively engaging in many projects, they are putting themselves at risk for hypomania and mania. One of the standard tenets of cognitive therapy is that doing things in moderation is generally the healthiest way to live, as is balancing rest, work, and play.

Cognitive Styles as Vulnerability Factors

In keeping with the cognitive model of emotional disorders (A. T. Beck, 1976), stressful life events do not possess universal power to trigger the physiological and emotional manifestations of affective disorders, at least not in an inevitable or stereotyped manner. Rather, there must be a mediating variable—the patient's cognitive style. There is strong empirical support for cognitive vulnerability theories of unipolar depression (e.g., Abramson, Alloy, & Metalsky, 1995; Abramson, Metalsky, & Alloy, 1989; Haaga, Dyck, & Ernst, 1991; Hollon, Kendall, & Lumry, 1986), but until recently there have been few studies on cognitive styles as factors in the onset and recurrence of hypomania or mania. However, some new research seems to indicate that certain attributional styles in combination with life events can predict hypomanic mood shifts (Alloy, Reilly-Harrington, Fresco, Whitehouse, & Zechmeister, 1999; Reilly-Harrington, Alloy, Fresco, & Whitehouse, 1999).

For example, Reilly-Harrington et al. (1999) found that individuals with negative attributional styles exhibited affective symptoms following stressful life events; interestingly, these symptoms could be either depressive or manic. Similarly, the prospective data of Alloy et al. (1999) suggest that those people who demonstrated abnormally negative mood problems, even in the context of occasional bouts of hypomania and mania, still had significantly more negative cognitive styles than those who had no clinically depressive episodes as part of their phenomenology. The authors noted that such findings are consistent with the conceptual view that bipolar patients' hypomanic and manic states are a defensive counter to their "true," underlying negative beliefs. In fact, Winters and Neale (1985) found support for the notion that mania is related to an ongoing sense of low self-worth, even though patients do not endorse this readily on self-report inventories.

PROGNOSTIC INDICATORS

Manic depression is a highly heterogeneous disorder, and it is difficult to describe a general prognosis for the illness. As Gitlin and Hammen (1999) stated, "Despite more than a century of careful observation by some of the most thoughtful clinical researchers in the field, it remains difficult to describe accurately the long-term outcome of bipolar disorder" (p. 39). However, certain statements can be made, such as this: Bipolar disorder (a) does not spontaneously remit and remain dormant; (b) requires pharmacological intervention as at least a part of the treatment in the vast majority of cases; and (c) tends to worsen over time if treatment is neglected, delayed, interrupted, or interfered with by alcohol and other drugs. Furthermore, it is accepted that bipolar I and II disorders, although highly related, represent different levels of severity, with bipolar II disorder being the relatively less virulent form, because it entails no episodes of full-blown mania.

Regardless of the subtype of bipolar disorder, however, it is important to assess the prognosis and outcome in a way that is most meaningful to the patients themselves. For example, if we limit ourselves to measuring extreme mood abnormalities alone, we may make the dubious judgment that a patient whose affect is stabilized on medications while he spends 6 months in a hospital represents a good outcome. Assessing the outcome from the patient's point of view alerts us to the need to look at variables that are more germane to the patient's overall quality of life. Such variables typically include the ability to engage in academic advancement, gainful employment, social activities—including the establishment and maintenance of long-term, serious romantic relationships—amiable ties to family members, and the absence (or minimization) of chronic, noxious side-effects from medications.

There is some evidence that the progress of bipolar patients across these salient variables lags behind their improvements in affective symptoms (Mintz, Mintz, Arruda, & Hwang, 1992). This finding has potentially enormous implications for long-term maintenance of therapeutic gains, because patients who are deemed to be "well" but who continue to suffer subjectively as a result of side-effects and life limitations may become hopeless about their future. This in turn may feed into a self-fulfilling prophecy, especially if the patients decide that the benefits of their treatment do not merit the perceived costs. Adherence to treatment regimens would decline in such instances, leading to a heightened chance of symptomatic recurrence, with its attendant problems. Regardless of the state of the patient's life overall, however, most would agree that a good prognosis includes long periods of time between depressive or manic recurrences, shorter episodes, no worse than subsyndromal symptoms at any time, and (in the ideal situation) no new cycles of maladaptive moods or behaviors whatsoever.

A number of factors pertinent to prognosis have been studied: (a) a history of prior episodes, (b) the presence or absence of psychotic symptoms, (c) the involvement of alcohol and other drugs, (d) the quality of family relationships, (e) long-standing personality characteristics, (f) a history of suicidality, and (g) the ability to recognize prodromes.

History of Prior Episodes

Even when a very young person—perhaps a high school student—presents with bipolar symptoms, it cannot be assumed that this represents the first episode of the illness. Taking a routine psychiatric history can clarify this issue. An initial episode of bipolar symptoms presents clinicians with a chance to formulate a coherent, coordinated, aggressive course of treatment that may have the best chance of helping the patient to achieve a durable remission.

On the other hand, some bipolar patients are not detected at the onset of their early episodes; thus, their first treatment may not occur until much later. Still others may be treated for previous periods of symptoms, but for one reason or another the treatment (or the patient's collaboration, or the patient's support from family) may be suboptimal, leading to a therapeutic failure. Patients who fit this description are more likely to experience relapses in the future (Tohen et al., 1990), although the initiation of a comprehensive, consistent treatment package can mitigate against this risk.

Psychotic Thinking

The presence of psychotic thinking during episodes of bipolar symptoms indicates a more guarded prognosis (Tohen et al., 1990). This class of symptoms has been at least partially responsible for the occasional diagnostic confusion between manic depression and schizophrenia. As a result, appropriate treatment for bipolar disorder may be delayed until two or more episode cycles have elapsed, and this delay alone may contribute to a poorer clinical course and outcome (Goldberg & Harrow, 1999b).

Clinicians can treat the symptoms of psychotic thinking in bipolar disorder with psychosocial means as one might treat these symptoms through talk therapy in disorders such as schizophrenia. This allows for a healthy cross-fertilization of techniques without the risk of inappropriate choices of pharmacotherapy. For example, the work of clinical researchers such as Chadwick and Lowe (1994) and Kingdon and Turkington (1994) can be applied with bipolar patients to help them engage in reality testing at times when delusions may be present. We would hypothesize that such strategies can help bipolar patients reduce impulsivity and improve decision-making and thus can break the vicious cycle of symptoms, social consequences, stress, and more symptoms that often drive the illness toward a worse outcome.

Alcohol and Other Drugs

All other things being equal, a bipolar patient who is clean and sober has a better chance of responding well to treatment than a patient who uses (abuses) alcohol and other drugs. This intuitive hypothesis is strongly backed up by the data. For example, Sonne et al. (1994) found that a group of bipolar patients who also abused alcohol and drugs reported twice as many hospitalizations as a group of bipolar patients who were not abusers. Furthermore, the former group experienced a higher frequency of problematic mixed states and additional Axis I diagnoses.

Unfortunately, as mentioned earlier in this chapter, there is a high comorbidity rate between manic depression and alcohol and other substance abuse (Regier et al., 1990; Strakowski, McElroy, Keck, & West, 1996). This is a most damaging interaction, in that either problem would be a challenge to treat effectively in isolation, much less in combination. Not only that, but the problems of bipolar disorder and alcohol and substance abuse probably exacerbate each other. The alcohol and drugs interfere with proper pharmacotherapy, worsen impulsivity, impair judgment, and increase the risk of suicide attempts. The mood problems inherent in bipolar disorder may serve as internal, high-risk stimuli that worsen the patient's cravings for alcohol and drugs (A. T. Beck, Wright, Newman, & Liese, 1993).

Because of the harmful effect that alcohol and drugs can have on the bipolar patients' functioning, course of treatment, and prognosis, it must receive high-priority attention in therapy. However, the therapist must exercise great care to communicate respect, empathy, and a recognition that patients are ultimately going to call the shots with regard to their own life. Otherwise, one may lose patients from treatment prematurely, because they may decide that they will not be told which drugs they should take and which drugs they should not.

In any event, it is important for clinicians to assess how much of the patient's substance use serves to enhance the sensation of being high (the hedonistic purpose) and how much serves as an attempt to find relief from troublesome affective symptoms. Ascertaining this distinction has implications for the case conceptualization and treatment. If patients want to perpetuate their mania, the therapist must focus the patients' attention on the damage that occurs when the mania is over and must help patients find safer alternatives for feeling content. If patients are trying to self-medicate, the therapist should focus more on teaching patients the coping skills they need to alleviate their distress.

Quality of Family Relationships and Social Support Network

The quality of relationships with close relatives has been shown to have predictive value in anticipating the course of bipolar disorder (Miklowitz, Goldstein, Nuechterlein, Snyder, & Mintz, 1988; Priebe, Wildgrube, & Muller-Oerlinghausen, 1989). Relapse occurs more frequently and social adjustment is poorer when bipolar patients are exposed regularly to a critical, hostile, family atmosphere. At the same time it must be remembered that the existence of bipolar disorder in the family has a significant impact on the way that its members interact. Thus, the question of how bipolar patients get along with their families requires looking at their interactions from a perspective of reciprocal causality (Lam et al., 1999). If we extrapolate to the clinical setting, this means that effective family therapy will need to address the attitudes, feelings, and behaviors of both the patients and their close relatives (Miklowitz & Goldstein, 1997). Changes that occur on both sides of the interaction are likely to result in the most robust improvements, thus giving the bipolar patients a better chance at reducing the sort of future family stressors that may trigger symptomatic relapses.

Similarly, it is very important for the long-term well-being of bipolar patients that they have a social support network of some sort (Lam et al., 1999). Bipolar patients who live in isolation (or perceived isolation) may be more prone to feel hopeless, to receive less support in seeking and remaining in treatment, and to have their signs of suicidality go undetected by others. These factors increase the risk of morbidity and mortality. On the positive side, a prospective, longitudinal study by Johnson, Winett et al. (1999) found that individuals with bipolar disorder recovered from their depressive episodes more quickly when they had more social support, and were less symptomatic at 6-month follow-up than their counterparts who had less social support. Individuals with manic symptoms were not found to be similarly sensitive to social support.

Presence of Personality Disorders

When bipolar disorder is superimposed on an existing personality disorder, prognosis for sustained remission of the former becomes clouded.

Personality disorders such as borderline personality disorder (which is commonly seen in clinical practice) and antisocial personality disorder (which is less often seen in routine practice) present formidable problems (see Layden, Newman, Freeman, & Morse, 1993; Linehan, 1993; Meloy, 1988). When these Axis II problems coexist with bipolar disorder, there is a higher frequency of life crises that can trigger bipolar relapses, a more consistent tendency toward recklessness, more problematic interpersonal relationships, a higher likelihood of suicidality, increased risk of alcohol and other drug abuse, decreased adherence to pharmacotherapy, more conflict with mental health professionals, and a general problem with instability and impulsivity that transcends bipolar episodes per se.

Suicidality

When patients have a chronic tendency toward suicidal ideation and parasuicidal behaviors (Linehan, 1993), this reflects problems in affect modulation that will have major implications for long-term functioning. On the basis of work from schema-focused cognitive therapy (A. T. Beck, Freeman, & Associates, 1990; J. E. Young, 1999), we hypothesize that chronic suicidality reflects hopelessness (A. T. Beck, Brown, Steer, Dahlsgaard, & Grisham, 1999), rigid thinking that impedes problem-solving (Ellis & Newman, 1996), and stereotyped ways of seeing oneself in pejorative ways called *early maladaptive schemas* (see Layden et al., 1993; J. E. Young, 1999). These problems, reflected in long-standing suicidal ideation, work against a favorable prognosis for bipolar patients, even when the worst of their symptoms are being managed by medication.

Additionally, there are significant life consequences for people who chronically express their wish to die through verbal or (more dramatically) behavioral means. These are the patients who are most apt to be seen as "problematic" by mental health professionals; as a source of strife, worry, and turmoil by loved ones; and as defective and fatally flawed by themselves. It is not uncommon for such patients to experience multiple hospitalizations (for suicidal gestures, not just manic–depressive symptoms), with its attendant heightening of life disruptions, stigma, shame, isolation, and medical–economic burdens. This scenario does not bode well for a fulfilling future. In summary, even if a bipolar patient manages to skirt the risk of death by suicide, chronic suicidal ideation (with or without parasuicidal behaviors) keeps the bipolar patient in states of mind that are not conducive to positive outcome. Furthermore, the practical consequences of suicide threats, attempts, and hospitalizations are anathema to the rebuilding of a desirable life. To improve a bipolar patient's prognosis, it is insufficient merely to strive to keep him or her alive. Clinicians must work actively against the suicidal ideation as well.

Subtypes of Bipolar Disorder

It is somewhat misleading to ask he question, "What is the prognosis for recovery from bipolar disorder?" because it falls prey to the "uniformity myth" (Kiesler, 1966), namely, that bipolar disorder represents a single entity. As noted earlier, the diagnostic classification of bipolar disorder includes a number of subtypes, including bipolar I disorder, bipolar II disorder, rapid-cycling bipolar disorder, cyclothymia, and bipolar disorder NOS, to go along with a number of different "states," such as the "mixed state." Therefore, it behooves us to ask questions about the prognosis for each of these subtypes, perhaps in relation to one another. Even beyond that, we need to be cognizant of factors such as patient age at onset and the issues mentioned above (latency until initial intervention, comorbid substance abuse, social support, suicidality and hospitalization), because these also influence the course of and prognosis for manic–depressive patients.

When mania strikes, the diagnosis of bipolar I disorder is indicated. When this occurs early in life, such as adolescence, the prognosis is somewhat guarded, because there is evidence of risk for future deterioration, rather than recovery (Geller & Luby, 1997; Post et al., 1999). Another red flag for long-term recovery is the existence of mixed-state mood episodes, which are associated with substance abuse and suicidality (Simpson & Jamison, 1999) and relative nonresponsivity to lithium (Post et al., 1999).

Similarly, rapid-cycling bipolar disorder poses difficulties across the board. Patients who experience this form of bipolar disorder must endure more frequent and unpredictable changes in their moods, ideation, and energy, thus leading to more frequent disruptions in their everyday life activities, along with increased negative consequences and resultant stress. Treatment is complicated in that lithium may not be the medication of choice, and the rapid changes in symptoms make titration of medication "cocktails" all the more difficult to navigate. As with mixed states, rapid cycling is related to increased risk of suicide (Fawcett et al., 1987). Therefore, greater vigilance is required in treating mixed states and rapid-cycling forms of the disorder, which itself necessitates more diligent and organized efforts to coordinate care between the nonprescribing and prescribing practitioners who often work in tandem (Moras & DeMartinis, 1999). Accordingly, more demands are placed on the patients themselves, who, in conjunction with their providers, must take an active, participatory role in their own care.

Although bipolar II disorder is considered to be a "milder" form of manic depression, with fewer, shorter, less dramatic disruptions in life functioning and better prognosis, the problems associated with this diagnosis are still significant and should not be minimized. For example, hypomanic episodes are frequently overlooked by patients and clinicians alike

(Coryell, 1999). Thus, patients who have experienced symptoms consistent with a diagnosis of bipolar II disorder may present for treatment (and may be assessed by their practitioners) as having a unipolar MDE. The result may be a course of antidepressant medication that inadvertently triggers a more serious episode of hypomania or even mania in some instances (Kupfer, Carpenter, & Frank, 1988b).

Along the same lines, patients who are in a state of hypomania may prematurely discontinue a course of psychosocial treatment for their mood-related difficulties, thus leaving themselves at greater risk for a recurrence of a depressive state. This would be consistent with data suggesting that bipolar II disorder has a shorter relapse time than unipolar depression (Coryell, Keller, et al., 1989). Additionally, this depressive state may be potentially more lethal than those depressive states encountered by patients who have never experienced hypomania or mania. This warning is suggested by the findings of two studies that indicate that patients with bipolar II disorder have a more significant history of suicide attempts than do patients with MDE (Endicott et al., 1985; Kupfer, Carpenter, & Frank, 1988a).

On the other hand, data show that bipolar II disorder (perhaps by diagnostic definition) is indeed less problematic than bipolar I disorder and demonstrates a better long-term outlook. For example, an examination of patients with bipolar I and bipolar II disorders in the 5 years following hospitalization has shown that bipolar II patients are significantly less likely to be rehospitalized than their bipolar I counterparts (Coryell, Keller, et al., 1989). Additionally, lithium discontinuation in bipolar II patients is highly unlikely to lead to manic episodes, whereas a nonadherence to pharmacotherapy in bipolar I patients leads to manic episodes more often than not (Faedda, Tondo, Baldessarini, Suppes, & Tohen, 1993). We also hypothesize that patients with bipolar II disorder have the best chance at using the cognitive therapy techniques that are geared to modifying problematic, undercontrolled behaviors (see chap. 3), because the subjective "pressure" to act on their desires and impulses is not quite as strong as that experienced by the typical patient with bipolar I disorder, for whom self-restraint is an ordeal.

Ability to Recognize Prodromes

An exciting area of study relevant to prognosis is the patient's recognition of the early warning signs of affective episodes, described collectively as *prodromes* (Joyce, 1984; Lam & Wong, 1997). Studies in this area offer evidence that manic–depressive patients who learn to spot the signs of impending mood problems, especially in the manic direction, are better equipped to make the attitudinal and behavioral preparations necessary to maintain adherence to medication and to moderate their activity levels.

In particular, Lam and Wong (1997) found that patients who recognized and actively coped with their prodromes of mania demonstrated relatively better social functioning than patients who were relatively less adept.

The findings presented above have significant implications for the potential efficacy of cognitive therapy, inasmuch as cognitive therapy strives to heighten the patients' awareness of their thoughts, feelings, and behaviors on the spot at critical times of stress. To the extent that cognitive therapy can succeed in improving manic–depressive patients' ability to recognize when their thought patterns, emotions, and behaviors are becoming too pronounced in one direction or another, coping can be improved, and so can prognosis.

CONCLUSION

Bipolar disorder is a heterogeneous illness comprising many subtypes, including bipolar I and II. The hypothesized causes of bipolar disorder are many and varied, including genetic–biochemical variables, socio–environmental stressors, and cognitive styles. Treatments have the best chance of succeeding if applied early and consistently. Comorbidity, especially with substance abuse disorders, poses serious complications and must be included on the therapeutic agenda. The risk of suicide in patients with bipolar disorder is significant and must be monitored. Treatment should be broad based (including pharmacotherapy, cognitive therapy, family interventions, and social support) and well coordinated between all practitioners treating the patient.

2

THE ROLE OF COGNITION IN BIPOLAR DISORDER AND ITS TREATMENT

An overarching, comprehensive cognitive model of bipolar disorder as yet remains elusive. Nevertheless, recent advances in theory and research from a number of quarters have converged to give the field a clearer understanding of the role that cognition plays in the development and course of bipolar episodes. Current research on bipolar disorder focuses on such cognitive factors as attributional styles (Alloy et al., 1999); perfectionism, problem-solving deficits, and elevations in sociotropy and autonomy (Lam et al., 2000; Scott, in press); decision-making biases (Leahy, 1999); maladaptive schemas (A. T. Beck, Freeman, & Associates, 1990; J. E. Young, 1994, 1999); and "modes," or integrated networks of cognitive–affective–behavioral functioning (A. T. Beck, 1996). These cognitive factors appear to be significant variables in the bipolar patient's vicious cycle of problematic functioning, including interactions with (a) abnormalities in brain chemistry, (b) deleterious changes in behavior (ranging from the vegetative to the impulsive), (c) reactions to and creation of psychosocial stressors (e.g., major life events and interpersonal problems), and (d) disruptions in optimal chronobiological functioning, and in responsivity and adherence to medications. These disparate factors appear to aggravate one another in ways that are not yet fully understood, although our appreciation of their interaction is leading the field toward the application of more comprehensive treatment packages, including cognitive therapy.

In this chapter, we endeavor to describe how the cognitive factors in bipolar disorder represent particularly fruitful areas for assessment and intervention. Understanding and using these factors can assist patients and clinicians in interrupting the cycles that otherwise might result in extreme affective symptoms and a deteriorating course (see Basco, 2000; A. T. Beck, 1996; Leahy & Beck, 1988; Lam et al., 1999; Scott, 1996a, 1996b, in press). First, we explain how the cognitive therapy treatment model can be explained to patients, and then we examine the current state of research and theory in this evolving, complex field.

PRESENTING THE TREATMENT MODEL TO PATIENTS

Therapists should not assume that patients who enter cognitive therapy already understand the cognitive model or the role that understanding cognition can play in helping them manage their disorder. Instead, it is wise for therapists to orient patients to the work of cognitive therapy, thus clearing up misunderstandings right from the start and helping patients to become effective and active participants in their own treatment (Basco & Rush, 1996).

"Diathesis–Stress" Nature of Bipolar Disorder

Therapists can start by acknowledging that bipolar disorder involves a "brain chemistry problem," a notion with which many patients are generally familiar. They can also explain that manic depression is a "diathesis–stress" disorder, which means that the biological problem does not stand alone; it interacts with stress. Although *stress* is a broad, vague term, cognitive therapists ought to zero in on the notion that it is based heavily on subjective perception. In other words, part of the patients' level of stress entails the psychological impact of their perceptions of themselves, their life events, and their future—the "cognitive triad" (A. T. Beck, 1976). Therapists can then emphasize to the patients that if they learn the skills of assessing and modifying their ongoing subjective interpretations (of these three important life areas), they gain efficacy in managing their bipolar illness in a host of ways, such as by

1. using cognitive skills to weigh against emotional waves and behavioral impulses,
2. improving hopefulness to reduce the risk of suicide,
3. weighing the pros and cons of important life decisions more methodically and with greater objectivity,

4. modifying perceptions of marital and family interactions, and
5. reducing the harmful sense of stigma and shame that is often associated with bipolar illness.

Teaching these skills is a significant boon to the overall treatment of bipolar patients and goes a long way toward improving the quality of their lives. That is precisely our intention in bringing an efficacious technology (cf. Dobson, 1989) and the human touch of cognitive therapy to the treatment of those with bipolar disorder.

Generally, the initial therapy sessions involve a mutual education process between patients and therapists, in which the patients (as part of their initial, diagnostic assessment) provide information about their personal history and the course of their illness. The therapists in turn offer information about bipolar disorder and the purpose and application of cognitive therapy for bipolar disorder, including what patients can reasonably expect. This can take the form of a verbal outline that includes the five points mentioned above or a formal, written handout (for excellent examples of patient education pamphlets, see Kahn, Ross, Printz, & Sachs, 2000; Lam et al., 1999). Identifying the hallmarks of cognitive therapy, including structure, collaboration, time effectiveness, and the use of homework, can be done in the first session, with repetitions for emphasis as therapy progresses. These areas are outlined below.

Collaboration, Structure, and Time Effectiveness

Patients in cognitive therapy quickly learn that their treatment is not a passive process. That cognitive therapy is a form of "talk therapy" does not mean it involves idle chitchat or stream-of-consciousness verbalization. Instead, cognitive therapy is an active collaboration between patient and therapist. Both parties should take great care to discuss high-priority issues, with an eye toward doing something about them, not just rehashing them.

Creating structure in therapy sessions is quite useful for bipolar patients, especially for those who have problems of low concentration and distractibility. Therapists might set up flexible routines in session, such as making an agenda, assessing the patient's moods during the week, reviewing assignments, discussing topics in order of importance, using open-ended questions to facilitate alternative ways of thinking about situations, asking for feedback, and assigning new homework. Aside from the benefits that structure brings to therapy sessions per se, such organizational methods serve as excellent models for patients to use during the week, as they try to manage their lives and stay focused on priorities.

Therapists should make it clear (through verbal instruction and by example) that therapy works best when both parties are equal participants. Bipolar disorder is a formidable foe and cannot be easily dealt with "one on one." It requires "double-" and "triple-teaming," with "defenders" including the practitioner, perhaps family members, and the patient. Two additional analogies might be used to describe the benefits of collaboration between therapist and patient. First, dealing with bipolar disorder is akin to moving a piano. One person probably cannot do it alone, but two or more people who are trained and coordinated can do the job. Similarly, therapy can be explained as being comparable to the "matching funds" concept in philanthropy, in which a single large contributor to a cause pledges to match the donations given by individual contributors. The more one side gives, the more the other pitches in, too. This is similar to therapy; the more the therapist works to help the patient, the more the patient must do to follow through. The more the patients do to help themselves, the more likely that the therapist is freed up to do more advanced cognitive therapy (rather than spend time in crisis management).

Time is a precious commodity in therapy, as in life, and therefore must be used well. Cognitive therapy is geared to manage time efficiently, by incorporating an agenda to shape each session, identifying a set of skills to be learned and practiced, and focusing on methods to enhance memory (e.g., taking notes, making summary statements, recording tapes of sessions for later review). With these techniques, patients accumulate knowledge and develop plans to use what they learn between sessions, through homework.

Therapy Homework

Therapy works best when it goes beyond social support and isolated revelations to include the learning of psychological skills that can be used at any time—in session and out of session, during the course of therapy and long after formal therapy has ended (Newman & Haaga, 1995). Although it is conceivable that these skills can be learned within the confines of the therapist's office in 1 or 2 hours a week, there is a high risk that maintenance of such skills is minimal. This is analogous to a person who takes violin lessons but only touches the instrument during lessons. It is possible that the student learns some rudimentary skills, but he or she cannot go far without practicing. The inactive violin student cannot learn advanced techniques, gain exposure to an interesting repertoire, or gain a sense of efficacy in playing the instrument. Interest in the violin will fade. Similarly, students who take a college course without taking notes, writing term papers, or studying for the exams cannot become knowledgeable in the subject material. They may find the class to be an entertaining, enjoyable experience, but they do not learn much. Similarly, therapy should be more than just an enjoyable, validating experience (not that there is anything *wrong* with that!); it should also provide an enduring learning experience for patients. This requires homework, one of the essential ingredients of cognitive therapy (A. T. Beck et al., 1979).

Although it is not absolutely necessary for patients to do therapy homework to benefit from cognitive therapy, it is in their best interest to practice cognitive therapy skills between sessions. For example, there is evidence (e.g., Burns & Auerbach, 1992; Burns & Nolen-Hoeksema, 1991; Neimeyer & Feixas, 1990; Persons, Burns, & Perloff, 1988; Primakoff, Epstein, & Covi, 1989) that unipolar depressed patients who do homework have quicker response to treatment and better maintenance of therapeutic gains than do patients who avoid it.

We acknowledge that these are predominantly correlational data. It may not be the case that homework causes positive outcome. Indeed, it may be that a third variable, such as motivation to change, causes both adherence to homework and overall responsivity to treatment. Nevertheless, the link between homework and good outcome has intuitive appeal and may be even more important with bipolar patients than with unipolar depressive patients. Clinical problems such as mania, involving emotional lability and behavioral impulsivity, may require that patients overlearn new cognitive–behavioral skills, so they can apply them automatically even under emotional duress and in the face of the urge to act without inhibition. Clearly, overlearning something requires a great deal of repetitive practice, which cannot easily be accomplished without between-session assignments.

Self-Monitoring

Perhaps the most common, straightforward, multipurpose, effective homework assignment is self-monitoring. One of the goals of cognitive therapy is to help patients become more objective observers of their own functioning, and self-monitoring is an indispensable technique to use between therapy appointments. Patients are taught to keep a written log, such as a journal of automatic thoughts along with corresponding emotions and behaviors in key situations (often in the form of Daily Thought Records; A. T. Beck et al., 1979), as well as a list of their daily activities (Daily Activity Schedule; J. S. Beck, 1995).

More germane to bipolar disorder per se are any one of a number of self-monitoring forms that have been developed specifically to increase bipolar patients' awareness of their symptoms, general functioning, and progress. For example, patients who use Mood Charting (Sachs, 1996) track depressive and manic mood shifts, hours slept, use of medications, and daily stressors. Over time, patients can view patterns in their functioning, noting their relation to such factors as seasonality, life events, and menstrual cycles. Similarly, Chronorecords (Whybrow & Bauer, 1991) involve daily (or twice daily) self-assessment of moods, sleep patterns, medications, and environmental triggers for mood problems. Along the same lines, patients can keep track of their prodromal symptoms. Adapted from the work of Smith and Tarrier (1992), the Early Warning Signs card-sorting task (Palmer & Williams, 1997) allows patients to identify their individual "relapse signatures." At the same time, the task provides an intellectually engaging way to learn about the norms for various symptoms, as experienced by those who are manic, depressed, and euthymic.

Advance Problem-Solving

Another important topic for homework assignments includes planning, preventing problems, and solving problems. For example, patients can be asked, as a homework assignment, to anticipate upcoming life events that will test their coping skills. To lower the risk of triggering a symptomatic episode, patients can (a) imagine the problem situation, (b) cognitively rehearse how they would have to talk to themselves to keep their emotional reactions within normal limits, (c) brainstorm and weigh the pros and cons of various courses of action they could take, (d) choose one or two of the best options, and (e) behaviorally rehearse their responses, perhaps through role-playing. Naturally, therapists help train and coach their patients to understand, develop, practice, and enact these kinds of advanced coping skills, and they do so with energy, enthusiasm, emotional support, and sometimes a bit of humor.

Maximizing Homework Adherence

Strategies to optimize homework assignments include the following:

1. Ask patients to rate their degree of confidence in following through with the assignment. If they say 0%, address their hopelessness. If they say 100%, ask them to consider the factors that might dampen their enthusiasm when they leave the office and how they would contend with them. If they answer with any figure between 0% and 100%, ask them to articulate the parts of their thinking that are confident and the parts that are not.
2. Suggest a few possible homework assignments and present the patients with a choice. Make the selection of homework a collaborative experience, and ask for the patients' input in tailoring the assignment to fit their needs.
3. For those patients who have negative associations with schoolwork, call the between-session task something other than "homework." If the patient has been involved in organized sports, call it *practice*; if the person is a musician or actor,

call it *rehearsal*; if the person is a scientist, call it a *personal experiment*. Aim for nonloaded terms.

4. Talk about the pros and cons of doing assignments between sessions and the pros and cons of not doing assignments (See Exhibit 2.1 for one of Trent's examples). Not only does this produce an interesting cost–benefit analysis of therapy homework, it also raises additional, clinically relevant issues such as low self-confidence, fear of facing issues, competition with the therapist, hopelessness, and other topics that are first-rate material for a therapy session.

5. Make sure that the instructions are clear. If helpful, suggest a specific day, time, and place where the patient may be most likely to follow through with the assignment.

6. Be willing to make a short telephone call to the patient during the week, as a prompt to do the assignment (if the patient does not think this is too intrusive or patronizing).

7. Engage in cognitive rehearsal in session, planning how the patients can follow through and discussing the steps they can take. In a role-play, the therapist can play the devil's advocate, telling the patients why they cannot or should not do

EXHIBIT 2.1
Trent's Analysis of the Pros and Cons of Doing and Not Doing Therapy Homework

Pro	Con
Doing Homework	
1. My therapist will stop reminding me.	1. It is drudgery; it is boring to do.
2. I'll get more therapy.	2. I'll feel inept.
3. I'll get better quicker.	3. It will be embarrassing showing it to my therapist.
4. I'll remember the important things from therapy.	4. It is time-consuming.
5. I'll have a sense of accomplishment.	5. I'll have to think about things that upset me.
Not Doing Homework	
1. I can pretend I know more than my therapist knows.	1. I'll be limiting what I can get out of therapy.
2. I can procrastinate, which is my area of greatest expertise.	2. Once again, my laziness will mess things up in my life.
3. I can relax instead.	3. I'll have nobody to blame but myself if I don't understand the self-help skills.
	4. My therapist will lose faith in me.

the therapy homework, and the patients can play the role of rational responder in favor of the assignment.

8. As with any intervention in cognitive therapy, ask the patient for feedback.

It is important that therapists not become discouraged when patients repeatedly choose to bypass homework. Many therapists are tempted to abandon the practice of giving homework to unreceptive patients. This is understandable but not therapeutically optimal. Therapists must not let their patients' nonresponsivity to homework extinguish their appropriate assignment-giving behaviors (Newman, 1994). Instead, therapists can show just how important the between-session assignments are by continuing to give them, even in the face of patients' noncompliance. Therapists can continue to address the issues of avoidance, hopelessness, lack of confidence, and so on. Furthermore, therapists can say, "I believe in the homework, so I am going to keep giving it. When you decide you want to give it a try, it will be there waiting for you."

Thus far, this discussion represents the basics of cognitive therapy, much of which can be used for a wide range of clinical populations. We provide more comprehensive reviews of intervention strategies for hypomania and mania in chapter 3 and depression and suicidality in the context of bipolar disorder in chapter 4. Now we turn our attention to some of the research and theory related to our treatment approach.

EMPIRICAL TESTS OF THE TREATMENT MODEL

Several studies that use treatment models closely related to the one presented in this text have provided support for the efficacy of cognitive therapy for bipolar disorder, both in group and individual modalities. For example, in a small, open pilot study in the United Kingdom, Palmer et al. (1995) used a repeated-measures design to study the benefits of an adjunctive 17-session group cognitive therapy for six bipolar patients. The four patients who successfully completed the treatment were assessed for changes in manic and depressive symptoms, as well as overall social adjustment. Although the pattern of change was not uniform for all patients, there was a significant general therapeutic change in the variables. A more recent group intervention was evaluated through a randomized, controlled trial at Massachusetts General Hospital (Hirshfeld et al., 1998). The group that underwent the adjunctive 11-session group cognitive–behavioral therapy had significantly longer periods of euthymia and significantly fewer new affective episodes than control patients treated with standard pharmacotherapy alone. This finding was maintained at follow-up as well.

In a randomized, controlled trial of individual cognitive therapy for bipolar disorder, Scott, Garland, and Moorhead (in press) studied the response of 29 treatment completers of the 6-month protocol (out of 33 who entered the program). The authors reported a number of encouraging findings. By and large, the patients had a highly favorable view of cognitive therapy; 26 patients indicated that they viewed cognitive therapy as a "highly acceptable" form of therapy and 23 patients agreed that they would recommend the treatment to others with bipolar disorder. Furthermore, over the course of the periodic self-assessments, medication nonadherence rates fell from 48% to 21%. Compared with patients receiving treatment as usual, those who received the additional cognitive therapy demonstrated improvements in global adaptational functioning as well as in several of their reported symptoms—especially the depressive symptoms. Scott and colleagues also noted that additional work is needed to improve the treatment, so that patients attend a greater proportion of their sessions, demonstrate improvements in manic symptoms that rival their improvements on depressive symptoms, and better maintain their gains at long-term follow-up. Given the cyclical nature of bipolar disorder, this latter criterion is especially important.

Perry, Tarrier, Morriss, McCarthy, and Limb (1999) used a brief cognitive therapy intervention (up to 12 sessions) with a large sample of bipolar patients, focused mainly on helping them to spot early-warning signs of relapse and to implement a self-help action plan. Perry and colleagues' trial succeeded in lengthening patients' interepisode intervals and in shortening hospital stays for manic episodes. Lam et al. (2000) ran a similar study using a somewhat longer period of treatment (up to 20 sessions over 6 months). The target group comprised bipolar patients who were experiencing relapses even though they were on mood stabilizers. Whereas the patients in the control group had treatment as usual, the experimental group received cognitive therapy, with great emphasis on relapse prevention. Lam and colleagues' data are extremely encouraging, in that the group receiving cognitive therapy was independently assessed to have fewer symptom episodes, better coping skills in response to early-warning signs of relapse, less hopelessness, and better medication adherence than the control group. Additionally, by the end of treatment the cognitive therapy group demonstrated significantly better general social functioning and a decreased need for neuroleptic medication than the control group.

CURRENT DIRECTIONS IN CONSTRUCTING A COGNITIVE MODEL OF BIPOLAR DISORDER

Developing a cognitive model for bipolar disorder involves reconciling a number of complications. For example, researchers have found that similar cognitive biases underlie both unipolar depression and bipolar disorder (e.g., internal attributions for causality, all-or-none thinking, sensitivity to signs of personal failure and interpersonal rejection; cf. Alloy et al., 1999; Hollon et al., 1986; Lam et al., 2000; Reilly-Harrington et al., 1999; Scott, in press). In contrast to patients with unipolar depression, however, bipolar patients are capable of showing extreme valence shifts in the content of their thinking. For example, a bipolar individual may believe that he is a complete failure when depressed and that he is the world's greatest genius when he is manic (Leahy, 1999). Thus, a cognitive model needs to account for the observation that bipolar patients demonstrate thought processes that look both like traits (i.e., long-standing predispositions) and states (responses to environmental triggers and biological activation). The cognitive model must also explain why some bipolar patients respond to stress by developing depressive symptoms whereas others become manic. Likewise, the model needs to explain why only certain kinds of positive events—namely, those involving goal-directed pursuits—have been found to predict mania, whereas general positive events have not (Johnson, Sandrow, et al., 1999).

A cognitive model also must take into account the biological processes that are inherent in extreme changes in mood and behavior seen in bipolar sufferers. One question is whether these patients' extremes of thought, faulty judgment, and difficulties in decision-making are merely the result of autonomous biobehavioral processes, are a part of a causal feedback loop, or perhaps are fundamentally tied together as different perspectives of the same mind–body process. The implications of this question are most important. We hypothesize that cognitive factors are not simply secondary peripheral signs of bipolar disorder but rather constitute their own diatheses for the development of symptoms (see Alloy et al., 1999) and are an integral part of the causal cycle of factors (see Basco, 2000). If this conceptualization is true—as we have posited for other psychological problems such as personality disorders (see A. T. Beck, Freeman, & Associates, 1990; Layden et al., 1993)—then it should be possible to design powerful cognitive interventions that can have a therapeutic effect on the biobehavioral course of the illness.

Yet another important topic that a cognitive model has to address is the role of life events and environmental stressors, whose links to unipolar depression and bipolar disorder (along with other diathesis–stress disorders) have been well documented (e.g., Ellicott et al., 1990; Hammen et al., 1992; Hammen, Ellicott, Gitlin, & Jamison, 1989; Johnson & Miller, 1997; Johnson & Roberts, 1995; Reilly-Harrington et al., 1999). In summary, a good, working cognitive model of bipolar disorder needs to provide a conceptual bridge among biology, beliefs, and behaviors; between environmental triggers and the patients' unique interpretations of these events;

and between cognitive "traits" and cognitive "states." This poses an exciting challenge. We hope to give a foreshadowing of the construction of this model in the review below.

Cognitive Traits: Beliefs, Schemas, and Modes

Our model of bipolar disorder proposes that patients' belief systems, or schemas, interact with their spontaneous perceptions of current, activating events (e.g., significant life events or other situations).[1] The result is a powerful subjective experience that interacts with the patients' biological state to determine their affect and behavior. When activated, long-standing schemas (cognitive traits) influence information processing by directing the individual toward information consistent with the schema and by overvaluing this information. Thus, a negatively valenced schema is activated during the depressed phase, directing memory retrieval toward events of loss or rejection and focusing current attention on the possibility of failure. In the manic phase, a positively valenced schema is activated, and it is likely to lead to problematic decision-making by selectively ignoring the need for appropriate caution and inhibition. The irritability so commonly seen in manic patients may indicate their simultaneous struggle with the implications of the opposite, negatively valenced pole of the schema. This irritability and awareness of both positively and negatively valenced schemas may be especially pronounced in mixed states.

When we understand the diagnostic issues pertinent to a given patient, we can draw important, general assumptions about the course of treatment that is required. A diagnosis alone, however, may not tell us much of what we need to know to provide individualized treatment to a given bipolar patient. This is where a cognitive case conceptualization comes to the fore. A solid grasp of the cognitive assumptions and schemas that comprise patients' perceptions of themselves, their worlds, and their futures—the cognitive triad—helps therapists to demonstrate accurate empathy for the patients' experiences. Additionally, knowledge about individuals' cognitive triad helps therapists to hone in on the assumptions and schemas that are causing the most distress and dysfunction. Furthermore, such knowledge can serve as a mental road map to predict how patients might change— for better or worse—if they modified their schemas in various ways. In summary, the best case conceptualizations allow therapists to understand

---

[1]Frequently used terms such as *beliefs, core beliefs, assumptions, schemas, early maladaptive schemas,* and so on have been used in varying fashion in the cognitive therapy literature, thus causing some confusion. All of these terms reflect cognitive processing and cognitive content that are "below" the level of spontaneous, surface, automatic thoughts. Our view is that the term *schema* is useful in describing fundamental, core, negative beliefs that implicitly guide patients' cognitive processing (and therefore their affective, physiological, and behavioral reactions). We also use the terms *beliefs* and *assumptions* interchangeably to reflect general points of view that patients maintain across situations.

patients' phenomenology (e.g., how they view the world through the lenses of their schemas), to empathize accurately, to identify problems to be solved (e.g., the unintended, negative consequences wrought by their schemas), and to make predictions about the patients' future functioning given therapeutic changes.

Etiologic and Descriptive Characteristics of Schemas

Early in life, people begin to make sense of their world by drawing certain conclusions about themselves and others and their relationship to the world (e.g., Rosen, 1988). This forms the first two parts of the cognitive triad; children's concepts of the future (the third part of the triad) arguably come later, as they begin to make abstractions about things they cannot grasp or see directly. These conclusions, such as "I am cared for and loved" and "I can do some things for myself," develop into general assumptions that developing children maintain as part of their ongoing, general cognitive processing. Such understandings are so basic and fundamental that they are not noticed by those who hold them—they are simply the underlying "truths" on which other conclusions about further life experiences are formed.

The above examples are positive assumptions, presumably based on a safe environment with secure attachments. These form the basis of a self-view and a worldview that may insulate children from undue anxiety and dysphoria as they develop and mature. Unfortunately, the early experiences of many children are not safe and secure. A host of life events, both acute and chronic, can lead children to draw much less favorable conclusions about themselves, their caregivers, and the world. When children face such problematic events, they become at risk for developing what J. E. Young (1994) has dubbed "early maladaptive schemas," which we refer to simply as *schemas*. The experiences that shape the formation of schemas are many and varied. The following are but a few examples (hypothesized schemas are in italics): (a) early loss of one or both parents, leading to a sense of *abandonment*; (b) emotional or physical neglect, leading to *emotional deprivation*; (c) early physical illness, leading to parental overindulgence, exaggerated *dependency*, and a sense of *entitlement*; (d) regular, harsh criticism received from unhappy, unempathic caregivers, leading to excessive self-criticism and a feeling of being *incompetent* or *defective*; (e) rejection by caregivers, such as when a child is shuffled between foster homes, with the child concluding that he or she is *unlovable*; (f) abuse by caregivers or others in whom the child placed his or her faith, leading to pronounced feelings of *mistrust*; (g) fear of a raging, chemically dependent parent, resulting in ongoing experiences of *subjugation*, *mistrust*, and fear of being *abandoned*; and (h) denial or invalidation of one's experiences and coercion into adopting the family's "party line" for the sake of public appearance, leading to a *lack of individuation* schema. This latter schema is often seen in the children of highly enmeshed families and may be prevalent in families that demonstrate high expressed emotion and negative affect.

The above examples, which may appear cut-and-dried or simplistic, are offered for illustrative purposes. The development of schemas is seldom tied so neatly to specific life events.[2] Some children experience traumas but have sufficient resources and support to avert the development of problematic schemas. Others experience stressors no different from the normal tumult of childhood and adolescence, yet they develop multiple maladaptive schemas. Some patients with bipolar disorder develop a number of maladaptive schemas; others develop fewer. Our point is to illustrate reasonable etiological factors that therapists and clients can discuss as part of their attempt to make sense of the patients' cognitive (and thus emotional) vulnerabilities.

That bipolar disorder runs in families increases the odds that children who are genetically at risk for bipolar disorder grow up in a household with parents or siblings who suffer from affective disorders, perhaps with serious comorbid disorders. This may increase the chances that at-risk children suffer the kinds of experiences that may make them more vulnerable to bipolar episodes later in life. We view the development of schemas and modes, or clusters of schemas, as being a particularly important vulnerability factor for emotional disorders.

As children develop into adolescents and young adults, their schemas may not only cause undue emotional distress that is not commensurate with the situation but also may create their own vicious cycles that are self-sustaining. In other words, schemas are hypothesized to contribute to people using faulty coping strategies (sometimes called *compensatory strategies*; J. S. Beck, 1995) that reinforce and perpetuate the very problems that support the formation of the schemas in the first place. This is known colloquially as the "self-fulfilling prophecy" and is a common clinical phenomenon observed in patients with serious affective disorders, anxiety disorders, personality disorders, and other psychiatric problems.

Although it appears clinically that maladaptive schemas that develop early in childhood have the most devastating consequences in adulthood, higher order belief systems that develop in adolescence or adulthood can also be damaging to the self-esteem and hopefulness of bipolar patients who have watched their psychological functioning decline or become erratic. For example, patients may have been self-confident and interpersonally successful prior to their first manic episode, only to have their self-image badly shaken by the consequences of reckless behavior. They may now believe that "My best days are behind me" and "I will be an emotional

---

[2]However, as we note, there is ample evidence that the *activation* of schemas and related modes of functioning is often related to specific life events.

invalid the rest of my life." Such beliefs that develop later in life may not be as "core" or pervasive as a "defectiveness" schema that emerges from childhood. Nevertheless, these beliefs may have deleterious effects on the patients' willingness to invest in the difficult work of therapy and to tolerate the side effects of medications. If cognitive therapists can help them to modify such self-condemning, hopeless beliefs, then they increase the chance that the patients are more active in pursuing a well-conceived course of treatment.

Modes

When bipolar patients are in the throes of a serious, symptomatic episode, their patterns of functioning seem to be all-encompassing and thus beg for a description of the phenomenon that goes beyond schemas alone. The concept of *modes* (A. T. Beck, 1996) is an important conceptual development in the cognitive conceptualization of psychiatric disorders. *Modes* are defined as integrated cognitive–affective–behavioral networks (e.g., powerful combinations of schemas; overlearned behavioral habits; and intense, difficult to modulate emotions) that produce synchronous responses to life demands and provide a mechanism for implementing internally driven goals. When schemas—and, at a more macro level, modes—are activated by life events, chronobiological disruptions, or other factors, the bipolar patients' predispositional "traits" become expressed as a "state," as evinced by extremities in emotional and behavioral functioning.

Although these states (whether they are depressive, manic, or mixed) are time-limited and thus may change, the underlying traits remain fixed unless met with powerful interventions. For example, psychopharmacological interventions can activate or inhibit modes and thus influence patients' states (A. T. Beck, 1996). Both cognitive therapy and pharmacological treatment can lead to improvements in patients' functioning, but we do not view them as equivalent in action. Our view is that medication can discharge or inhibit a dysfunctional mode, thus leading to an improved state of mind, but it cannot produce durable changes in the meaning structures that patients ascribe to themselves, their worlds, and their future. Thus, even with medication, a patient with bipolar disorder retains cognitive traits, which remain as vulnerability factors for future activation of symptomatic episodes (cf. Scott, Stanton, Garland, & Ferrier, 2000). Altering these traits is an important goal of cognitive intervention. By doing so, we hypothesize that we can therapeutically alter the more all-encompassing modes of functioning in an enduring fashion.

Intensity of the Charge

The activation of schemas and modes does not occur with uniform intensity for all patients or for a given patient in all situations. The intensity of the "charge" determines the power of the activation (A. T. Beck, 1996). A very intense negatively or positively charged activation may result when schemas were developed at an earlier age and when the patient encounters a life situation that provides a particularly apropos "match" with the schema. This intense activation likely is worsened by biological factors, which are themselves exacerbated if the patient experiences early onset of symptoms without prompt or adequate treatment. Alternatively stated, a schema's or mode's charge is a combined function of the patient's historical experiences regarding the etiology and maintenance of cognitive traits, the salience of the situational stressors at a given time, and the extremity of the patient's biological dysregulation.

Bidirectionality in the Expression of the Schemas

It is important to assess patients' schemas regardless of their presenting symptoms. The patient who presents with manic grandiosity may have the same maladaptive schemas of "unlovability" or "incompetence" as a depressed patient but presented in inverse fashion. Bipolar patients seem to maintain consistent, maladaptive schemas that simply shift polarity (i.e., into a new state) along with their moods. Therefore, when individuals who have an unlovability schema (cf. Layden et al., 1993; J. E. Young, 1999) are in the throes of deep despair, they may think that they are hated by all humanity, but when they become manic, they may switch to believing that they are worshipped universally. Later, as a result of successful cognitive therapy that modulates the unlovability schema, we would expect a reduction in the breadth of this cognitive and emotional swing, because both poles would be somewhat moderated.

It is the cognitive therapist's responsibility to assess and conceptualize patients' unique patterns of schemas (and the historical events linked to them). This enables both therapists and patients to begin to predict when patients are at greatest risk for significant shifts in modes of functioning. After the schemas are identified, they can be modified, and as the amplitude of the dysfunctional swings in bipolar patients' functioning is reduced, therapeutic progress is made.

Assessing Schemas: Targeting Long-Standing Cognitive Vulnerabilities

Maladaptive schemas are associated with strong, negative affect across a wide range of situations, as well as difficulties in therapeutic change. There is evidence, at least with unipolar depressive patients, that changes in the deeper, negative beliefs can reduce the likelihood of symptomatic relapses in the future (Evans, Hollon, et al., 1992; Hollon, DeRubeis, & Seligman, 1992). With bipolar patients, we hypothesize that modification of schemas helps delay the onset of new episodes and reduces the duration and severity.

An inventory designed to measure beliefs—some maladaptive, some not—is the Dysfunctional Attitudes Scale (Weissman & Beck, 1978). This 40-item self-report inventory is designed to detect dysfunctional belief systems that are believed to increase patients' vulnerability to affective disorders. Participants are asked to agree or disagree with each belief on a 7-point Likert scale. Clinicians can peruse the maladaptive beliefs that patients endorse and the adaptive beliefs with which they strongly disagree and can look for patterns that may suggest the existence of problematic schemas. Examples include, "If I fail partly, it is as bad as being a complete failure," "I am nothing if a person I love doesn't love me," and "If I am to be a worthwhile person, I must be truly outstanding in at least one major respect." When patients agree with a belief or two (in the extreme) in isolation, this is not necessarily a compelling indicator of schemas. Likewise, when patients agree with clusters of beliefs but in moderation, this, too, is a weak sign of schemas. However, when patients agree with clusters of dysfunctional beliefs, this is a red flag for the existence of maladaptive schemas.

Within the past decade, questionnaires have been designed to assess schemas commonly associated with personality disorders. Two of these are the Schema Questionnaire (J. E. Young, 1994) and the Personal Beliefs Questionnaire (A. T. Beck, Butler, Brown, Dahlsgaard, Newman, & J. S. Beck, in press). The former examines how patients weight certain categories of predefined schemas, such as unlovability, mistrust, abandonment, and incompetence, whereas the latter looks for patterns in beliefs that are hypothesized to map onto the various personality disorders. Taken together, these self-report inventories can make therapists aware of the long-standing patterns of patients' fundamental understanding of themselves and their world. Thus, therapists can spot areas of vulnerability and can devise treatment plans to modify these problematic beliefs.

Regardless of the psychometric instrument or interviewing technique used, cognitive therapists assess the extremity and strength of endorsement of their patients' belief systems. One of the central strategies of cognitive therapy is to moderate patients' beliefs, so that the patients take a broader perspective, reduce the magnitude of affect (e.g., dysphoria, anger), and improve their ability to deal constructively with stressors. As bipolar patients accomplish these general goals, their level of perceived stress is diminished. As patients practice the psychological skills they learn over time, through therapy homework, they become less vulnerable to affective episodes in the future, even when significant stressors occur.

Life Events and Their Interactions With Cognitive Factors

What are the psychosocial factors that contribute to the activation of bipolar symptoms, including strikingly polarized thinking? There are compelling data that significant life events, such as those bringing hardship or major life changes, are linked to an increased onset of affective episodes in bipolar disorder (Ellicott et al., 1990; Hammen & Gitlin, 1997; Johnson & Miller, 1997; Johnson & Roberts, 1995). However, it appears that patients' cognitive styles play an important interactional role (Alloy et al., 1999; Reilly-Harrington et al., 1999). For example, in combination with negative life events, people with maladaptive thinking styles are more apt to develop affective symptoms, including both depressive and manic episodes.

The finding that negative life events can trigger mania—not just depressive episodes—is most intriguing (Johnson & Roberts, 1995; Reilly-Harrington et al., 1999). Manic–depressive people may be particularly vulnerable to stressful life events, especially if they maintain problematic schemas that serve to magnify the negative implications of these triggers. They may respond to these negative life events by drawing excessively harsh conclusions about themselves and hopeless interpretations for their future. The resultant stress could then lead to a combination of deleterious biological reactions, along with behaviors that may tax their physical well-being even further (e.g., loss of sleep, giving up, allowing problems to accumulate). The outcome of this process may well be expressed in the sort of biological dysregulation that results in manic symptoms, even though the environmental triggers were negative. One hypothesized mechanism is that troublesome life events that trigger sleep disruption are more apt to lead to mania than those that do not (Malkoff-Schwartz et al., 1998). It is vitally important for cognitive therapists to teach their bipolar patients to identify and respond adaptively to stressors and to identify early warning signs of symptoms. With prompt intervention, it is possible that manic responses can be circumvented or at least attenuated.

Attributional Styles

Research from attribution theory has found empirical support for a mediating link between life events, predispositional cognitive factors, and the activation of the bipolar symptoms (whether depressive or manic). This connection is particularly evident for bipolar patients who tend to make internal, global attributions for significant life events (Alloy et al., 1999; Leahy, 1999; Reilly-Harrington et al., 1999). This may lead people with manic depression to see themselves as being in greater control of (and more responsible for) their important life events than objective evaluation would warrant. A clinical implication of these findings is that it is potentially corrective to help patients understand that some life situations are outside of their direct control and not reflective of their characters. When balanced against an accurate appraisal of their problem-solving skills, such external, specific attributions may help patients take situations "in stride" and keep more of an even keel. This militates against undue mood swings.

Interestingly, there is some evidence that negative thinking patterns in patients with unipolar and bipolar depression are quite similar to each other and are stable over time (Alloy et al., 1999; Reilly-Harrington et al., 1999). Therefore, when bipolar patients switch from their depressive to their manic phases, they still maintain the negative attributional styles they exhibited when they were in their depressed phase. Alloy and colleagues (1999) wrote, "These findings are compatible with traditional psychodynamic formulations suggesting that cyclothymics' and bipolar individuals' hypomanic or manic periods are a 'defense' or counterreaction to underlying depressive tendencies . . ." (p. 36). It also highlights the importance of teaching patients to be as objective as possible in appraising their life situations, so that their cognitive styles do not unduly magnify their levels of affect that are already so difficult to manage in the context of the bipolar illness.

Another interesting clinical and research question to ask is, "In the absence of obvious, normative life stressors, do patients' maladaptive cognitive styles create the subjective equivalence of significant life changes?" In other words, is it possible that the onset of depressive or manic episodes may appear to be spontaneous—as in the case of relapses in the middle and latter course of the illness—yet be at least partially attributable to the self-induced stress of viewing everyday situations as hopeless, catastrophic, requiring "100%, driven effort," or the like? If support is found for this hypothesis, it has potential implications for the kindling hypothesis of bipolar disorder, in that the seemingly physiological "autonomous" nature of later symptomatic relapses may be postponed, muted, or avoided altogether through the use of cognitive coping skills. If we help bipolar patients reduce their tendency to think in ways that create self-induced stress, we may be able to decrease the likelihood (and amplitude) of mood problems.

Sociotropy–Autonomy Dimensions

Another area of potential convergence of research on patients' personality characteristics, schemas, and stressful life events is the study of the sociotropy–autonomy continuum, using the scale that bears its name (Sociotropy–Autonomy Scale; A. T. Beck, Epstein, Harrison, & Emery, 1983). Patients with high degrees of sociotropy are hypothesized to be vulnerable to affective disorders when they are confronted with interpersonal difficulties and losses, whereas those with a high degree of autonomy are thought to be more vulnerable when their sense of freedom and achievement is thwarted. Hammen and colleagues (1989) found support for this theoretical assumption in a sample of unipolar depressive patients, but found ambiguous results in a smaller sample of bipolar patients who had become symptomatic during the course of the study. The authors argued that a clearer picture may develop only over a longer period of time, when more of the bipolar patients experience recurrences. Fingerhut (1999) followed up on this line of research and found that bipolar patients with a high degree of sociotropy required minimal interpersonal stress to influence their time to relapse. By contrast, patients with low sociotropy did not show this vulnerability. Instead, only high levels of interpersonal stress influenced the course of their illness. In general, when patients with low and high levels of sociotropy were combined, the median time to relapse for participants with interpersonal life events was more than 4 months shorter than it was for participants without interpersonal life events. Although these findings are not statistically significant, they represent a statistical trend in support of the general hypothesis that interpersonal life stressors can influence affective relapse. Lam and colleagues (2000) reported that bipolar patients demonstrated an interaction between their perfectionist beliefs about achievement and autonomy, and life events in which they found themselves having to work hard to compensate for previous failures. The result was overdriven behavior that risked spurring on new symptomatic episodes, including mania.

The constructs of sociotropy and autonomy are not orthogonal, and patients can load heavily on neither or both, as the bipolar patients in the Scott et al. (2000) study demonstrated (they were high in both the need for social approval and perfectionism). The tendency toward a high degree of sociotropy may be associated with the schemas of unlovability, abandonment, and dependence. Therefore, we would expect that patients with an unusually high need for interpersonal affiliation are especially vulnerable to rejection, so that they may experience situations involving interpersonal discord and loss as representing personal catastrophes. The result may be an elicitation of affective symptoms hypothesized to be associated with a sense of being unloved, alone, and helpless. Because this represents an area of particularly high subjective stress for markedly sociotropic individuals, we would expect that it would bring about relapse in this type of bipolar patient.

In like fashion, the tendency toward a high degree of autonomy may be associated with schemas of incompetence, defectiveness, and perhaps mistrust as well. For example, when a highly autonomous bipolar patient witnesses the business that she created while manic fail and go bankrupt, she may experience more than simply the stress that goes along with financial loss. She may be prone to feeling supremely incompetent, and her personal sense of failure may be a further trigger for significant affective symptoms, such as a deep depression. In addition, patients who believe that their relatives and therapists are needlessly discouraging them from pursuing their flight of ideas and goals may react with a schematic level of mistrust. In other words, they may not see others as showing concern in their best interest; rather, they may interpret others' cautionary comments as stemming from jealousy and a deliberate attempt to sabotage their success. The resultant anger and frustration may become the emotional stressors that further hasten or exacerbate the manic symptoms, especially the characteristic irritability.

Decision-Making and Goal-Directedness

One of the most obvious and salient ways in which bipolar patients demonstrate the contrasts between their negatively and positively biased modes of thought, affect, and behavior is in their decision-making. Leahy (1997, 1999, 2000) has explicated a risk management model to highlight these differences. Using a financial portfolio analogy (cf. Bodie, Kane, & Marcus, 1996), Leahy demonstrated how depressive thinking is characterized by an extreme aversion to risk, to the point where patients cut themselves off from opportunities to improve their lot, even if it means accepting an unfavorable situation. Patients who are deeply dysphoric may be loath to try to take action to improve their situation, fearing that they can only make things worse by changing course. These patients present as being helpless, see no point in putting themselves out to do therapy homework, and do not show up for sessions that they see as doing nothing more than stirring up trouble. At the other extreme we have manic individuals who crave excitement and thus minimize or deny the existence of risk in a frantic attempt to attain and use all possible opportunities for gain. These patients feel so in control of their lives as to make therapy seem superfluous, and they interpret their therapists' attempts to collaborate in problem-solving as being tedious, unimaginative exercises in conformity and mediocrity.

Of course, the situation would be difficult enough if the bipolar patients remained in just one of these extreme, biased states of decision-making. For example, unipolar depressive individuals may be "stuck" in old self-preservation modes that give them little joy but are predictable. Manic individuals may be wreaking havoc on their lives, but at least they experience the thrill of the moment and the hindsight bias of thinking that the fun made it all worthwhile despite the trouble. Unfortunately, the shifting from depressive decision-making mode to manic decision-making mode is even more problematic.

Anecdotally, we have heard bipolar patients complain that when they feel high, they feel pressured to make up for lost time—the time they had spent in depressive, inert states, letting their lives stagnate (cf. Lam et al., 2000, for similar findings). This just fuels the pump of emotions and stretches their extremes of risk-taking even more. Similarly, patients in the depressive state have lamented to us that they rue the days when they made their mania-driven choices, as they now try to hold onto what little semblance of resources and order remain in their lives. In other words, manic–depressive individuals do not even get to have the "luxury" of holding on to their old, familiar dysfunctional ways of coping. Each mood swing brings with it its own set of maladaptive decision-making processes that go against the grain of the previous state of mind. They cannot "settle in." One of our patients likened herself to Sisyphus, who was forever doomed to push the boulder up the hill, let it fall back, push it back up the hill, watch it fall down, on and on, for all time. Clearly, our cognitive interventions must target the extremes of decision-making that support this demoralizing process and must offer a technology of problem-solving that splits the difference between risk denying and risk aversion.

Bipolar disorder is sometimes characterized in terms of the dysregulation of the affective, or more precisely the hedonic, system, which plays a major role in the initiation, maintenance, and inhibition of behavior. Some intriguing and important research relating to the above pertains to the role of the "behavioral activation system" (Depue & Iacono, 1989; Gray, 1990; Johnson, Sandrow, et al., 1999; Meyer, Johnson, & Winters, 1999) in bipolar disorder. The behavioral activation system is a hypothesized neurobehavioral system that has been linked to dopaminergic pathways in the ventral tegmental area (Depue et al., 1996). Dysregulation of the behavioral activation system, specifically excessive activity, may be associated with a person's becoming too focused on incentives and goal-related activities. Thus, patients in the throes of a manic state could scarcely turn down the opportunity to strive for achievement and pleasure, even at the expense of their health, financial standing, and social reputation. In fact, the manic patient would not perceive these risks as being significant, and therein lies a major part of the problem. Hence, the cognitive therapist's role here is to assist hypomanic (and even manic) patients in making more normative appraisals of the costs and benefits in pursuing their identified, ambitious goals. The intent is to give patients cognitive "brakes" to slow down their over-responsive behavioral and hedonic systems, perhaps just enough to stave off further life consequences that could lead to more stress and exacerbated symptoms. Because cognitive processing is part of the hypothesized vicious cycle of factors that drives manic depression, cognitive therapists constantly look for ways to break this cycle through a wide range of standard and specialized interventions (see chapters 3 and 4).

CONCLUSION

Cognitive factors represent a significant part of the vicious cycle of interacting variables that comprise the syndrome of bipolar disorder; other factors include neurobiochemical dysregulation, behavioral extremes, and psychosocial stressors (both causal and consequent). The cognitive varia-bles have been described in a number of ways in the literature, from attri-butional styles to schemas to all-encompassing modes of functioning that become activated under certain conditions. Regardless of how cognitive factors are presented, their assessment and modification can serve as en-during, therapeutic brakes to attenuate the overall bipolar process, espe-cially if patients learn to implement cognitive self-help skills at the early signs of symptom onset.

The cognitive therapy treatment model is most effective when pa-tients are full partners in the process. This is accomplished best when therapists educate patients about the diathesis–stress nature of bipolar dis-order, structure the sessions in a time-effective manner, socialize patients into the model of cognitive therapy, apprise them of the rationale for in-terventions, and collaboratively design homework assignments that in-crease their sense of skill and autonomy. A growing number of outcome studies are providing evidence of the efficacy of cognitive therapy in im-proving the condition of bipolar patients significantly above and beyond treatment as usual.

An assessment and understanding of beliefs and schemas (e.g., using in-ventories such as the Dysfunctional Attitudes Scale, Sociotropy–Autonomy Scale, Personal Beliefs Questionnaire, and Schema Questionnaire) can help advance therapists' individualized cognitive case conceptualization, thus assisting them in identifying the cognitive traits that comprise areas of personal vulnerability in bipolar patients.

3

MODERATING MANIA
AND HYPOMANIA

Many clinicians have observed that it is exceedingly difficult to use psychosocial interventions effectively when patients with bipolar disorder are in a manic phase. Patients themselves often maintain that after they exceed a certain level of heightened mood state and impulsivity, there is little that anyone can say to stop them. Indeed, when patients experience a full-blown manic episode, they are almost always in need of heightened supervision and medication adjustment. However, it is needlessly pessimistic—not to mention an example of all-or-none thinking—to conclude that talk therapy has no role in helping bipolar patients at such times.

The rates of bipolar patients' shifts in mood, cognition, and behavior are not uniform across cases, and sometimes they evince a gradual process. When the change is not rapid, it allows time for the alert clinician to make psychosocial interventions while the patients are hypomanic and arguably still responsive to cognitive and behavioral techniques. Recent work on the recognition of prodromes (early warning signs of symptoms; Lam & Wong, 1997; Smith & Tarrier, 1992) represents a promising new area in which to devise interventions to subvert the full impact of a manic episode before it begins in earnest. In this chapter we review a wide range of clinical strategies for just such scenarios. Bear in mind that the techniques below are meant to be used in the context of a treatment plan and that alterations in level of supervision and medication may be required.

EDUCATING PATIENTS ABOUT HYPOMANIC
AND MANIC ONSET

Knowledge is power. Given that bipolar patients need all the strength they can muster in managing their disorder, it is incumbent on therapists to use a psycho–educational model as much as possible. For example, some patients report that their mania "sneaks up" on them insidiously, and therefore they fall prey to its effects before they take preventive or corrective action. Other patients tell us that they are well aware of the impending state of mania, but are at a loss as to how to impede or otherwise mitigate its onset. Still others note that they have some ideas as to how they might reduce the full effects or consequences of their manic episodes, but do not use their ideas out of a sense of fatalism and helplessness (e.g., "What's the point of trying to curb my mania? If you can't beat it, join it!"). Of course, there are some instances in which patients welcome their periods of mania, believing that it is a desirable state, that no precautions are necessary, and that risks are irrelevant. In each type of case, cognitive therapists can educate their patients about ways to use their experience, knowledge, and hopeful thinking to put a cap on the negative impact that an unbridled manic episode might otherwise produce.

Recognizing Early Warning Signs of Hypomania and Mania

As the saying goes, "forewarned is forearmed." We want bipolar patients to become adept at spotting the prodromes, or the early-warning signs, of an impending manic episode. If they can recognize this process, they are in a better position to reduce the sorts of behaviors that drive the mania. In other words, we argue that the process of cycling into mania is not simply a stereotyped biological process; rather, it is interactive with the patient's life situation, cognitive processing, and general level of coping skills. To the extent that we can help patients practice advance problem-solving and "damage control" on recognizing that their moods are becoming too expansive, we can teach patients how to curtail vicious cycles. In this manner, biological and environmental factors are less likely to feed off each other, and the full effects of the mania can be muted.

It should be noted that although there are some signs that are common to most bipolar patients, there can be high variability among patients (Molnar, Feeney, & Fava, 1988). Fortunately (at least from an assessment standpoint), individuals often show consistent intra-individual "relapse signatures" (Smith & Tarrier, 1992) from which they can take cues about the onset of mania or depression. This reinforces the importance of an individualized case conceptualization, which takes into account the symptomatic factors that are unique to each patient, including his or her beliefs and schemas (see Needleman, 1999).

Therapists can assist bipolar patients in modifying some of their basic beliefs about their disorder, so that they become more apt to see the value in recognizing and heeding the early-warning signs of hypomania and mania. For example, if patients maintain the all-or-nothing belief that "My mania will play itself out, no matter what I do," it is unlikely that they will take active steps to help themselves. Even more dangerously, the patients may deliberately throw caution to the wind, reasoning to themselves that they might as well take their mania to the limit rather than engage in an anticipated futile struggle against it. This maladaptive belief is akin to the phenomenon in the substance abuse literature known as the "abstinence violation effect" (Curry, Marlatt, & Gordon, 1987; Marlatt & Gordon, 1985). Given that there is a high incidence of comorbid substance abuse with bipolar disorder (Brady & Lydiard, 1992; Brady & Sonne, 1995), this analogy is especially apropos. Despite the compelling nature of euphoria, bipolar patients can be taught that each new behavior is a new decision over which they have some measure of responsibility, even if control is limited. This counteracts the maladaptive belief that the onset of manic symptoms gives patients license to engage in further manic behaviors.

Having explained our position above, what in fact are the early-warning signs of hypomania and mania (see Exhibit 3.1)? How can patients distinguish between these problematic signs and normal good mood? After all, we do not want them to fear their own feelings of happiness, as some patients sadly learn to do. (Additionally, we do not want the loved ones of patients to express disapproval when patients demonstrate normal good moods. We want them to be skilled in making a differential assessment. Therefore, they, too, must be educated about the early-warning signs of mania.)

Aside from those listed in Exhibit 3.1, there are other early-warning signs as well. We encourage therapists to work with bipolar patients to compile more complete lists of such cues that fit the individual patient's experiences (see Lam et al., 1999). By noticing these signs, patients have a better chance of using the skills that we describe in this chapter. In this way, patients can preempt some of their actings out and thus may avoid incurring significant consequences. Additionally, by interrupting their manic vicious cycles, patients can buy some time to allow for greater degrees of supervision and adjustments in their medication. This makes it possible to do some significant "harm reduction."

Therapists can also keep track of the status of patients' hypomanic and manic symptoms over time by making self-report measures available to patients, who may complete these on a regular basis (perhaps as often as every therapy session). For example, the Internal State Scale (Bauer et al., 1991) is a questionnaire that assesses for the severity of both manic and depressive symptoms. The Halberstadt Mania Inventory (Halberstadt & Abramson, 1998) is a 28-item self-report inventory designed to measure

EXHIBIT 3.1
Typical Early-Warning Signs of Hypomania and Mania

1. Sleep disruption, including a decrease in the subjective need for sleep, and behaviors that interrupt the normal sleep–wake cycle (such as when a patient feels compelled to stay up late to take care of some chores that are not really urgent).
2. An unwarranted, marked decrease in anxiety. For example, patients begin to express a devil-may-care attitude about missing an important deadline at work, appear less than concerned about money owed to others, or do not feel concerned that final exams are approaching, even though they have not studied.
3. High levels of optimism, not backed up by good planning and problem-solving. The patients believe that their ideas will pan out in positive ways. However, when pressed for details, they will not have thought things through carefully, made contingency plans, or considered the risks and the down side. They may become annoyed and irritated if this is brought to their attention.
4. A high degree of social gregariousness, combined with relatively poor listening skills. That is, patients subjectively feel very affiliative, but they are not well attuned to what others are saying, nor are they highly aware of social cues. For example, the hypomanic individual may begin talking at length to a person who obviously is in a hurry to leave. However, the hypomanic person does not pick up on this and continues to banter. The other person may feel trapped, especially if he or she is unassertive or is just trying to be kind. The hypomanic person takes leave of this conversation without being aware that he or she has annoyed the other person.
5. Diminished concentration. This shows itself in any number of ways, such as difficulties in reading, following through on tasks, and remembering things from moment to moment. The person seems more disorganized than usual.
6. Libido increases to the degree that it begins to "spill over" into unusual ideation or behavior that the patient would otherwise find embarrassing, such as dressing too provocatively or using far too much make-up and perfume. Overall, this may be a warning that the patient is at risk for engaging in excessive flirtatiousness, unsafe sex, or other sexual improprieties (including ribald humor that may come off as harassment in some settings).
7. Goal-directed behavior markedly increases (Johnson, Sandrow, et al., 1999), to the point that patients appear driven and unaware of the drawbacks of their activities. In many instances, the time and effort expended in such endeavors go for naught; patients do not complete the tasks, switch to extraneous tasks midstream, or choose projects that are impulsively conceptualized and therefore have little chance for success.

the severity of affective, cognitive, motivational, and somatic symptoms characteristic of hypomania and mania.

In addition, the therapist may choose at times to administer an interview-based questionnaire. For example, the Young Mania Rating Scale (R. C. Young, Biggs, Ziegler, & Meyer, 1978) rates the intensity of symptoms associated with mania. It inquires about elevated mood, increased motor activity, sexual interest, sleep changes, irritability, speech (rate and amount), distractibility, racing thoughts, questionable new interests or plans, thought disorder, disruptive and aggressive behaviors, appearance, and insight. Likewise, the Bech–Rafaelsen Mania Scale (Bech, Bolwig, Kramp, & Rafaelsen, 1979) is a 12-item measure in which the clinician interviews the patient about such manic symptoms as euphoric mood, heightened self-esteem, irritability, increased motor activity, reduced need for sleep, and others. Each item is rated on a 5-point scale, with the total score indicating the presence and level of severity of mania. The use of measures such as these can assist therapists in spotting patients' prodromal (as well as more advanced) hypomanic and manic symptoms.

Regulating *Zeitgebers* (time-givers)

Bipolar patients are highly sensitive to biological rhythms. There is some evidence that even a modest disruption in sleep–wake cycle, including that caused by jet lag, can trigger mood swings (Ehlers et al., 1988; Malkoff-Schwartz et al., 1998; Wehr, Sack, Rosenthal, & Cowdry, 1988). Along the same lines, changes in daily routines, such as the time a patient eats dinner, may also have an impact on his or her moods.

Therefore, it is important to educate bipolar patients about the need to strive for regularity in their daily schedules and activities. Of course, this requires advance planning, attention to detail, and self-restraint from spontaneous actions—some of the very qualities that patients have the most difficulty demonstrating. Needless to say, therapists must gently guide and coach patients in such matters. It also helps to have a significant other, such as a spouse, assist in this area.

As with many of the interventions we mention in this volume, this approach risks making bipolar patients feel unduly monitored and controlled. Therapists must be highly sensitive to the patients' attempts to preserve their dignity, including the right to make decisions about such basic human functions as sleeping and eating.

Differentiating Normal Good Mood From Hypomania

We have described some of the early-warning signs of hypomania and mania. This helps bipolar patients to enact interventions and safeguards to stave off the full effects of a manic episode. However, by taking this approach we sometimes incur "false positives," in that the patients' good moods are simply indicative of normal happiness. How can we reduce such confusions and therefore not teach patients to unduly fear their own positive states of mind (see Exhibit 3.2)?

Obviously, the criteria of Exhibit 3.2 are not all-or-none phenomena. Therefore, it is useful to demonstrate to patients how they can rate each of the above factors on a continuum. By doing so, bipolar patients can do

EXHIBIT 3.2
Typical Indicators of "Normal" Good Mood

1. The patient is able to sit down and enjoy reading a newspaper or book, for a significant period of time, without becoming bored or terribly distracted.
2. The patient is capable of doing most of the listening and less of the talking in a social conversation.
3. The patient does not feel the urge to "push limits" or otherwise do something risky, just for the sake of "stirring things up."
4. The patient shows the ability to complete tasks without repeatedly becoming side-tracked by other ideas or projects.
5. The patient experiences a modicum of anxiety and concern about the demands on his or her life, including responsibilities, deadlines, financial obligations, and so on.
6. The patient can experience and enjoy moments of quietude and serenity.
7. The patient is able to sleep well at night and for normative periods of time.
8. The patient is able to accept well-meaning, constructive criticism from another person without becoming unduly irritated.

an informal self-assessment of the adaptiveness of their mood. This allows them to balance the need to catch early-warning signs of hypomania with the importance of finding satisfaction and peace of mind in everyday life. Of course, therapists need to be aware of those times when patients are all too willing to rate their own moods as "normal," even when other people (including the therapist) strongly believe otherwise.

Understanding the Consequences of Hypomanic and Manic Behavior

Perhaps the most important source of education for bipolar patients about their illness comes from their own life experience. Therapists who work with bipolar patients usually can expect that some of their patients have already been through multiple mood cycles (and perhaps multiple trials of treatment) in the past. There is valuable information to be gained from looking at these past episodes.

The following are some questions that therapists can ask to learn more about the patients' history of manic episodes and to remind their patients of important facts about their illness:

1. "In your experience, what situations typically are associated with the onset of a hypomanic or manic episode?"
2. "During those times, what were some things you thought, felt, and did?"
3. "What are some of the things that you did while you experienced a manic high that you now regret, looking back?"
4. "In your experience, how does your hypomanic or manic mood 'trick' you into believing that everything is okay, and that you do not have to take any precautions?"

5. "What are some things that you now remind yourself of, so as not to fall prey to the allure of the 'high' while there is still time to keep yourself in check?"

6. "What are some of the valuable lessons that you have learned as a result of going through hypomanic and manic episodes?"

7. "Based on the above, what strategies are you willing to adopt now, so that you can lessen the chances of ever having to suffer such consequences again?"

As one can deduce from examining these questions, it is useful to phrase the questions in as respectful a manner as possible, because the topic of mania and its consequences can be quite shaming for individuals with bipolar disorder. Prefacing questions with the phrase, "In your life experience . . ." is one way to communicate this respect. It is also helpful to acknowledge that the experiences of hypomania and mania can be very seductive and difficult to resist. Nevertheless, by focusing on the negative consequences of these past episodes, therapists can use evidence from the patients' own lives to help dissuade them from doing things that would otherwise drive their euphoria and related actings out. It is typically more powerful for patients to take instruction from their own experiences than to have to follow the edicts of authority figures such as mental health professionals.

Bear in mind, however, that the phenomenon of state-dependent learning (Bower, 1981, 1987) may operate here: Patients who are in a very good mood may have difficulty remembering the negative things associated with their moods. When this happens, continue to gently probe and perhaps use the secondary retrospective reports of the patients' loved ones. Additionally, it is useful to encourage patients to record events in a daily journal, so that they are not dependent on long-term free recall but rather can jog their memories through recognition of recorded events.

TESTING THE REALITY OF HYPERPOSITIVE THOUGHTS AND BELIEFS

Cognitive therapists routinely help depressed patients test the reality of their thinking. Having said this, we wish to clarify that we do not believe that there is one true "reality" to which everyone should subscribe. The constructivist viewpoint in cognitive psychotherapy maintains that each person actively creates his or her own reality, through perceptions, interpretations, idiosyncratic memories, and narrative stories (see Mahoney, 1995; Ramsay, 1998). Our view takes the constructivist approach into account while still maintaining that there are reasonably definable, objective standards of reality of which people must be aware if they are to function adaptively in society. We strive to help depressed, bipolar patients ascertain this standard through self-assessment, observations of others' viewpoints and actions, problem-solving, and thinking in more productive ways. The goal is not to make patients think idle positive thoughts but rather to help them weigh evidence more fairly and objectively, against a backdrop of general hopefulness (see Newman & Haaga, 1995).

When patients show signs of hypomania and mania, cognitive therapists try to show them how to do reality-testing of their extremely positive thinking. The goal is not to make them feel sad or to "burst their bubble," but instead to help them weigh the facts more carefully and perhaps seek outside opinions before acting on their beliefs.

It is very important to find respectful, face-saving ways to help the euphoric or highly agitated bipolar patients to achieve some balance in their viewpoints. One way to do this is to emphasize the patients' autonomous role in keeping themselves in check.

Using Daily Thought Records

Toward this end, Daily Thought Records (DTRs; see J. S. Beck, 1995) represent a central technique. DTRs are a structured method through which patients can do the work of reality-testing on themselves, thus enhancing their self-efficacy and preserving their need for a sense of control.

The following are some informal categories of hyperpositive thinking that we and our patients have assessed:

- overestimations of one's capabilities ("I can do no wrong" statements),
- overreliance on luck ("It will all work out somehow" statements),
- underestimations of risk ("I can get away with it" statements),
- minimization of life problems ("I don't have a care in the world" statements), and
- overvaluing of immediate gratification ("I need it right now!" statements).

Therapists can teach patients to monitor and identify these classes of hyperpositive thinking in the same manner that they teach them to spot and change depressotypic thinking. Some errors of inference are common to both dysphoria and euphoria (although with the opposite valence; see Leahy & Beck, 1988), such as all-or-none thinking, jumping to conclusions, overgeneralization, emotional reasoning, mind-reading, personalizing, and others.

For example, the following two automatic thoughts both may be characterized by the errors of jumping to conclusions and mind-reading:

- "She wants to work with me on the project. She must be attracted to me. I think I'll make a play for her. I can't miss!"
- "She wants to work with me on the project. She must think I'll do all the work for her. She must think I'm a poor, stupid fool. I guess I am, because I let people like her take advantage of me."

Patients associate emotional problems with the latter of these automatic thoughts but not necessarily the former. Therefore, it is important that therapists assist euphoric patients in recognizing the maladaptive potential of the first example above. A rational response that would fit both automatic thoughts above is the following:

"It is nice that she wants to work with me. Perhaps she likes me. Perhaps she thinks well of my work. Maybe she thinks she can learn from me. Then again, maybe she wants to prove something to *me* about her skills. Then again, I could be making a big deal over nothing. Maybe it would simply be convenient for the two of us to share this project. I'll just do my job responsibly and see what happens."

Bipolar patients who are in a "high" emotional phase may construe this use of the DTR as an attempt to make their lives dull and to spoil their fun. It is vital that therapists address this concern when it arises (as tipped off by the patient's nonverbal displeasure or reluctance to practice the technique) and work to generate rational responses that clearly engender a healthy degree of optimism and contentment. The patients then can write these responses on a series of flashcards that they can use at their convenience during the week as prompts. The following are examples of such flashcards:

- "Take it one step at a time. You don't have to do everything at once."
- "I can be more in control of the situation if I think things through slowly and carefully."
- "It is okay to consult with others about my ideas and plans. It does *not* mean I am weak, or indecisive, or insecure. It just means that I value certain other people's ideas."
- "Sleep on it. Then decide tomorrow."
- "Don't make a scene. Show some quiet dignity."

Flashcards are quite useful when the patients are more responsive to their own reminders to themselves than they are to others' reminders. In this way, they can slow themselves down and feel that they are controlling their own lives.

Using Behavioral Experiments

A behavioral experiment involves patients engaging in real-life experiments to test out the veracity of their automatic thoughts and beliefs. For example, a dysphoric person who believes that it is "pointless" to try to work on his dissertation may be encouraged to test this assumption by spending a designated hour at his computer. The patient's subsequent involvement in the activity may increase his sense of mastery and lift his mood, thus refuting the hypothesis that the task has no merit. This is a tried-and-true method with depressed patients, whose negative expectations, inertia, and hopelessness often discourage them from acting on their environment to bring about positive reinforcement and change.

With bipolar patients who are in an "up" phase, however, this powerful technique must be used judiciously and with caution. This is so because unlike dysphoric patients, euphoric patients tend to experiment with their beliefs in an excessive manner. For example, if a hypomanic patient contends that "no harm will result" if he takes a spontaneous trip and misses a few days of work without telling his boss, it is unwise to set up a behavioral experiment that encourages him to test his theory. The therapist may prove a point about the patient's underestimation of risk, but the patient may lose his job in the process.

Instead, therapists can use behavioral experiments to test the plausibility of *not* following through on a hyperpositive idea. For example, the patient above may contend that he will "suffocate" if he doesn't escape from his job for a few days. The therapist can entreat the patient to see what would actually happen if he remained at work. Likewise, the therapist and patient also could test the advisability of the patient's requesting a vacation sometime in the near future. The patient might think, "I can't wait that long; and besides, telling my boss up front would take all the sport out of it." This too becomes a belief that may be tested. Will asking his boss for a vacation instead of sneaking away really take all the fun out of the trip? This can be tested, with reduced risk to the patient's job. In summary, behavioral experiments are to be used to test negative beliefs about "playing it safe" or "being responsible."

Consulting With Trusted Others

Bipolar patients who are in an expansive state often believe that they are able to generate new plans and ideas that are exciting, profitable, and guaranteed to lead to success. One example is a working father of four who enthusiastically told his therapist that he wanted to quit his job so he could go to law school. This patient's wife did not work, and the patient's lack of success in college 15 years earlier did not bode well for his acceptance into a professional school. Another example is a young woman who planned to purchase a highly powerful motorcycle, even though she had no experience driving even a moderately sized machine.

In both of these cases, the therapist surmised immediately that the patients' ideas and plans were ill-conceived and would likely lead to trouble. The therapist also knew that he would be unsuccessful in dissuading the patients from following through on their plans if he merely gave them negative feedback. This is so because euphoric patients commonly have strong drives to feel in control of their own fates; they do not appreciate outside interference, and they certainly do not take kindly to therapists who rain on their parade.

At the same time, therapists in such cases are remiss if they say nothing. Although it is important to do everything possible to preserve the positive, collaborative nature of the therapeutic relationship, therapists also have an important responsibility to provide their patients with corrective feedback. If the therapist says nothing, this may communicate (by omission) tacit agreement with the patients' risky plans.

To minimize this sort of problem, therapists should help their patients see the benefits of making use of their social support system for consultative advice. The *two-person feedback rule* is a helpful technique along these lines. During periods in the patients' treatment when their mood is euthymic, therapists make a collaborative agreement with the patients: Any patient idea or plan that the therapist cannot safely endorse will be shelved until at least two other people are consulted on the matter. The results of this polling of two independent observers are discussed in the next therapy session.

For example, the above-mentioned father of four who wanted to sacrifice his sole source of income to attend law school was asked to consult with both his wife and his best friend. The therapist, in turn, agreed to ask his clinical supervisor what she thought of the idea. The therapist and patient agreed to discuss the results of their respective consultations the following week. In the end, the patient was quite displeased at the discouraging feedback that he received. However, after following through with this assignment, he was more willing to listen to the compelling reasons against his ill-advised idea than he would have been had the therapist flatly given him a directive to abandon his plans.

The two-person feedback rule alerts the patient to the need for feedback as a general rule. This is noteworthy because many hypomanic and manic patients impulsively enact their ill-fated plans without first sharing their notions with others. If patients believe that they would be losing a sense of control and dignity by asking others for advice, we nicely remind them that the most successful people in life generally have a cadre of personal advisors and consultants. We ask patients to ponder why this is so. Put this way, they often can articulate that it is wise and constructive to nurture these kinds of relationships with trustworthy, sensible others. It is a smart way to get vital information and to make ample use of inter-personal resources.

Using Productive Potential vs. Destructive Risk Ratings

As mentioned previously, one of the signs indicating that bipolar patients are going into a hypomanic or manic phase is that they begin to take undue risks. This happens either because they underestimate the harm that their behavior can cause, or because they overestimate the benefit or entertainment that they would derive from their activities (Leahy, 1999).

When therapists assess that their bipolar patients are engaging in unwise risk-taking behavior, they need to find a diplomatic way to ask their patients to spell out the pros and cons of the behavior in question. One such vehicle for this strategy is the *productive potential vs. destructive risk rating technique*. This is done by creating two columns on a sheet of paper or by using both sides of an open spiral notebook. On the left side the patient is instructed to write about the productive potential of the plan in question. On the right side the patient is to list the ways in which the intended plan creates destructive risk (Exhibit 3.3 is a sample exercise in which a hypomanic patient evaluates his intention to quit his job in favor of making a living through online trading).

This technique allows patients to make useful discoveries for themselves and therefore reduces the likelihood that they will be annoyed at others (including the therapist) who they perceive are trying to control them. If patients are unable to generate items under the destructive risk

EXHIBIT 3.3
"Productive Potential" vs. "Destructive Risk" of Quitting Job and Doing E-trading All Day as a Source of Income

Productive Potential	Destructive Risk
1. I could make a small fortune.	1. The trading fees could "nickel-and-dime" me to death.
2. I could sharpen my analytic skills by doing daily research of stocks.	2. If I get the least bit depressed, I could lose my edge. I might even stay in bed and miss out on important opportunities.
3. I could become the envy of my working-stiff friends.	3. I might become obsessed with the computer and never socialize again.
4. My parents would finally have to reckon with the superiority of my ideas.	4. I could take a financial hit because of unexpected market forces in these volatile times.
	5. If I regretted leaving my job and my friends there, it would be too late to go back and I'll be majorly bummed.

column, therapists should volunteer to offer some examples. They then suggest negative consequences that the patients are asked to ponder. With each item that the therapist generates, patients are asked how much they believe these drawbacks are true, on a scale of 0 to 100. The higher the degree of belief, the more successful the technique.

If patients maintain that the risk is low, therapists must persevere with the technique by asking them again to try to generate their own list of cons. One way to facilitate this strategy is to ask the patient,

> "In your experience, how has this idea *not* worked out in the way you wanted it to in the past? How have other really exciting ideas that you have had in the past *not* panned out for you? What commonly goes wrong? What can you learn from these unfortunate past experiences that you can apply now in this situation, *before* you suffer any consequences?"

A variation of this technique is the *benefit to others vs. cost to myself rating*. This technique follows the same format as above but specifically targets those situations in which euphoric patients are maladaptively generous with their money, time, and efforts. Examples include the patient who routinely lends his playboy brother large sums of money with which to go out on the town and the patient who devotes tremendous amounts of time and energy to a political or social cause at the expense of his social life and health.

In each of the above hypothetical cases, it is readily demonstrable that the patients' actions lead to moderate benefit (at most) to others, while incurring huge costs to themselves. This inequity can be solved if patients agree to diminish the lengths to which they go to be excessively generous. When bipolar patients resist using this intervention, it is common to find that they harbor a schema of unlovability (cf. J. E. Young, 1994). In their elated and driven states, they believe that by making great personal sacrifices they will obtain love. Furthermore, they may believe that if they do not go to these martyrlike extremes, they will be rejected, shunned, forgotten, or otherwise devalued. In such cases, the patients' unlovability schemas become an important focus of treatment. A central goal is to help the patients to see that they do not have to go to extremes to prove their worth.

Yet another variation of the technique of assessing the pros and cons of extreme behavior is the opposite of the above, namely, the *benefit to myself vs. cost to others method*. This form of the pros and cons strategy can be used when patients are acting out in such a way as to cause great inconvenience or harm to others. Examples include a person who repeatedly cheats on his wife and does not inform her about his herpes infection and a fellow who rapidly squanders all of the money from the inheritance that had been earmarked for his children's college education.

We often find that patients who are "high" and "racing" do not focus on the harm that they are causing others. They believe that they are merely having fun or living life to the fullest. Sometimes they may profess to be having so much fun that they do not care about the consequences for themselves. In these instances, therapists may gain some leverage in persuading patients to change their destructive behavior by focusing their attention on the negative consequences to others.

Using Devil's Advocacy Role-Playing and Debating

Hypomanic and manic patients often maintain overvalued ideas. An example is a college student who believed that his philosophical discussions with others in his dormitory were much more important than doing any of his assignments or studying for exams. Consequently, he spent hours going from room to room in his dorm, engaging anyone who would listen in discussions on the meaning of life and other transcendental issues. As a result, "Lanny" was in danger of failing two of his four courses.

Consistent with typical euphoric ideation, Lanny held that his ideas were unassailable and that his powers of logic were formidable. He also showed no obvious signs of anxiety that his point of view may lead him down the wrong path. The therapist therefore chose not to challenge Lanny's ideas directly. Instead, he challenged him to a debate, but Lanny had to take the devil's advocate position. In other words, Lanny's job was to argue why it is important to spend at least as much time studying as talking about the meaning of life with friends, whereas the therapist was to defend the premise that schoolwork was superfluous and unimportant in comparison to the sharing of existential ideas with his friends.

At first, Lanny demurred, saying that he did not believe in the devil's advocate position and therefore could not debate in its favor. The therapist retorted in a way that was intended to appeal to the patient's inflated confidence and euphoric grandiosity. He argued that Lanny should have no trouble debating from any point of view. In fact, the therapist added, the mark of a truly great mind is the ability to make compelling arguments from both sides of an issue. Lanny then accepted the challenge and engaged in the devil's advocacy debate, whereby he argued against his own overvalued ideas. A condensed version of the reverse role-play dialogue is as follows:

> *Therapist:* I think that grades are meaningless. The only important aspect of a college education is talking to other people and discussing the deep topics of life.
>
> *Lanny:* Well, grades are important, too.

Therapist:	Oh, don't tell me you buy into that whole business of grade-point averages and all that meaningless numerical stuff!
Lanny:	Well, it's what gets you a diploma.
Therapist:	What good is a diploma if all you are is a trained robot who can spit out facts, but you can't think for yourself, and you can't relate to other people at the most meaningful level?
Lanny:	I think you can get good grades and still learn to think for yourself and have intelligent conversations.
Therapist:	How are you supposed to do *that*? Studying for exams and writing papers takes all your time! All you would do all day is stay in the library, all by yourself, and probably sleeping in the carrels half the time. You would have no friends and no life!
Lanny:	Other students manage to study, and write papers, and still have a life.
Therapist:	How do they do *that*? Darned if I know how.
Lanny:	They just balance their time. They study hard when they're supposed to study, and they socialize "hard" when they they're relaxing. They just find a way to do both.
Therapist:	I don't think I can do that.
Lanny:	Well, then you have a problem with all-or-none thinking!

At this point, the therapist stopped the role-play and asked Lanny what he thought. Lanny's first response was, "Do I *really* sound like that?" The therapist nodded. Lanny came back with the question, "Don't people get annoyed with me?" The therapist, trying not to shame Lanny, shifted into problem-solving mode and asked, "What can you do about it, Lanny?" The discussion then shifted into a search for methods of good time management, so that Lanny could study, write, *and* socialize.

It is interesting and perhaps predictable that what emerged from these discussions was Lanny's fear that his bipolar illness would prevent him from succeeding academically in the traditional manner. He believed that he was likely to flunk out of college, because he was unable to study and write as well as was required. Lanny came to realize that his arguments about the primacy of existential discussions and the unimportance of grades was an example of sour grapes. It was a cover for his incompetency schema (see Winters & Neale, 1985). This is a modest example of how the case conceptualization invariably plays a role in determining the power of a given technique.

The *devil's advocate role-play technique* can be an eye-opener for patients such as Lanny. In the course of proving their debating prowess, patients force themselves to verbalize alternative points of view that they had previously refused to consider. The result is that they become more credulous of competing (adaptive) hypotheses. Following the completion of the role-play, therapists ask their patients to experiment with behaving in ways (between sessions) that are consistent with the new, improved mindset.

A further benefit of this technique, as demonstrated by Lanny, is that patients get to hear what they themselves sound like to others. By listening to the therapists' respectful impersonations, patients may become more open to hearing the flaws in their overvalued ideas. Additionally, they may gain some understanding into why others have shown impatience with them. Moreover, when bipolar patients hear their therapists accurately re-creating their views in the debate, they achieve a better sense that their therapists are listening carefully.

As with any rational restructuring technique, the devil's advocate role-play should be discussed fully following its completion. Ideally, therapists can persuade their patients to write down the principles that have been derived from the exercise and ideas regarding their implementation in everyday life. In the case of Lanny, he was willing to experiment with studying additional hours in the following week. This was quite helpful in its own right, in terms of Lanny's scholastic productivity. However, it also proved to be fertile ground for discussing Lanny's insecurities as a student. When in a normal or depressive mood, Lanny believed that he was a failure as a student. In his more euphoric states, he disguised this fundamental self-doubt by maintaining that his philosophical discussions transcended "mere schoolwork." The reverse role-play and resultant homework assignment brought this problem into the open for discussion in therapy.

REDUCING IMPULSIVITY AND RECKLESSNESS

Closely related to the set of techniques that helps bipolar patients test the reality of their hyperpositive thoughts is the following series of interventions that help them slow down and think before acting. On the surface, these strategies look more "behavioral" than those previously mentioned, but it will become apparent that this division is artificial. The following techniques naturally combine and overlap with those that seemingly are more "cognitive" or "affective."

Using the "Wait 48 Hours Before Acting Rule"

Bipolar patients who are in an "up" phase tend to be quite impatient, if not impulsive. They may benignly interpret their behavior as "spontaneous," but this just serves as permission-giving for behaviors they wish to enact right now but may regret later. A stark example comes from Lanny, who got the "thrilling" idea of skating down a partially frozen river during an extremely cold spell in Philadelphia. He reported that he would have carried out this action right away but that his roommate was present to talk him out of it.

A simple behavioral technique, the *wait 48 hours before acting* rule, asks that patients agree to keep a log of the day and times when they entertain notions about doing something bold, risky, wild, or out of the ordinary, such as Lanny's plan to skate the Schuylkill River. Then, they are to wait 48 hours before taking any action on the idea. In the meantime, they are encouraged to use the two-person feedback rule as well. The purpose of this technique is to give patients a chance to reconsider acting on their affect-driven temptations and to avoid the often-made human error of making life-altering decisions when in a state of high emotional arousal (e.g., quitting a job immediately after a disagreement with the boss; proposing marriage during the heat of passion with a new partner).

In explaining the rationale for this 2-day delay, therapists tell their patients that,

> "If it's a good idea now, it will still be a good idea in 2 days. If it's not a good idea now, it may take you a couple of days before you start having second thoughts about the matter—the kinds of thoughts that may save you a lot of trouble. The 2-day wait is insurance."

Furthermore, therapists can challenge their patients to show the ability to delay gratification by demonstrating restraint. If patients can succeed in putting off something they really have the urge to do, then this is a sign that they are not succumbing to the impulsivity that is characteristic of mania. Instead, they are making their most important decisions after a period of cool deliberation, which minimizes the chances of acting in ways that bring about regrets.

Therapists also must stipulate that patients wait until they have had at least one good night's sleep before they carry out their plans. This is very important when patients are in a full-blown manic episode and therefore sleep very little. A 2-day wait may be insufficient if no significant sleep has taken place in the interim. Because patients in this state resist following this rule, they should be encouraged to contact their therapists if they believe they will not be able to delay their actions for the requisite period of time.

Foreseeing Negative Consequences Through Imagery

In stark contrast to depressive states, euphoric and impulsive states make it very difficult for patients to envision worst case scenarios. Euphoric patients expect that their impulsive, thrill-seeking behavior will not cause appreciable harm. They may foresee only positive results, or they simply may be so enamored by the process of their actions that the outcome seems inconsequential by comparison (e.g., engaging in sexual intercourse without a condom). In such instances, the person is taking the adage "live for the moment" to maladaptive extremes.

For example, when Lanny wanted to skate down a thinly frozen river, he could focus only on the feelings of power and freedom he anticipated from the activity. He even went so far as to contend that such a stunt would make him a "legend" to his friends (which might have been true). Lanny did not envision the possibility that he might freeze, drown, or be arrested. This example represents manic patients' deficits in controlling their own behavior. However, one skill that can help compensate for this problem is the mental imaging of negative outcomes.

When a therapist ascertains that a hypomanic or manic patient intends to do something reckless, the therapist can elicit the patient's cooperation in undergoing a guided-imagery exercise. Here, the therapist's job is to present a number of plausible but terrible outcomes for the patient to picture. In Lanny's case, some examples were as follows:

- taking two strides and falling through the ice, then freezing for 10 minutes before going under. Lanny envisioned his funeral, with his parents sobbing, his siblings stone-faced, and his roommate cursing himself for letting him go to the river without telling anyone;
- skating for a while, then partially falling through the ice, extricating himself, and later developing a nasty illness from toxic chemicals in the water (perhaps going on to imagine suffering from diarrhea, nausea, fever, and painful skin sores);[1]
- skating for a few minutes, then exiting into the hands of the police, who immediately handcuff him; and
- completing the skate, only to have word get back to the school, whereupon he is placed on academic probation.

On completion of this exercise, therapists should probe for the patient's thoughts about the images. Therapists can ask these questions:

- "How much do you believe that this image could really occur?"
- "How much did you consider the likelihood of this potential outcome before?"

---

[1]This imagery example represents the therapist's taking "poetic license," as the Schuylkill River, the renowned site of national and international regattas, is (as far as we surmise) far more appealing and less polluted than the imagery technique would suggest.

- "Now that you have envisioned this possible outcome, how does it affect your desire to carry out the behavior?"

These questions help therapists assess how much the imagery technique has made a therapeutic impact on the patients and serve to reinforce further the main points of the intervention.

Scheduling Activities

Hypomanic and manic patients are active to a fault. Their actions may be excessively goal-directed (Johnson, Sandrow, et al., 1999), such as staying up for three straight nights rebuilding an engine in the garage, or scattered and disorganized, such as continually starting projects and then abandoning them to start other ill-fated tasks.

Engaging in excessive activities can lead to a further driving of the mania, leading to a vicious cycle of poor decision-making, greater problems, more ineffective activities, and further absence of thoughtful deliberation before acting. Ultimately, the patient crashes because of exhaustion, becomes depressed, and then has to face a slew of newly hatched problems. In such cases it is clearly advantageous to help patients slow down and do fewer activities.

The Daily Activity Schedule (DAS; J. S. Beck, 1995) helps patients chart their activities each day. The value of this technique goes beyond mere assessment. First, it focuses the patient's limited or scattered attention on something specific and important. Second, the act of monitoring activities alone may subtly influence a "speeding" patient to slow down. Third, the DAS can be used prescriptively to plan a reasonable amount of work and other activities for the coming week. If the patient greatly exceeds the plan, then evidence will have been gathered demonstrating that he or she is overextended.

It is usually a good idea to ask patients to plan their activities first and then eliminate the lowest priority items from the schedule. If patients are unable or unwilling to do this, their beliefs about the task must be assessed. Sometimes, their explanation is that "everything is important." This lays bare the nature of their all-or-none thinking, because it is statistically impossible for everything in life to be of equal priority.

Sometimes, patients believe that they would be remiss or lazy if they were to eliminate some items from their DAS, or that they would experience overwhelming regret if they denied themselves any opportunity for living life to the fullest (Leahy, 1999). These are hypotheses that can be tested. For example, the therapist and patient can set up a behavioral experiment whereby the patient schedules some "down time" into the DAS and then assesses the effects of some rest and relaxation on his or her mood, well-being, and productivity on other tasks. When patients follow the true spirit of this assignment, they sometimes find that, when they curb their frenetic pace, they actually accomplish more and with fewer problems.

Patients who use the DAS also can rate the degrees of mastery and pleasure they derive from each listed activity. In general, doing things that give one a sense of joy and accomplishment improve one's quality of life. However, in the case of hypomania and mania, caution must be exercised. Patients in these states may view *mastery* as synonymous with acts of daring. The results may be something far less than a true accomplishment. Similarly, euphoric patients may interpret *pleasure* as consisting of all manner of hedonistic pursuits, no matter what the risk. Therefore, therapists should be very clear with patients that mastery activities can involve the "achievement" of showing restraint in the face of temptation. For example, it is a useful homework assignment for patients to chart all the times that they were "masters of their impulses." Along the same lines, therapists should define *pleasure* as consisting of the simple, everyday joys of life, usually involving creating something rather than consuming something. We encourage patients to plant gardens; write letters, stories, poetry, and journals; paint and sketch; sing and dance; knit and craft; do yoga and tai chi chuan; and so forth. These are much more powerful, enduring, and self-esteem enhancing pleasures when compared to consumptive behaviors such as excessive gambling, spending, eating, drinking, recreational sex, and other behaviors that produce addictive potential, social consequences, and shame.

Increasing Sitting and Listening

Bipolar patients in a high phase seem to be on their feet a great deal. Moreover, in conversation they tend to be poor listeners. This is partly so because their bodies and minds are in overdrive. Their sympathetic nervous systems seem to be in high gear, and they are continually prepared to act with extreme energy. Additionally, they are experiencing flights of ideas and therefore are not very capable of focusing their attentions on other people's comments or ideas (including their therapists').

Two surprisingly simple techniques can be helpful in providing for a temporary break from these problems. The first is that patients are to sit down when they notice that they are speaking or gesticulating rapidly when interacting socially, in person or on the telephone. This simple behavioral maneuver tends to interrupt the acceleration of motor activity and to reduce the risk of acting in socially inappropriate ways.

Second, therapists instruct patients to focus their attentional energy on listening to other people speak. This helps patients deploy their attention away from their own racing thoughts and keeps them engaged in their interpersonal interactions. If they report that they have a difficult time concentrating on the other person, they can rehearse a number of self-statements that orient them to the importance of what the other person is saying. Such covert prompts may include the following:

- "Pay attention. Listen to [name of the other person]."
- "This is a meaningful conversation. Don't miss it!"
- "Show that you care about [name of the other person] by paying attention."
- "Be a friend. Be aware. Be *with* [name of the other person]."
- "Keep listening to and talking with [name of the other person]."

At times, we have stimulated the patients' interest level in this technique by hinting that it is a trade secret of psychotherapists. After all, therapists are only as effective as their listening skills. The message is clear: Sitting and listening looks professional.

Using Anticipatory Problem-Solving

There are two major classes of problems that bipolar patients need to learn to anticipate and trouble-shoot in advance:

1. general life stressors that agitate patients and put them at risk for a recurrence or an exacerbation of symptoms (Johnson & Miller, 1997; Johnson & Roberts, 1995) and
2. early signs that warn of an impending dysfunctional elevation of mood (Lam & Wong, 1997).

When bipolar patients are under stress, that is, when their coping resources are heavily taxed, they are at increased risk for mood abnormalities. Therefore, therapists must help patients become more effective problem-solvers and copers. Because the onset of a hypomanic or manic episode impairs the individual's capacity for adaptive coping (the aforementioned techniques notwithstanding), it is wise to teach patients to identify and begin to address problems before they become full-blown.

This teaching process involves several components:

- retrospectively evaluating past crises—how they started, how they became unmanageable, and what could have been done to avert their occurrence;
- setting short-term goals in major life areas, such as work, relationships, and recreation, with patients monitoring their progress on a regular basis;
- mapping out the steps that are necessary to achieve these goals;
- hypothesizing or spotting potential obstacles to taking these steps; and

- dealing with these obstacles using standard problem-solving techniques (defining the problem, brainstorming solutions, evaluating pros and cons of each solution, choosing the most advantageous or most conservative of these options, implementing the choice, and monitoring the outcome; Nezu, Nezu, & Perri, 1989).

Therapists instruct their patients to take stock of their most common early-warning signs of a hypomanic or manic episode. Family members may help if patients allow them to be "spot-checkers" of their mood and behavior. One patient was very successful in recognizing her warning signs because she was willing to let her husband cue her regarding potential problems. For example, when she stayed up late at night more than two nights in a row, her husband called this to her attention and encouraged her to get a full night's sleep; when she began to make so many plans that she barely had any time in her schedule, he entreated her to stay at home for a leisurely night of watching movies, and worked with her to figure out a way to eliminate lower priority items from her schedule; and when she began to drink (which potentiated her mood swings), he "allowed" her one drink and then suggested a "fun" alternative such as a milkshake, hot cocoa, or a special tea.

These interventions worked because the patient had given her husband her blessing in giving her such feedback. Therefore, she did not feel that he was infringing on her freedom (see chapters 6 and 8 for more on spousal and family involvement in treatment). However, this type of assistance is not always welcomed by patients. In such cases, the meaning of the situation for the patient should be discussed. This may lead to fruitful therapeutic discussions about the patient's sense of autonomy, dependency, trust, fear, shame, and other significant emotions and beliefs about the self.

Therapists have to walk a fine line between patients and their loved ones who are looking out for them. On the one hand, therapists must support their patients' attempts to self-regulate and show respect for their knowledge and awareness of themselves. On the other hand, therapists must remember that patients who are on a high often need an outside reality check and that loved ones often can provide this. Furthermore, loved ones who have suffered as a result of the actings out of the patient warrant empathy as well. If they react with alarm to changes in the patients' behavior, this is understandable. This is a tricky balancing act when involving family and other loved ones in treatment.

Using Stimulus Control

Bipolar patients would do well to minimize or avoid altogether certain situations and activities:

- alcohol and other unprescribed drug use;
- unsupervised expenditures of large sums of money (e.g., going to auto dealerships, taking part in online stock trading, going to the race track or casinos, shopping at expensive boutiques, making purchases from the home through the Internet or the television);
- daredevil hobbies, especially those in which they have had insufficient experience (e.g., skydiving, deep sea scuba diving, auto or motorcycle racing, rock climbing, or other such activities in which the taking of excessive risks can lead to death);
- exaggerated acts of generosity, friendship, trust, or gregariousness with relative strangers (e.g., casual sex, befriending street people, lending money willy-nilly to acquaintances or distant relatives, being overly friendly with police officers and other public employees, trying to contact famous celebrities); and
- activities that entail the use of a lethal weapon (e.g., hunting, target shooting, archery, launching fireworks).

These are but a few of the activities that are contraindicated in the lives of patients who are prone to act impulsively, with inflated self-confidence, and without giving negative consequences due consideration in advance. In addition to the aforementioned examples, there are other problematic situations that can put bipolar patients at risk for dysfunctional mood shifts and energy surges:

- making contact with the person or people who typically collude with the patients in reckless behaviors (e.g., former extramarital lovers, drug cohorts, gambling buddies);
- taking on jobs or responsibilities that require extreme hours or disruptions in sleeping and eating habits (e.g., working three jobs, switching to graveyard shift, agreeing to work on too many projects, traveling incessantly); and
- doing things that test limits just for the thrill factor (e.g., deliberately waiting until the last minute before leaving for important appointments or before starting critically important tasks, provoking high emotionality in significant others, experimenting with the limits of significant lying, being cavalier about taking the appropriate medications in the prescribed dosages at the required times).

Generally speaking, it is neither necessary nor wise for therapists to present bipolar patients with a pat list of prohibitions, such as those listed above. As mentioned previously, euphoric, irritable patients are highly reactive to the sense of being under someone else's control. Therapists must remember to take as collaborative a stance as possible, lest patients wind up doing the very things that they have been advised not to do.

One way for therapists to be collaborative is to ask patients to assess and list their own contraindicated situations and to take part in the task of monitoring themselves. When patients who are on a high get the sense that they are being treated respectfully instead of in a patronizing manner, they may become more willing to be forthcoming with the truth about their activities. Furthermore, they may be more receptive to feedback from therapists who openly admit that they cannot force the patients to do anything (or stop doing anything) against their will.

Another way therapists can maximize collaboration is by compromising on setting limits. Some of the stimulation-seeking behaviors in which bipolar patients engage are not necessarily reckless, and they may serve the function of keeping them satisfied with normal everyday living. For example, a patient may concede that it is inadvisable to gamble, or to go car shopping on a whim, or to frequent prostitutes. He may be willing to relinquish these activities if he can compensate for the loss of stimulation by doing exciting things such as playing in paint-ball competitions, taking guided canoeing trips, attending rock concerts and sporting events, planning unusual day trips, visiting with friends who are out of town, and so on. Therapist and patient can decide as a team at what point the interesting activities cease serving a satiation function and start potentiating problematic craving for further stimulation.

MODULATING AFFECT

The following are methods that specifically and directly target the bipolar patients' problems with euphoric and irritable mood. Many patients contend at first that their moods are completely autonomous of their volition. They maintain that when their moods are "driven up," there is "nothing that can be done." We agree that it is quite difficult to rein in an expansive and grandiose mood state. However, we also have seen how certain techniques can curb the patients' moods just enough to allow for a reduction of impulsivity, an increase in the patients' willingness to engage in cognitive and behavioral interventions, and a potential "softening" of their otherwise inevitable crash-landing moods.

Using Relaxation and Breathing Control

The hypomanic and manic patients' excessive euphoria and irritability can be modulated somewhat by physical exercises that slow down sympathetic nervous system activity. Standard relaxation exercises (e.g., Jacobsonian "tense and relax" method; see Goldfried & Davison, 1994) can help patients diminish their adrenaline surges and thus decrease the intensity of their arousal. This, in turn, feeds into a reduction in the risk that patients will act out their extreme emotions.

In a similar way that patients with panic disorder benefit from learning to control their breathing (Salkovskis & Clark, 1989), patients with bipolar disorder can slow themselves down by noticing and decreasing their tendency toward hyperventilation. Patients can be taught to use their intense emotionality as a cue to get themselves to sit down, close their eyes, and to breathe slowly and smoothly but not too deeply. Therapists instruct the patients to breathe in "gentle, wavelike fashion," as opposed to fits and starts. Inhaling should crest lightly into exhaling, which in turn should flow almost imperceptibly into inhaling. These cycles should be slow—not more than 8 to 10 per minute for the average person with healthy pulmonary functioning.

Using "Longevity vs. Intensity of Feelings Ratings"

It is well established that hypomanic and manic patients often demonstrate temporary, high-intensity affect. Examples include sudden, marked irritability that is excessive for the situation and emotional expansiveness typified by an impulsive outpouring of love for another person. In these instances, patients are at risk for acting on these emotions, potentially causing social embarrassment and harm to important relationships. Aside from challenging the patients' beliefs that they must demonstrate their feelings overtly (which is addressed by techniques such as the DTR), the technique below teaches patients to rationally evaluate their emotions directly.

Intense emotions are very compelling; they seem to act as drives that force patients to express them. Additionally, their very intensity is such that patients cannot imagine ever having felt (or ever again feeling) another way. This is especially true when emotions such as anger and romantic ardor are involved. People are very apt to maintain the belief that "the more *intense* the emotion, the more *real* it is, and the more I must act on it without delay." Given that the strong emotions of the patient fluctuate, the fallacy of this belief is soon laid bare, but not before significant damage may be done. Examples include a man who quits his job at the height of anger, only to be remorseful and regretful the next day, and a person who engages in an impulsive sexual encounter at a party and then worries about HIV/AIDS for months to come.

Therapists must explain to such patients that they must test out the *longevity* of their emotions before deciding whether to consider acting on them. Patients are asked to keep a daily log of their level of emotionality about a given subject or person. The ratings are made on an intensity scale from 0 to 100, where 0 = *no feelings at all; numbness, indifference*; 20 = *some feelings, but mild*; 40 = *moderate intensity of feelings, but no compulsion to express*; 60 = *strong feelings that you would like to express verbally*; 80 = *very strong feelings that you wish to act upon*; and 100 = *overwhelming feelings that consume you and force you to act.*

The patient charts these emotional intensity ratings at least twice a day, every day, between therapy sessions. The patient's task is to discover how the intensity of the feelings holds up over the course of a week or longer. If the patient complies with this assignment, it will provide therapeutic benefits no matter what the data indicate. If the intensity of the feelings wanes over the course of the week, then the patient learns an important lesson about the advantages of waiting to test the staying power of an emotion before acting on it. If the feelings persist at a high level, the patient benefits from the reflective delay brought about by self-monitoring. Additionally, the therapist gains valuable data as to whether this topic should become a central focus in the therapy session. Patients learn a useful skill when they learn to make distinctions between the intensity and longevity of emotions and therefore put less stock in their beliefs and intentions about high-powered but short-lived feeling states.

Using Therapist Modeling and Role-Playing

One of the most obvious (yet subtle) ways that therapists can help their euphoric or irritable patients modulate their emotions is by consistently maintaining their own expressed affect within a safe, neutral zone. Therapists potentially are extremely important models in their patients' lives and therefore have an important responsibility to act in a manner that they would have their patients emulate.

When patients become angry and aggressive in session, there may be great temptation for therapists to attempt to restore control and order by raising their voices (or by using other forceful gestures). By and large, this is an inadvisable strategy. If therapists react angrily, the risk of a rupture in the therapeutic relationship increases significantly (Newman, 1997). Also, therapists will be providing their patients with less than sterling examples of how to act when under stress. On the flip side, patients who act giddy in session may amuse their therapists into acting silly themselves. Again, such actions are contraindicated, because this serves only to provide positive social reinforcement for the patients' inappropriate elation.

We are not suggesting that therapists should act as lifeless, humorless dullards in session. There are many examples of therapists being both stern and humorous that are well within the bounds of appropriate therapeutic behavior. What we are suggesting is that therapists refrain from trying to maintain control in sessions with intensely emotional patients by unwisely trying to match their patients' fevered pitches. Instead, therapists can adopt a "conservation of energy" policy, whereby they respond to patients' racing speech, laughing, and yelling by remaining cool and collected. At the same time, therapists should give direct feedback and demonstrate their ongoing involvement and interest in their patients. The strong, sedate, dignified approach serves the best calming influence and solidifies the therapists' positions as important, healthy role models.

Addressing Patients' Desire to Experience the "Highs"

Bipolar patients who profess to obtain great joy and meaning from life while in their hypomanic or manic phases pose serious challenges to their therapists. This is so because such patients often do not wish to relinquish their euphoric moods, thoughts, and behaviors. Therefore, they are most apt to resist interventions that are geared to encourage them to slow down, reflect, and plan things carefully. In addition, these patients also are likely to be the least willing to take their medications.

The experiences of bipolar patients who wish to remain elated are similar to those of patients who abuse illicit stimulants (e.g., cocaine, amphetamines). In both cases, the high is immensely gratifying, and patients may be convinced that nothing else in life can ever produce such a wonderful rush. The immediate reinforcement of the high is so great that it temporarily blinds them to the horrors of the crash that inevitably occurs, as well as the significant negative consequences that occur as a result of their erratic behaviors while "under the influence."

As in the treatment of substance abuse, it does little good for therapists merely to point out the dangers of the high, and it certainly does no good to disparage the patients' desired experiences. Instead, therapists can rely on their collaborative skills—they can ask the patients themselves to spell out the advantages and disadvantages of being euphoric and of being on an even keel. More specifically, the patients can use this technique to evaluate the pros and cons of specific destructive behaviors that are potentiated by the hypomania or mania, such as reckless spending, indiscriminate sexual behavior, driving at great speeds, and other harmful activities.

Next, therapists assist bipolar patients in re-evaluating and testing their beliefs about the high feelings themselves. Some of these beliefs are strikingly similar to those that are espoused by substance abusers (see A. T. Beck, Wright, et al., 1993) and include the following:

- "Life is boring if I stay in control of my moods."
- "I can't be creative unless I am in a high state of mind."
- "Being manic enables me to overcome my shyness."
- "I wouldn't be able to cope with life if I weren't so happy once in a while."

- "My moods are not a problem. I could control them if everybody just got off my case."
- "I can't get things accomplished unless I'm racing."
- "Why shouldn't I do wild and crazy things? It's my life!"

These represent just a few of the problematic beliefs we have elicited from patients who wish to remain euphoric and energized. To modify these beliefs, we use five main strategies (aside from the pros and cons technique mentioned above):

1. We discuss the phenomenon of "crashing," whereby euphoric patients suddenly lapse into abysmal depression. This includes graphically reviewing the times that the patients themselves have gone into the depths of despair following a euphoric run and discussing the means of averting such mood swings, including the importance of doing all that one can to stay within normal limits in the first place.
2. We review past negative results of the patients' euphoric and irritable behaviors, for themselves and for their loved ones.
3. We search the past for evidence of times that a normal mood was associated with self-satisfaction and contentment, and help the patients reminisce about such times in great length and detail.
4. We begin to brainstorm about ways to enjoy life within reasonable limits of mood and behavior. It is not sufficient merely to eliminate maladaptively intense responses; therapists need to help patients replace their hypomanic and manic reactions with alternative, adaptive means by which to feel good.
5. We use bibliotherapy, especially the authoritative and gripping works of Kay Jamison (e.g., 1993, 1995). In *Touched With Fire*, Jamison presented evidence against the notion that writers and artists needed their manic highs to produce great and prolific works. Indeed, she demonstrated that creative masters lost much more than they gained as a result of their bipolar disorder—in terms of concomitant substance abuse, years lost because of suicide attempts and suicide itself, and the progressively dementing process of an untreated disorder. In *An Unquiet Mind*, Jamison acknowledged the powerful allure of mania. However, she went on to argue persuasively —as both a professional and as a person with manic–depressive illness—that there is much to enjoy about life in a more sober state of mind, without the hellish risks of life disintegration brought about by mania.

Additionally, for those patients who have had negative experiences growing up in households in which a parent had bipolar disorder and acted out, a review of the patients' memories and feelings toward the parent (and the negative experiences themselves) serves as a stark reminder of the ugly side of manic highs. The goal is not to reopen old wounds but rather to learn from past experience in as vivid a way as possible.

COMBATING DISORGANIZATION AND DISTRACTIBILITY

One of the less dramatic but considerably problematic symptoms of hypomania and mania is scattered, unfocused thinking. This is typified by flights of ideas and speech, difficulty remaining on task, tangentiality in responding to questions, and the tendency to start and then discontinue personal projects and therapeutic homework assignments alike. Hence, the cognitive styles of bipolar patients sometimes resemble those of people with marked attention deficit disorders (West et al., 1995).

Therapists witness this phenomenon firsthand when patients do not follow session agendas, have difficulty setting priorities, show deficits in their ability to understand the therapists' comments, remember very little of the contents of therapy sessions when they leave the office, and complain to their therapists that "everything is so confusing and overwhelming." One middle-aged patient cried as she told her therapist that she could not "think like an adult ... everything is too hard to comprehend or remember."

Needless to say, these cognitive deficits pose serious obstacles to the work of therapy. The beneficial structure that cognitive therapy ordinarily provides the bipolar patients is compromised when they feel frustrated and hopeless about ever learning to apply such structure to their lives on their own. The first step is for therapists simply to point out that an improvement in concentration, memory, planning, and problem-solving skills represents one of the goals of therapy. Toward that end, therapists collaboratively elicit agreements from patients that they will work together to help them become more organized and structured in their thinking. When this agreement is reached, therapists are free to use a good deal of repetition, summary statements, and frequent questions to check for understanding, without inadvertently insulting the intelligence of the patients.

The bipolar patients' medication regimens sometimes provide relief from the problem of disorganized thinking and distractibility. We see this most frequently in patients who have a premorbid history free from problems such as attention deficit disorder and hyperactivity. When medication helps patients improve their cognitive skills, this becomes a motivator for them to continue taking the medications. One of our patients said, "Generally speaking, I don't like the idea of having to be on medication, but at least it helps me think clearly and use my intellectual skills to the fullest." The therapist respectfully added that the patient's creative ideas also seemed more practical and safe when she was taking her lithium faithfully.

When patients are less vigilant about taking their medication or continue to have difficulties in staying cognitively focused despite their medications, the work of therapy can become bogged down. In such cases, therapists should make use of as many structure-facilitating techniques as possible. These include the following:

- repeating of important points of discussion,
- frequent open-ended questioning to ascertain the patients' level of understanding,
- having the patients take notes in session,
- asking patients to listen to audiotapes of their own therapy sessions numerous times during the week (and to take notes as well),
- practicing the art of completing one task before starting another,
- steadfastly and vigilantly bringing patients back to the topic at hand if they digress excessively,
- teaching patients to increase the amount of time they spend sitting and writing and decrease the amount of time they spend standing and talking, and
- placing heavy emphasis on learning the skills of planning and problem-solving in therapy as a prerequisite to addressing major life decisions.

It is important for therapists to pay close attention to the patients' verbal and nonverbal behaviors in session to identify difficulties in concentration and focusing. Such signs include the following patient behaviors:

- making very little eye contact,
- nodding as if they understand, but with a blank stare,
- responding to therapist comments with statements that are unrelated to the discussion at hand,
- asking frequent questions that seem repetitive, and
- demonstrating great difficulty in making summary statements about what has transpired in the session.

When these signs occur, therapists can help by slowing the pace of the session and by carefully reviewing the information that the patients are having trouble comprehending. Although taking this tack means that the quantity of material covered in a session is decreased, the quality of the patients' retention of that material is increased. This is a much more favorable outcome than would occur if the therapists' numerous interventions went in one ear and out the other. Furthermore, by helping patients learn to process information more accurately, therapists are assisting patients in improving their concentration in everyday interactions with other people.

CONCLUSION

The period of time that elapses during a bipolar patient's ascent into hypomania or mania allows for the application of prompt, effective, psychosocial interventions to attenuate this process. Patients benefit from learning to identify their personal "signature" signs of impending mania. While hypomanic, patients can use a wide range of cognitive restructuring techniques to test the adaptiveness of their hyperpositive thoughts, assumptions, and plans. Techniques that reduce physiological arousal (e.g., relaxation; breathing control; the therapist's calm, reassuring demeanor) can help patients modulate and moderate their affect. Methods that encourage and teach patients to reduce their level of activity, keep their sleep–wake cycles regulated, and institute a period of reflective delay can reduce impulsivity. The use of summary statements, written notes, audio- and videotapes of sessions, and other structured methods for improving the retention of therapeutic material helps patients reduce distractibility in session and therefore learn more. When instituting all of the above, therapists must be mindful of the patients' desire for respect and autonomy. Therefore, therapists must skillfully guide patients toward the recognition of the wisdom and benefits of applying their cognitive therapy self-help methods rather than risk engaging in a power struggle over what the patients should or should not do.

4

CLINICAL MANAGEMENT OF DEPRESSION, HOPELESSNESS, AND SUICIDALITY IN PATIENTS WITH BIPOLAR DISORDER

People who have bipolar disorder often experience demoralization and despair. Simply put, bipolar disorder not only wreaks havoc on people's emotions, it also engenders hopelessness, a factor that is strongly associated with suicidality (A. T. Beck, Brown, Berchick, Stewart, & Steer, 1990; A. T. Beck, Brown, & Steer, 1989; A. T. Beck, Steer, Beck, & Newman, 1993). This is true for a number of compelling reasons. First, the mood swings and concomitant behavioral problems typically create many problems in people's lives. Bipolar patients routinely have to "pick up the pieces" after bouts of both manic impulsivity and depressive withdrawal. Second, the cyclical nature of the disorder makes it very difficult for patients to trust their euthymic moods. They are prone to worry about when the next devastating episode will occur. Third, patients face stigma and shame associated with their disorder (Lundin, 1998), which compounds their misery and makes them less likely to take advantage of social support. Fourth, and most fundamental, the mood swings themselves (especially the crushing lows that are so common in bipolar disorder) are difficult to bear. Add to these factors the fact that manic–depression is a highly relapsing disorder—long-term remission of symptoms is often difficult to achieve (Goldberg & Harrow, 1999b)—and one can see why patients begin to give up hope of recovery. All in all, the phenomenology of bipolar disorder involves painful and unstable affect, extremes of thought, behavioral excesses and deficits, and a general sense of exhaustion and depletion that does not go away on its own.

As a result of these problems, bipolar depression can be extremely severe and dangerous. The lifetime suicide rates of bipolar patients (including those who have been treated) have been found to be as high as 15% (Simpson & Jamison, 1999). The overall figure for premature death in patients is even higher when one includes the large numbers of accidents and medical problems that patients incur (Bowden, 1999). Needless to say, bipolar patients comprise a very high-risk population, requiring a high level of vigilance and competence from their therapists. An assessment of suicidality—in the past, at the present, and on an ongoing basis across therapy sessions—needs to be a routine part of the treatment of bipolar patients. Therapists should show that they have an appreciation for the level of pain and suffering that patients go through, yet be able to model hopefulness and an unfailing determination to help the patients build a better, more stable, more rewarding life. In a nutshell, therapists have to help patients make sound decisions about their treatment, to stick to a plan that works, to build an array of psychological skills (e.g., communication, problem-solving), to facilitate their relationships in everyday life, and to aim for the future with hope and enthusiasm.

In this chapter, we review some of the fundamentals of cognitive therapy for depressive episodes, with special emphasis on suicide prevention. We do not reiterate the full range of cognitive therapy interventions for depression that are so well explicated in other texts, including the basics of rational re-evaluation using Daily Thought Records (DTRs; e.g., A. T. Beck et al., 1979; J. S. Beck, 1995; Greenberger & Padesky, 1995). Instead, we concentrate on selected methods that enable therapists to maximize the safeguards for bipolar patients and to boost their sense of hopefulness at times when they might otherwise experience despair.

ASSESSMENT

There are three basic ways that therapists keep tabs on their patients' levels of depression and suicidality:

1. direct verbal questioning,
2. self-report measures, and
3. reports from concerned third parties, such as family and other professionals on the case.

Verbal questioning, including between-sessions crisis telephone calls, can be done at any time and therefore is the method that is most readily mastered. Self-report measures are also helpful; although they are subject to patients' idiosyncrasies in responding, they nevertheless serve a medical–legal function that cannot be underestimated (see Bongar, 1991). Finally, third-party input may be the least convenient assessment method but sometimes the most accurate and most meaningful, especially in cases in which patients are not entirely forthcoming about their feelings and intentions.

Direct Verbal Questioning

It is appropriate and necessary to ask patients about their attitudes toward life and death on a regular basis. Such questioning does not have to be overly intrusive, nor does it have to be incongruous with the context of the session's agenda. Therapists can let their patients know that they understand that bipolar disorder is a serious problem, that it has major emotional repercussions, and that it is quite common for patients to entertain thoughts of suicide. As a result, therapists can prep their patients to expect that questions about depression, hopelessness, and suicidality, will come up rather routinely, as part of good clinical care.

When conducting a verbal interview about the patient's suicidality, a number of areas should be covered thoroughly. This involves asking patients about factors such as the following:

- level of desire to die (weak, moderate, strong);
- level of desire to live (weak, moderate, strong);
- frequency and duration of suicidal ideation;
- subjective sense of control over suicidal behaviors;
- deterrents to suicide;
- reasons for wanting to commit suicide;
- specific plans for committing suicide;
- methods available for killing oneself;
- arrangements made in anticipation of death, if any; and
- degree to which they have been forthcoming about revealing their feelings and intentions.

This is not an exhaustive list, but it is thorough by any clinical standard. To formalize this process of questioning, the clinician may choose to use the Beck Scale for Suicide Ideation (BSSI; A. T. Beck, Steer, & Ranieri, 1988), which is a structured interview that covers the issues listed above and more.[1] Even more important, the BSSI assesses the patients'

---

[1]Clinicians can obtain the BSSI and additional Beck inventories from the Psychological Corporation, 555 Academic Court, San Antonio, TX, 78204-9990, USA; 1-800-872-1726; *www.PsychCorp.com*.

level of suicidality both in the present and at the worst time in the past. The BSSI directly asks patients if they have attempted suicide in the past, by what methods, and with what level of intent to die. Such information is telling indeed, because previous suicide attempts and their levels of potential lethality are indicators of present and future risk (Bongar, 1991).

There is evidence that patients who have made multiple suicide attempts exhibit qualitatively different responses to both stressors and treatment than those who have attempted suicide once or not at all (Joiner & Rudd, 2000). Specifically, multiple attempters seem to require less and less provocation from external stressors to become suicidal. Although this phenomenon is not limited to bipolar disorder patients who are suicidal, it does bear a striking resemblance to the kindling phenomenon found in bipolar patients with repeated affective episodes. In addition, Joiner and Rudd note that multiple attempters tend to experience psychological states of crisis for longer durations, are more likely to drop out of treatment, and are more apt to reject or negate the help of others.

Therefore, therapists who ascertain extensive histories of suicidal behavior in their bipolar patients gain valuable information about the increased risk. Therapists will need to pay special attention to patients' feelings and beliefs about being in treatment (to reduce the risk of sudden, unexpected flight from therapy), and will have to expect that periods of crisis will probably require more extensive and intensive intervention until the danger abates. From a cognitive standpoint, we would hypothesize that multiple attempters are more apt to respond to mild to moderate stressors with the activation of schemas and modes of schemas. This could account for the tendency of multiple attempters to seem to "overreact" to unremarkable provocations with increased suicidality. Therapists who are aware of the full scope of their bipolar patients' histories of suicidal behavior are best equipped to prepare for such frightening scenarios.

Self-Report Inventories for Depression and Hopelessness

It is very quick and convenient for patients to complete self-report questionnaires such as the Beck Depression Inventory (BDI; A. T. Beck, Ward, Mendelson, Mock, & Erbaugh, 1961) and the Beck Hopelessness Scale (BHS; A. T. Beck, Weissman, Lester, & Trexler, 1974). Although the subject matter is weighty, the time commitment required to fill out these questionnaires is light. This makes it possible for patients to complete questionnaires for each and every session, thus making it a straightforward task for therapists to assess the level of patient depression and hopelessness on an ongoing basis. In addition, using questionnaires at each session enables therapists to collect data on the patients' levels of suicidality, which can be measured over the course of treatment and at follow-up points as well.

In addition to its intended role of measuring the level of severity of a diagnosed mood disorder, the BDI is useful as a self-report measure of suicidality. Although this 21-item measure broadly covers symptoms associated with depressive disorders, Items 2 and 9 provide uniquely useful information about current suicide risk. These items tap into the patients' level of hope for the future and intent to commit suicide, respectively. When the patients' responses are strongly positive on either item, it is a red flag. When both items are strongly endorsed, therapists need to put the topic of suicidality at the top of the agenda for the current therapy session.

Even when patients do not report feelings of hopelessness or suicidality, the BDI cues the therapist about other symptoms that have important implications for treatment, including the choice of topics of discussion in the session. For example, the BDI taps into the patients' sense of being a "failure" and propensity for self-criticism. The BDI raises the issues of the patients' subjective levels of guilt, worthlessness, and the feeling that they are being punished, as well as symptoms of indecisiveness, anhedonia, and a host of other useful indicators of depression. When patients endorse such items on the BDI, it is very important to follow up with further questions to tease out the personal meaning.

To get a more comprehensive picture of patients' level of hopelessness, the BHS (A. T. Beck et al., 1974) should be used in conjunction with the BDI. The BHS is a 20-question true–false inventory, focusing on patients' beliefs about the future and related issues. The following are two representative items:

- "I might as well give up because there is nothing I can do about making things better for myself."
- "I never get what I want, so it's foolish to want anything."

If a patient answers with nine or more hopeless responses, this is an indication of elevated suicide risk (A. T. Beck, Steer, et al., 1993; A. T. Beck, Steer, Kovacs, & Garrison, 1985), especially if there is concurrent depression (cf. BDI).[2] Clearly, the patient's view of the future has a great deal to do with how much he or she is willing to invest in the sometimes arduous work of therapy. The more hope patients have, and the more they expect a pay off for their efforts, the more they collaborate with their therapists. Under such conditions, the chances of a favorable treatment outcome increase. Conversely, patients who are mired in hopelessness may be more prone to take a maladaptive, apathetic attitude toward therapy. This, in itself, becomes a therapeutic issue.

It should be noted that hopelessness when patients are *not* depressed may be an even stronger predictor of long-term suicide risk than it is when

---

[2]In assessing elevations in suicide risk, false positives are the norm. Nevertheless, this is acceptable in that excessive caution may be clinically warranted when a client's life may be endangered.

they are depressed. In other words, some patients maintain a high baseline level of hopelessness regardless of their mood state, which indicates vulnerability to suicide (M. A. Young et al., 1996). Later, when these patients become dysphoric, their hopelessness increases further still, giving them a "double hopelessness" that is analogous to "double depression" (acute major depression superimposed on long-standing dysthymia). Thus, it would be prudent for therapists to continue to have patients fill out questionnaires such as the BHS each session (ideally), especially when they are euthymic. Clearly, patients' baseline levels of hopelessness, along with their sensitivity to increases in hopelessness, should be topics of discussion in their own right in cognitive therapy.

Reports From Family Members and Other Professionals Providing Services

There are times when patients do not fully report the extent of their self-destructive thoughts and wishes for more deliberate reasons. For example, patients may not trust the therapist, thinking that the therapist will have the knee-jerk reaction of summarily hospitalizing them if they so much as utter the "s" word (suicide). Some patients are averse to the idea of an inpatient stay, fearing the stigma involved and the social and vocational repercussions of such a stay. In other cases, patients feel ashamed to admit that they have felt suicidal, fearing that the therapist may judge them and perhaps even relinquish responsibility for their care. In the most dangerous cases, patients resist divulging their suicidal thoughts, feelings, and intentions because they do not want to be prevented from following through with the act.

In all of these situations, therapists can use the following strategies to help patients become more willing to express their suicidal ideation:

1. They can communicate respect for the patients.
2. They can express empathy for their hopelessness and suicidal feelings.
3. They can explain that hospitalization is used only after all reasonable outpatient interventions have failed, and the patient is at imminent risk.

However, sometimes even these interventions do not convince patients to open up about their intentions to harm themselves. Therefore, it is potentially life-saving to have the informational input of others who are involved in the patients' lives (e.g., family, other professionals on the case). In the case of other professionals, it is important to gain the patient's written consent at the beginning of treatment to share clinical information among the interdisciplinary team that is working with the bipolar patient. Needless to say, if the patient declines to give this consent, it presents a significant red flag for secrets, hidden agendas, and potential danger. Therefore, the patient's refusal should become an immediate therapeutic issue, even at the risk of straining the therapeutic relationship.

Therapists who establish rapport with the patient's family members gain important safeguards. For example, family members can learn some of the therapist's interventions through modeling, which may help defuse critical situations with the patients at home. Second, therapists who form a bond with the family of the patient gain allies in the process of potentially hospitalizing the patient to save his or her life. Third, one of the therapist's best protections against potential lawsuits in the aftermath of a patient suicide is a healthy alliance with the patient's family during the course of treatment (Bongar, 1991).

Because bipolar patients often have multiple professionals working with them, it is useful and necessary for those professionals to be in contact with one another. The nature of bipolar disorder is that patients exhibit extremes of behavior, affect, and cognition in a somewhat unpredictable fashion, so it is helpful for professionals to share information about the best and worst examples of the patient's functioning that they have witnessed.

For example, it is possible for a bipolar patient to deliberately withhold feelings of active suicidality from his nonphysician cognitive therapist but readily to express such sentiments to the prescribing psychiatrist. When the two clinicians consult, the psychiatrist can inform and warn the cognitive therapist of the patient's active risk. Similarly, the cognitive therapist may be able to notify the psychiatrist that the patient has admitted to stockpiling medications for a future suicide attempt. These are healthy examples of mental health professionals collaborating on a case, serving as each other's eyes and ears, backing each other up to reduce the chances of a tragedy, and generally improving the accuracy of the suicidality assessment (cf. Moras & DeMartinis, 1999).

INTERVENTIONS

To be diagnosed with bipolar disorder is to face a lifelong vulnerability to cyclical suffering, along with the necessity of vigilant, long-term treatment, often including medications that are not easy to tolerate. Thus, bipolar patients are prone to feel hopeless about their future—a state of mind that unfortunately is quite conducive to suicidality (A. T. Beck, Steer, et al. 1993). To sincerely validate the plight of bipolar patients, therapists must acknowledge that patients have to contend with significant challenges for years to come. At the same time, is it absolutely vital that therapists demonstrate a dogged determination to help patients manage their bipolar disorder well enough to have hope for a better future. As such, therapists of bipolar patients are purveyors of hope.

Therefore, therapists have to be prepared to help patients deal with setbacks and must be undaunted in their effort to help patients who have symptomatic relapses. When patients are in euthymic states, therapists can model an outlook of "cautious optimism" by reminding them that their normal mood state does not indicate that they can now terminate their treatment. Bipolar disorder must be treated over the long term, and therefore it would be a mistake to state that patients who feel better are no longer in need of professional care and monitoring. However, it is important to communicate to patients that their ongoing adherence to the treatment regimen increases their chances of leading a higher quality life than would be possible if treatment were sporadic or absent. The message is clear: Active, collaborative engagement in treatment, even when things are "going well," improves prognosis. Therefore, there is reason to have hope.

Contracting for Safety

When patients express their thoughts and feelings of suicidality, it is sometimes useful to try to negotiate an antisuicide agreement (see Ellis & Newman, 1996). Although such "contracts" (whether verbal or written) do not provide actual guarantees of the patients' safety (Kleepsies & Dettmer, 2000; Silverman, Berman, Bongar, Litman, & Maris, 1998), they do bring relevant issues to the fore and strengthen the therapeutic alliance (Stanford, Goetz, & Bloom, 1994). For example, good antisuicide contracts should address the following topics:

- concrete self-help steps patients should take if they feel suicidal and cannot reach the therapist or their support system;
- the arrangements that the therapist will make to provide emergency coverage (e.g., a telephone number for a colleague on call or the telephone number and location of a nearby emergency room);
- a list of people comprising the patients' support system whom they can contact when they feel suicidal and need supervision; and
- a statement of the patient's intent to live, to engage in therapy in good faith, and to adhere to the spirit of the contract even when unforeseen complications make the specifics of the contract difficult to uphold.

Antisuicide contracts should be drawn up collaboratively between therapists and patients. Ideally, they should not be presented to patients as a generic set of rules to which they must adhere. Compliance is facilitated to the extent that patients believe they had a hand in constructing the items on the contract. Therapists guide this process, so that the contract supports the safety of the patients and spells out each party's roles and responsibilities in a clinical crisis.

From time to time it is prudent to review the contents of the antisuicide contract, if for no other reason than to refresh the patient's memory. Such periodic reviews also allow for the contract to be revised in accordance with changes made over the course of treatment. Furthermore, therapists can encourage their patients officially to renew the contract. (See Exhibit 4.1 for a sample contract.)

We should emphasize that antisuicide contracts are not a substitute for the usual and customary methods for closely monitoring patients' levels of risk and responsivity to treatment. Therapists should not assume that they can relax their levels of vigilance when patients sign an antisuicide contract or verbally consent to the spirit of such a contract. The contract is simply a part of the treatment and a vehicle for organizing a response to a clinical crisis situation.

Counteracting "Suicidogenic Beliefs"

When depressed bipolar patients experience suicidal ideation, they often evince one or more negatively biased beliefs that seem to support the notion of killing themselves as a viable option. It is the therapist's job to help elucidate these dangerous beliefs and to engage patients in an exploration of alternative, life-affirming beliefs. Some suicidal patients emphasize one belief more than another, whereas other patients hold multiple suicidogenic beliefs. The greater the number of suicidogenic beliefs, the more arduous—and more vital—will be the process of responding to them rationally.

Belief 1: "My problems are too overwhelming. The only way to solve all my problems is to kill myself."

As we have mentioned earlier, bipolar disorder can cause major disruptions in people's lives. The real-life consequences of the patients' manic behaviors, as well as their depressive neglect in solving problems, can lead to patients' being overwhelmed by their predicament. To make matters worse, the patients may view their bipolar disorder itself as a problem that cannot be overcome unless they die.

To address this belief, therapists will need to demonstrate that it is possible for the patients to engage in problem-solving, and to reduce the breadth and depth of their life difficulties, within the context of life. Although patients sometimes view suicide as "the solution to end all prob-

EXHIBIT 4.1
Sample Antisuicide Contract

Therapeutic Contract

- I agree that although I am in emotional pain, it is important not to give up hope, and instead to continue to search for ways to improve my lot in life.
- I understand that therapy is sometimes difficult to go through, but I will nonetheless collaborate with my therapist(s) in finding ways to manage my symptoms and life problems.
- I declare that my life is worth preserving, and I will not act in ways to put my life at risk.
- I realize that I may be tempted to do harm to myself at certain times, but I will refrain from such actions.
- In times of emotional crisis, instead of isolating myself, I will try to contact Dr. X at 555-2467, my sister Val at 555-4982, my friend Bernice at 555-0471, my AA sponsor Joanne at 555-3119, and my neighbors Hal and Sue at 555-6483.
- If I can't reach any of the above people, I know that I can contact the Crisis Hotline at 555-1095 or Dr. X's emergency on-call person at pager number 555-7857, or I can get myself to the emergency room of St. Elsewhere Hospital on Maple Street (either by driving or calling "911" for the police).
- Before I assume that I am helpless and defeated, I will try many of the cognitive therapy skills I have learned in working with Dr. X, such as relaxation, self-soothing, engaging in productive activities, writing up Daily Thought Records, writing in my journal, or engaging in pleasant distractions such as watching movies or reading a good book. If all of these fail, I know I can still rely on my support team.
- I know that my therapist is in my corner, and I will continue to work with her faithfully. I also understand that she is trying to teach me the skills and strategies to help improve my life. I will use these techniques, rather than try to hurt myself.
- I have been told that Dr. X typically will try to be available for impromptu therapy sessions if I am in crisis. If she can't be available, she will let me know who her back-up doctor is, and I will contact this person if the need should arise.
- I am realistic enough to know that every contact has unforeseen loopholes, but Dr. X and I will not take advantage of these loopholes. In the interest of my short- and long-term well-being, both of us pledge to follow the life-affirming spirit of this contract.

_____
Patient's Signature

_____
Dr. X's Signature

_____
Date

lems," it is more accurately seen as "the problem to end all solutions" (Ellis & Newman, 1996, p. 125). When a person is dead, the chance to solve problems is ended forever, and the survivors inherit even worse difficulties, compounded by grief and guilt. To live is to have a chance to make things better. It is vitally important for therapists to help their patients reach this more hopeful conclusion, because the level of expectancy that suicide can solve one's problems is predictive of higher suicide intent (Linehan, Camper, Chiles, Strosahl, & Shearin, 1987).

Belief 2: "I am a burden to others, and they would be better off if I killed myself."

Bipolar disorder can be a burdensome illness, for the sufferers themselves as well as their loved ones. However, if patients have the notion that suicide is the preferred method to unburden others, this needs to be challenged in a most powerful way. One can argue that the suicide of a loved one is one of the worst burdens of all—one that can never be "fixed" or undone and that perpetuates feelings of anger, helplessness, guilt, and grief in those left behind.

Although bipolar patients do indeed place certain demands on their caregivers and support systems, their commitment to life and to treatment gives them the chance to lift others' burdens in a productive, hopeful way. Suicide does not achieve this end. Patients who maintain this particular suicidogenic belief should be asked the following question: "Would others rather that you kill yourself, or that you invest yourself in your treatment to the fullest?" Sometimes the patient's response will be along the following lines: "It doesn't matter if I invest myself in my treatment, because I am never going to get better, so I might as well cut my losses and end it all right now." On hearing this, therapists should impress on patients that while this is an understandable lamentation given their illness, it is nonetheless an example of fortune telling. The patient is willing to die based on a subjective expectation, which is the worst kind of gamble. Instead, the patients should be entreated to live long enough to test hypotheses about their future prospects for improved condition.

Belief 3: "I hate myself, and I deserve to die."

Patients who espouse the belief that they deserve to die often feel a great deal of shame and regret as a result of past behaviors and incidents. Their self-loathing, aside from being inherently depressogenic, also makes them prone to discount, minimize, negate, or sabotage their therapeutic progress. As a result, patients who profess to hate themselves are most difficult to treat and pose significant suicide risks.

Although there is no single foolproof method for helping such patients to like and respect themselves again (or for the first time), there are some general strategies that may lessen the degree of self-hate. Such methods include:

- discussing the past shameful events, toward the goal of a more benign conceptualization,
- exploring ways for patients to devote their lives to "turning over a new leaf,"

- striving to make "penitence" and gain "absolution" (if they are religious), and
- imploring patients not to "execute the victim," as they would surely do if they leveled capital punishment on persons who have been suffering from a terrible disorder.

Additionally, although patients may profess to hate themselves, they cannot include a fair judgment of their future self-image in this assessment without relinquishing the suicide option. In other words, only by living out their lives to their natural conclusion—and seeing how they grow, change, contribute to the world, and make peace with themselves—can patients get the big picture of their self-worth.

Belief 4: "I am in intractable emotional pain, and only suicide can end it."

Here, patients are looking for an anesthetic for their emotional hardship. Believing that their bipolar disorder can only get worse and that no relief is in sight, they may truly believe that suicide is a "humane" act.

The best way to address this belief is to start by validating the patients' sense of anguish in the present, as well as their battle fatigue in dealing with bipolar disorder for many years. It is best to acknowledge that to a person in deep pain, each day can seem like an eternity, whereas eternity can seem like a haven. Nevertheless, there is always hope that bipolar disorder can be treated, and suicide does not have to be the patient's only means of respite from agony.

It is very useful to collaboratively review all of the patient's emotional palliatives—both the tried-and-true methods of the past and the new ideas for today and beyond. It goes without saying that alcohol, illicit drugs, self-mutilation, and impulsive sex should not be among these "remedies," because these invariably worsen the patient's condition. Rather, the therapist and patient should search for healthy, self-soothing distractors, from momentary pleasures such as a warm blanket and a good book to more enduring salves such as the project of writing a self-help journal for other bipolar patients. The key is to help the patients immerse themselves in meaningful life experiences (see Frankl, 1960) that provide an oasis of comfort while they do the difficult work of therapy.

Belief 5: "I'm so angry at everybody. I'll just kill myself because that's the best way to teach everybody a lesson."

The view that suicide is a way to teach others a lesson is the ultimate example of "cutting off your nose to spite your face." When patients are very angry, at least partly because they believe they have been mistreated by others, they sometimes resort to threats of self-harm to make a strong statement of interpersonal protest and control. The appropriate therapeutic response to this type of dangerous beliefs is threefold:

1. understand and empathize with the patients' anger,
2. engage the patients in an attempt to find and use more adaptive methods of expressing anger, and
3. continue to assess and treat the aspects of the patients' suicidality that are based on despair, shame, and hopelessness.

Furthermore, it is worth exploring what the patients' past suicide attempts have actually "taught" others. Often, patients do acknowledge that their self-destructive acts (especially when precipitated by anger) were most apt to teach their loved ones that patients were sick, fragile, not to be trusted with medications, impulsive, contrary, and even manipulative. Is this the "lesson" that suicidal individuals want to convey to those closest to them? We should imagine not. Instead, we would like to help patients learn prosocial ways to express their feelings, including the darkest of the lot.

The above beliefs represent just a sampling of bipolar patients' suicidogenic beliefs; they provide a conceptual template that helps therapists more quickly assess and treat patients before they harm themselves. More of the specific interventions to which we allude appear below.

Focusing on the Pros and Cons of Suicide, for the Patient and for Others, Now and in the Future

At first blush, this clinical strategy might seem either overly simplistic or needlessly hazardous. It is neither. Patients who are actively suicidal already have concluded on the basis of their subjective assumptions that the future holds only misery for them and that it is best to cut their losses now by dying. In other words, they are highly focused on the apparent "benefits" of suicide. Getting these patients to articulate such opinions does not heighten the risk. To the contrary, it brings heretofore unchallenged morbid, biased thoughts into the light of day for serious inquiry and dialogue. This is therapeutic.

Likewise, patients who wish to die typically have given too little thought both to the drawbacks of dying prematurely and to the advantages of continuing to live. Furthermore, they may not have put sufficient thought into predicting the long-term effects that their suicide would have on loved ones. Similarly, suicidal patients rarely allow themselves the normal indulgence of fantasizing about a better future. With all these cognitive gaps causing further negative bias to the patients' decision-making process about suicide, it behooves therapists to call attention to these "missing data."

There is striking evidence that the suicide of a loved one has significant impact on those left behind (e.g., Brent, Moritz, Bridge, Perper, & Canobbio, 1996; Van Dongen, 1991). Suicidal patients tend not to appreciate this fact, and therefore it is useful for therapists to bring this up for discussion. As mentioned above in Belief 2, it is important to look at how the patient's suicide would likely be a far greater (and irrevocable) burden for loved ones than his or her continuing to live, even with an active bipolar disorder. The key is to encourage the patient to imagine a better outcome, one in which the patient's condition ultimately improves through cognitive therapy and pharmacotherapy—a future in which the burdens to both the patient and loved ones are lessened.

We acknowledge that this may be a hard sell for some patients who have had chronic difficulties. They may profess the desire not to get their hopes up for a better future, only to have those hopes dashed once again. Therapists can find a middle ground between validating the patients' despair and expressing blind optimism by giving empathy for the patients' current feelings while insisting that the future is unknowable and therefore open to all possibilities. Then, therapists can encourage the patients at least to visualize and describe what a better future might look like, even if they do not expect that this will occur. There is an adage stating that in order to do something grand, you have to be able to dream it first. This intervention (sometimes called "positive future imaging") is just such a strategy. In the same way that pessimism can lead to a negative self-fulfilling prophecy, it is possible that imagining the specifics of a healthier future can increase the chances of more favorable outcomes (cf. Seligman, 1991).

In Exhibit 4.2, patient "Lanny" hypothesizes the pros and cons of committing suicide, both for himself and for his parents and siblings. Although he was quite convinced that his suicide would relieve him of his shame and take away his family's daily worrying in the short-term (pros of suicide), he professed to have never considered the long-term drawbacks of his suicide. For example, Lanny considered the likelihood that his parents might suffer a variety of long-term consequences if he killed himself, such as

- losing friends, who would be too horrified to deal with a couple who lost a child to suicide;
- becoming overbearingly protective to the other two children, for fear of losing them as well;
- marital dissolution, which sometimes happens after the death of a child; and
- unending guilt.

Lanny also noted that his self-inflicted death would rob him of the chance ever to get married, to travel, and to see what his life might become. In summary, although the intervention did not suddenly make Lanny disavow suicide forever, it raised reasonable doubt in his mind about the relative merits of killing himself. In other words, it gave him pause. Such indecision and delay can mean the difference between life and death at moments of extreme affect.

EXHIBIT 4.2
Lanny's List of the Pros and Cons of Living and Dying
(for Himself, His Loved Ones, Now, and Later)

Pros of Dying	Cons of Dying
1. Pain ends right away. 2. Parents no longer have to worry about me. 3. I'm ashamed of the things I've done. Suicide is the honorable way out. 4. People will really understand how bad things were for me.	1. My mother would freak. 2. I might linger and suffer before dying. 3. I would never have a chance to get better. 4. I would always be remembered as the crazy person in the family who "offed" himself. 5. My parents might get divorced because of my death. 6. My parents would feel guilty forever. 7. My brother and sister would never get any freedom, because my mother would be so afraid of losing them too that she would never let them out of her sight. 8. My parents would become social outcasts because their friends won't want to deal with talking about my suicide. 9. I'll never travel the world. 10. I'll never have sex again or get married.
Pros of Living	Cons of Living
1. My parents won't have to pay for a funeral. 2. My mother's worst nightmare won't come true. 3. I might get married someday. 4. I could do some traveling in the future, like I always planned. 5. I would find out what my life could possibly be if I get better.	1. I have no guarantee that I'll ever get better. 2. I have to suffer with this disorder. 3. I'm making my parents waste money on my treatment. 4. I'm always making my parents worry. 5. I can't keep friends, and I'll keep failing with girls.

Increasing Mastery and Pleasure

One of the ways that patients can reconnect with life, improve self-efficacy, and boost morale is to take part in productive, enjoyable activities. Granted, when patients are feeling depressed, anhedonic, inert, and withdrawn, they are not likely to spontaneously fill up their calendars with interesting things to do. However, with a little encouragement and guidance from the therapist, patients can learn to follow a basic principle—

namely, that it is vital to do the things that you would normally do if you were in a good mood, even if you are in a bad mood.

Therapists and patients can take inventory of the kind of activities that the latter have traditionally found meaningful and agree to do as many of these activities as possible as part of the antidote against suicidality. The rationales are clear:

1. Being active breaks the vicious cycle of hopelessness, helplessness, withdrawal, exacerbated mood, and increased hopelessness.
2. Physical activity has natural antidepressant effects (Tkachuk & Martin, 1999).
3. Involvement in activities keeps patients in contact with other people, whose presence can be safeguarding, if not downright enjoyable.
4. Doing things in spite of ill mood can increase the patient's sense of self-efficacy.
5. Being physically activated can trigger positive outcomes such as finishing important tasks, thinking things through more fully and clearly, getting positive feedback from the environment, and reducing general lethargy.

Therapists need to show compassion for patients who have a markedly difficult time in getting themselves to take part in such activities. Nevertheless, it is useful to continue to encourage them to focus on performing the life tasks that have helped them feel a sense of mastery and pleasure in the past.

A novel way to look at the tactic of staying active is to construe it as an attempt to "procrastinate suicide" (Ellis & Newman, 1996). In other words, patients are instructed to take stock of their unfinished business in life and to begin to take care of this business as a prerequisite to entertaining notions of suicide. Such ventures might include taking a certain trip, finishing a project, completing an educational degree, or reconciling with an old friend. As patients attempt and accomplish more and more of these tasks, further unfinished business is assessed. This pattern is continued until they find that they are now more engaged in life by virtue of all the things in which they have been partaking and accomplishing.

When patients cannot or will not consent to become more active, it is still useful to support this strategy and to generate a list of tasks that they could do if their level of energy were to increase. In the meantime, therapists can focus on modifying patients' suicidogenic beliefs.

Teaching Problem-Solving Skills

It is extremely useful for bipolar patients to understand and use the principles of problem-solving (Nezu et al., 1989). As patients tend to get into downward spirals of functioning, accompanied by worsening environmental consequences, it is especially helpful if they can implement the principles of "damage control" to minimize harm. All too frequently, the extreme moods of the patient work in concert with equally extreme thoughts, such as, "I have made such a mess of things, now it no longer matters what I do." Such thoughts can lead a patient to throw caution to the wind, wreaking havoc on an already troubled life situation and precluding the implementation of problem-solving strategies that might otherwise mitigate the person's difficulties. It is evident that patients who compound their problems with further dysfunctional behaviors (borne of hopelessness) put themselves at relatively greater risk of suicide than those patients who try to make repairs, especially if they lack efficacy in the formal skills of problem-solving (Schotte & Clum, 1987).

By contrast, patients who adopt the mindset that it is useful to try to mend fences and build new bridges, no matter what has previously transpired, are in a better position to cope and to be hopeful. This reduces the risk of a downward spiral toward suicide.

In her review of the cognitive risk factors in suicidality, Weishaar (1996) cited findings suggesting that suicidal patients often perceive more problems but generate fewer solutions than their nonsuicidal counterparts. This seems to be the case for both impersonal and interpersonal problems. People who are suicidal are also more likely to avoid actively dealing with their problems than those who are nonsuicidal. Intuitively, this phenomenon seems to be related to hopelessness, as typified by patients' comments such as "I can't see a way out of this problem." Taken literally, the suicidal patient who makes such an assertion is implying that if he or she cannot perceive a solution, with satisfactory clarity, right now, then no solution exists. They then do not put in the necessary time and effort to engage in effective problem-solving. Therapists can respond by asking their patients, "If you cannot immediately think of a way to improve your life situation, does that necessarily mean that it is useless to think about it? Would you be willing to work with me to explore some possible ways to deal with your problems, even if the solutions are not obviously apparent?" The therapist's intent here is to induce patients into engaging in active problem-solving.

It has been hypothesized that factors such as "cognitive rigidity," perfectionism, and poor autobiographical recall play a role in hindering the problem-solving abilities of patients who are suicidal (Blatt, 1995; Ellis & Ratliff, 1986; J. Evans, Williams, O'Loughlin, & Howells, 1992; Hewitt, Flett, & Weber, 1994; Scott, 1996b; Williams & Broadbent, 1986; Williams & Scott, 1988; Scott, et al., 2000). *Cognitive rigidity* refers to a tendency to see things in black and white, all or none. For example, a person whose bipolar illness has forced him to leave medical school may say to himself, "If I can't be a doctor, then there is no point in going on living." He may have a very difficult time comprehending or accepting that there may be other ways to find vocational fulfillment and that his self-esteem can be maintained by more than one particular professional identity. As long as he takes this maladaptive approach, he is disinclined to try to solve his problem through a creative search for alternatives. Therapists have to walk gingerly as they try to help such patients to expand their sense of positive possibilities in their life, lest patients conclude that their feelings are being invalidated. Nevertheless, it is advisable for therapists to focus on patients' inflexible cognitive style as a risk factor for poor problem-solving at best and hopelessness and suicidality at worst. Therefore, cognitive rigidity is a necessary area for therapeutic intervention.

Similarly, *perfectionism* comprises a set of beliefs that can make someone vulnerable to dysphoria and despair. In a clinical sense, perfectionism does not pertain to a healthy, ambitious striving toward goals and success. Rather, it refers to a more punitive, unreasonable demand that things must work out *just so*, along with a mindset that nothing else is satisfactory. Thus, perfectionism is going to impede good problem-solving, which otherwise would necessitate the exploration of the relative pros and cons of various courses of action that patients can take, some being less than optimal. Looking at pros and cons and weighing the relative merits of options requires a tolerance for a "good enough" solution, a position that the perfectionistic patient may eschew at first glance.

Existentially speaking, nobody's life can be perfect; thus, a demand for perfectionism is a set-up for frustration, disappointment, and anxiety. As we have often said to our patients, "Perfectionism entails a futile, life-long struggle to break even (after all, you can never exceed your expectations or be pleasantly surprised!)." As part of her homework in generating "anti-perfectionism flashcards," one of our patients penned this gem: "You can't be at your best all the time, because if you could be at your best all the time, it wouldn't be your best; it would be your average!" For bipolar patients, who encounter more than their share of bumps and hurdles in life, it is even more deleterious to maintain an unflinchingly perfectionistic stance.

In fact, there is evidence that perfectionism in patients can even interfere with the development of an optimal therapeutic relationship (Zuroff et al., 2000): "perfectionism was specifically associated with the failure of patients to increase their contribution to the alliance as therapy progressed" (p. 120). Zuroff and colleagues also cited additional data suggesting that perfectionistic attitudes are related to self-criticism, perceived stress, and increased interpersonal problems, all of which can impede the process of therapy and self-help. These issues can be fruitfully addressed with depressed bipolar patients.

Additionally, the phenomenon of *poor autobiographical recall* has been implicated in problem-solving deficits in patients with unipolar depression (Evans, Williams, et al., 1992; Williams & Broadbent, 1986) and bipolar depression (Scott et al., 2000). Patients who show the most difficulty in recalling, imagining, and describing the specifics of past, meaningful events in their lives have been found to be the least effective in providing solutions to social problems. Such patients give vague, nondescript overviews of past events, but not as a result of poor general intellect or medication effects. Rather, they evince a cognitive style that reduces their ability to learn optimally from past experience. Thus, their emotions and behaviors are more apt to be driven by old, dysfunctional beliefs rather than be shaped by their personal experience in what has served them well and what has failed. Personal growth is stunted under such circumstances, along (perhaps) with progress in therapy.

To counteract this cognitive deficit, cognitive therapists place great emphasis on teaching patients to

- look for specific evidence to support or refute their beliefs,
- generate as many answers as they can to questions that probe for alternative ways to look at situations,
- list and evaluate numerous potential solutions to problems, and
- keep written records (e.g., DTRs, journals) of personal experiences and audiotapes of therapy sessions to provide patients with a data bank of specific memories to assist them in recall.

It may also be possible and useful to encourage patients to use imagery exercises (perhaps involving a relaxation induction) to facilitate the recall of salient life events. The goal certainly is not to "recover repressed memories," and this should be spelled out at the start. Rather, the intent is to use more of the patients' senses in trying to perceive the richness of their life experience, both in the present and in the past. We hypothesize that such therapeutic activities can assist patients in learning from their mistakes, appreciating their successes, and getting a more fair appraisal of the ratio between the two.

Maximizing Social Support

A good support system is a boon to any patient's treatment, general well-being, and recovery (see Johnson, Winett, et al., 1999). To ascertain the extent of the patient's support system, a thorough, initial assessment should include a psychosocial history and should take inventory of the extent and quality of the patient's familial and social relationships. If patients report that they are lonely and isolated, it is almost guaranteed that one of the primary goals of therapy is to help them establish and maintain healthy ties to others, regardless of their diagnosis or concurrent problems.

Unfortunately, the depressive symptoms of bipolar disorder have a high potential to damage or otherwise compromise the patients' psycho-social relationships. The anergia, inertia, anhedonia, and withdrawal common in the depressive phase easily can make bipolar patients drop off the social map. People who try to encourage deeply depressed patients to engage in social activities are often rebuffed or ignored, leading the former to give up trying to socialize with the patients. Patients in turn use this outcome to "prove" and "justify" their ongoing self-imposed isolation. Furthermore, as noted above, patients who are depressed, self-critical, and perfectionistic tend to have fewer healthy interpersonal relationships.

The above are significant obstacles to achieving the goal of a stable social support system. Given this reality, the first place to start is with the people who already have the greatest previous investment in the patients: namely, parents and spouses (and sometimes adult children and to a lesser extent siblings). These are the people who are most involved with the patients and who would be most likely to serve as therapists' allies in situations in which the patients needed to be hospitalized. Improving the quality of patients' relationships with their parents and spouses reduces stress and increases their motivation to live.

It is also important to examine the patients' relationships with friends, acquaintances, neighbors, and coworkers. Although these people—all things considered—are likely to be less invested in patients' well-being than are parents and spouses, they can represent a useful network. Here, quantity is arguably as important as quality, because it is generally not realistic for patients to get all their affiliation needs met by one or two friends. It is therapeutic for bipolar patients to keep in touch with a wide range of people who have been in their lives. Some may not be responsive, but others will be, and these people then become part of the patients' lifeline. When friends are scarce, it is time to start helping patients find formal support groups for bipolar disorder, such as their local chapter of the National Depressive and Manic Depressive Association (NDMDA), the National Alliance for the Mentally Ill (NAMI), and the Depression and Related Affective Disorders Association (DRADA) (see Exhibit 4.3). As social isolation is one of the risk factors for suicide (Jamison, 1999; Trout, 1980), it behooves therapists to make social attachments one of the top priority agenda items for therapy with bipolar patients.

Bipolar patients can take stock of the people in their lives who have been most understanding of their episodes of dysfunction. These are the people with whom bipolar patients may still be able to have good relationships, even after mania-induced conflicts and depression-induced estrangements. They are also the people who are least likely to reject the patients outright when they make overtures to reconcile. Still, patients have to use their rational responding techniques to gird themselves for the possibility that former friends will continue to distance themselves. Rejec-

tion of this sort is difficult to take, but it does not have to devastate
patients' present and future social lives.

Finally, it is important for bipolar patients to develop conversation
topics that do not necessarily involve their disorder or their treatment.
Role-playing can be useful to build such a repertoire. Although patients
may profess to wish to be honest about their troubles, there is no inherent
dishonesty (in most casual social situations) in keeping one's psychiatric
condition to oneself.

CONCLUSION

The cyclical pattern characteristic of bipolar disorder can cause patients to have their high hopes for recovery disappointed time and time
again, leading to demoralization and hopelessness. As a result, bipolar patients are especially prone toward suicidality, especially when in the throes
of the depressive phase. It is vital for therapists to assess patients for suicidal
ideation and intent. This can be accomplished periodically throughout the
course of therapy through direct verbal questioning; self-report measures
such as the BSSI, BDI, and BHS; and reports from patients' relatives and
other treatment providers. To combat patients' dysphoria and hopelessness,
therapists must strive to increase patients' sense of hope for a better future.
This approach is most credible when the patients are learning new coping
and life skills during the course of therapy, thereby increasing their chances
of having success experiences, including positive feedback from loved ones.

It is sometimes necessary for therapists and patients to devise a contract for safety. Although this does not ensure that patients will never
attempt to harm themselves, it provides a forum for an open discussion of
all the relevant issues pertinent to the risk of suicide. It is particularly useful

to identify and modify patients' maladaptive, "suicidogenic" beliefs, such as, "I am a burden to my loved ones, and therefore they would be better off if I killed myself." Additional interventions include a thorough review of the advantages and disadvantages of living and dying, identifying and using social support, and learning and practicing psychological skills such as communication and problem-solving. Anything that increases patients' sense of self-efficacy supports their decision to live and to strive to make their lives better.

5

PHARMACOTHERAPY IN THE CONTEXT OF COGNITIVE THERAPY FOR PATIENTS WITH BIPOLAR DISORDER

It is of the utmost importance for cognitive therapy and pharmacotherapy to be partners in the battle against manic depression. We hope that pharmacologists are able to learn and use the principles of cognitive therapy to maximize patient adherence and to heighten their own sensitivity to the experiences and beliefs of bipolar patients that typically scare them away from their treatment. Similarly, we have written this chapter in the hope that cognitive therapists will familiarize themselves with the state of the field of pharmacotherapy. Thus, in the first half of this chapter we offer the following brief, nonexhaustive summary of the current state of knowledge in the field.

In the second half of the chapter, we explicate the use of cognitive therapy in the service of increasing the patient's ability to make optimal use of pharmacotherapy. However, we endeavor to go beyond the facilitation of simple adherence to medication. We also hope to show how the skilled, caring, informed therapist can assist bipolar patients in making peace with medications.

STANDARD DRUG THERAPIES

Lithium

Interestingly, the medication that served as the first serious "break-through" in the pharmacological fight against bipolar disorder continues to be generally at the center of the standard of care (Goldberg & Harrow, 1999b). When patients faithfully take lithium, a body of evidence suggests that it has powerful protective value against the threat of suicide (Isometsä, 1993; Isometsä & Lonnqvist, 1998; Jamison, 1999; Nilsson, 1999; Tondo, Jamison, & Baldessarini, 1997). Lithium is considered a first-line agent for treating mania, both for acute episodes and for prevention of future oc-currences (Bauer et al., 1999).

One of the most important functions of lithium is to keep a euthymic patient from entering into new affective episodes. This represents both a benefit and a sticking point in taking lithium. Lithium has been shown to have a good prophylactic effect when used early in the course of a "classic" bipolar I disorder that does not involve significant comorbidity or mood incongruent psychotic features (Bauer et al., 1999). However, patients sometimes miss the point of taking a medication when they are feeling well. They are mindful of the side-effects and conclude that they are need-lessly putting themselves through aversive symptoms for no apparent ben-efit (Jamison & Akiskal, 1983). Therefore, there is always the risk that patients will reason to themselves that they are asymptomatic and therefore can safely go off their lithium. Clinicians must let their patients know that lithium is not just for active symptoms, but also for preventing future symp-toms. Nevertheless, as Solomon, Keitner, Miller, Shea, and Keller (1995) noted, taking lithium by no means guarantees that future symptoms are warded off. Additional medications may be required to stave off bouts of mania, and antidepressants may need to be added judiciously to the med-ication regimen in cases of the recurrence of depression. It is important that patients understand this, even though it is yet another reason they may become less than enchanted with lithium maintenance therapy.

Clearly, lithium has its limitations. Lithium's efficacy is muted when the illness is most virulent (Maj, 1999), in the prevention of episodes of bipolar II disorder, and when there is significant comorbidity (Greil, Klein-dienst, Erazo, & Muller-Oerlinghausen, 1998). The same is true when patients exhibit mood-incongruent psychotic features (Miklowitz, 1992), rapid cycling (Dunner & Fieve, 1974), and mixed episodes (Himmelhoch, 1986; 1994). Nonresponse to lithium can be counteracted in some cases by the addition of carbamazepine (Tegretol), divalproex (Depakote), or other mood stabilizers (Maj, 1999).

Whereas the preponderance of data supports the efficacy of lithium in reducing morbidity, it often does not eliminate mood episodes altogether, and the patients' overall levels of functioning are not always optimal (Maj, 1999). This finding cries out for the concurrent use of a psychosocial treatment such as cognitive therapy, so that patients can learn coping skills that improve the quality of life and where the development of a therapeutic relationship can provide additional support against hopelessness at times of symptom recurrence.

A poor quality of life can also predispose otherwise stabilized bipolar patients to relapse despite compliance with lithium (Maj, 1999), consistent with the findings that stressful life events serve as potential triggers for both depressive and manic episodes (e.g., Johnson & Miller, 1997; Johnson & Roberts, 1995). This is an important finding, because bipolar disorder itself can create a diminished quality of life, through losses in academic and vocational standing, rifts in relationships, financial strain, hospitalizations, stigma, and other problems (see chapter 7). Clearly, coordination of cognitive therapy and biological treatments is necessary to reduce the intrusiveness of bipolar disorder on the lives of patients.

Divalproex (Depakote)

The second medication approved by the Food and Drug Administration (the first being lithium) for the treatment of mania is divalproex (Depakote; Post et al., 1999). Depakote is in the class of drugs used as anticonvulsant agents. In addition to the placebo-controlled trials that support Depakote's efficacy, there is some preliminary evidence in support of its prophylactic effects (Bowden, 1998). Additionally, Walden, Normann, Langosch, Berger, and Grunze (1998) have indicated that Depakote may be especially useful in the treatment of mixed mania and rapid cycling, two forms of bipolar disorder that are difficult to treat with lithium. Depakote and lithium should not necessarily be viewed as rivals; in fact, they are often used in concert (Solomon, Keitner, Ryan, & Miller, 1998).

Carbamazepine (Tegretol)

Originally used for the treatment of seizure disorders such as epilepsy, carbamazepine is often used in the treatment of bipolar disorder for patients who do not have good responses to lithium alone. Considerable evidence (including numerous double-blind studies) supports carbamazepine's acute antimanic efficacy (Post, Ketter, Denicoff, & Pazzaglia, 1996; Post et al., 1999).

Highly treatment-resistant bipolar patients may benefit from a triple combination of carbamazepine, Depakote, and lithium (Denicoff et al., 1994). Rapid cyclers in particular have been found to respond better to a combination of anticonvulsants and lithium than either medication alone (Denicoff et al., 1994). Similarly, there is some evidence that anticonvulsants combined with lithium during euthymic periods provide better protection against the recurrence of affective symptoms (Solomon, Keitner, Ryan, & Miller, 1996).

Antidepressant Medications

Bipolar depression can be a particularly crushing and debilitating form of the family of depressions. In general, over the life span of individuals with bipolar disorder, depressions tend to be of longer duration than manias, and they occur with more frequency than recurrent depressive episodes in unipolar depressive individuals (Roy-Byrne, Post, Uhde, Porcu, & Davis, 1985). In clinical practice, it is very important to be aware that any given depressed patient who presents for treatment may have had a previous episode of hypomania or mania. This emphasizes the obvious need for a thorough history. Otherwise, antidepressant medications may be prescribed naively in isolation, thus putting the patient at risk for a manic breakthrough.

It is interesting that the use of antidepressants with depressive bipolar patients is not that uncommon. Antidepressants can be used legitimately in the treatment of bipolar depression when combined with mood stabilizers (Frances, Docherty, & Kahn, 1996). If patients exhibit severe or recurrent bipolar depression, it may be necessary to take the calculated risk of administering antidepressant medication. Nevertheless, when such patients begin to show signs of hypomania, mania, or a mixed state, the use of antidepressants should be discontinued (Bauer et al., 1999).

Because the use of antidepressant agents has been associated with switching to hypomania and mania, their application in bipolar depression remains the subject of ongoing debate (Goldberg & Kocsis, 1999). There is some evidence that selective serotonin reuptake inhibitors, bupropion (Wellbutrin), and venlafaxine (Effexor) may be somewhat less likely to evoke hypomania and mania than tricyclic antidepressants (TCAs; see Frances et al., 1996). Nevertheless, Goldberg and Kocsis (1999) summarized the current thinking in the field by stating that clinicians at large often recommend using "smaller-than-usual doses of antidepressants for shorter-than-usual periods of time during depressive phases of illness . . . [while] ensuring the presence of a 'therapeutic' blood level of a primary mood stabilizer before adding any anti-depressant medication . . ." (p. 136).

The use of monoamine oxidase inhibitors (MAOIs) is an intriguing option. A controlled study by Himmelhoch, Thase, Mallinger, and Houck (1991) found tranylcypromine (Parnate) to be superior to the TCA imipramine in treating bipolar depression when hypersomnia and hyperphagia were prominent symptoms. From a clinician's standpoint, the difficulty with MAOIs is the often-heard complaint that dietary restrictions present particular hazards in a population such as bipolar patients, where diminished concentration and impulsivity can lead to dangerous nonadherence. Medical consequences such as hypertensive crises can scare patients and therapists away from even the most promising medications. Not surprisingly, this is another area where cognitive therapy plays a potentially vital role in helping patients manage their approach to their pharmacotherapy properly and safely. For example, cognitive therapy emphasizes the importance of patients learning to monitor their own thoughts, feelings, and actions. Patients practice "taking data" on their functioning, and this can be extended to their diets and their routines of taking medication. This important skill can reduce potentially harmful mistakes and oversights. Additionally, cognitive therapy helps patients identify and test their beliefs and fears about medications, including those related to side effects and potential hazards.

Antipsychotic Medications

Psychotic symptoms sometimes are part of the clinical presentation of bipolar disorder. This refers to the presence of either delusions or hallucinations and may also include bizarre behavior or dysfunction in formal thought process (Bauer et al., 1999). Not surprisingly, neuroleptic medications have been used in clinical practice to treat bipolar patients who exhibit these features. The more recently developed antipsychotic medications, such as risperidone (Risperdal) and olanzapine (Zyprexa), seem to present bipolar patients with a somewhat reduced risk for tardive dyskinesia. There is some evidence that when risperidone is added to one or more mood stabilizers in response to a breakthrough episode, the global adaptational functioning of patients can be improved (Ghaemi, Sachs, Baldassano, & Truman, 1997).

RECENT DEVELOPMENTS IN PHARMACOTHERAPY

There has been a proliferation of new anticonvulsant (and other) medications that are being tested in the treatment of bipolar disorder. The field is advancing rapidly in terms of the development of these agents. However, tests of their efficacy require painstaking, systematic (and sometimes long-term) attention to methodological detail that requires years of study and replication. Nevertheless, these recent pharmacological applications have resulted in a surge of hope that is tempered somewhat by a bottleneck of uncertainty as the data are gathered carefully and slowly evaluated. The following is a nonexhaustive review of a sampling of these medications.

Lamotrigine (Lamictal)

A recently developed anticonvulsant, lamotrigine has had very posi-tive effects in the treatment of refractory epilepsy (Post et al., 1999). This outcome has led to a number of clinicians and researchers reporting its efficacy—especially when used adjunctively—in treatment-resistant bipo-lar depression (Labbate & Rubey, 1997), rapid cycling (Calabrese et al., 1999; Fatemi, Rapport, Calabrese, & Thuras, 1997), and mixed phases (Calabrese, Rapport, Shelton, & Kimmel, 1998).

According to Calabrese et al. (1999), the most common side-effects of lamotrigine include dizziness, tremor, somnolence, headache, and nausea. However, the most noxious side-effect arguably is a rash, which was cited by the patients in their study as the primary reason for discontinuation. Indeed, this rash can be downright dangerous in a pediatric population (Freeman & Stoll, 1999; Lovell, 1999). Fortunately, Kusumakar and Yatham (1997) demonstrated that these rashes can be reduced through a slow escalation of the dose of lamotrigine.

Some patients who have been on lithium for many years develop problems in renal functioning. The typical treatment for this medical prob-lem involves steroids, which unfortunately can trigger mania. This puts patients in a terrible bind. However, a positive finding in the use of la-motrigine is that it apparently reduces the likelihood of steroid-induced mania in such patients (Preda, Fazeli, McKay, Bowers, & Mazure, 1999).

Topiramate (Topomax)

Goldberg and Kocsis (1999) advocated further controlled trials of the anticonvulsant topiramate (Topomax), yet another promising agent that is becoming more prevalent in clinical practice. Normann, Langosch, Schaerer, Grunze, and Walden (1999) published a case study illustrating the apparent antimanic effects of topiramate. This must be balanced against findings such as those presented by Martin et al. (1999), who warn that topiramate may produce more neurocognitive side-effects than lamotri-gine.[1]

Anticonvulsant and Antianxiety Medications

When bipolar patients experience insomnia and agitation, the anti-convulsants clonazepam (Klonopin) and lorazepam (Ativan) are now

---

[1]There are many additional medications, including recently developed anticonvulsants, antipsychotics, calcium channel blockers, and other agents whose discussion goes beyond the scope of this volume on cognitive therapy. For a more complete review, the interested reader can refer to the Expert Consensus Guideline report *Medication Treatment of Bipolar Disorder* (Sachs, Printz, Kahn, Carpenter, & Docherty, 2000).

widely used. They do not induce mania or rapid cycling in the manner that has been suspected with alprazolam (Xanax; Arana, Pearlman, & Sahder, 1985). Clonazepam and lorazepam are relatively safe and are generally well tolerated by patients. Therefore, they are excellent alternatives to neuroleptics at times when patients complain that they cannot relax or rest (Chouinard, Annable, Tumier, Holobow, & Szkrumelak, 1993; Edwards, Stephenson, & Flewett, 1991; Post et al., 1998). Additional medications such as Ambien or a low dosage of trazodone (Desyrel) may also be used in an attempt to regulate the sleep of patients who can ill afford to have disrupted sleep cycles that may trigger mania. Clearly, such medications must be used judiciously, and patients must be educated about the differences between their mood stabilizers (which are not addictive) and their antianxiety drugs, which may be quite habit-forming.

Some basic principles that guide the field of pharmacotherapy for bipolar disorder appear in Exhibit 5.1. These are simple guidelines that can help orient patients and therapists. However, they should not be used in isolation, but rather in conjunction with a thorough consultation with a psychiatrist.

SPECIAL ISSUES IN THE PHARMACOTHERAPY OF BIPOLAR DISORDER

Challenges of Rapid Cycling

When lithium began to achieve standard, widespread use in the 1970s, clinicians and researchers noticed that a subgroup of bipolar patients was considerably less responsive than others to lithium. Dunner and Fieve (1974), in a highly cited study, noticed that this subgroup comprised mostly people who exhibited four or more affective episodes each year. This became the central criterion for the designation *rapid cycler*. Prien, Caffey, and Klett (1974) supported the Dunner and Fieve (1974) assertion by finding that patients with frequent attacks of depression and breakthrough mania tended to do relatively poorly on lithium maintenance therapy.

There have been many hypotheses about the etiology of rapid cycling. Among these are such diverse factors as substance abuse, history of head trauma and brain injury (Krauthammer & Klerman, 1978), and psychosocial and psychiatric histories consistent with borderline personality disorder (Dunner, 1999). However, one of the most significant biochemical distinctions between non–rapid cyclers and rapid cyclers is that the latter (especially the female patients) tend to have either a history of thyroid disease or a marked thyroid sensitivity to lithium treatment (Dunner, 1999; Joffe, Kutcher, & MacDonald, 1988). This has led to important developments in the use of thyroxin to treat rapid cycling (Bauer & Whybrow,

EXHIBIT 5.1
Some Basic Principles of Pharmacotherapy for Patients With Bipolar Disorder

- Use of a mood stabilizer, particularly lithium or divalproex (Depakote), is advisable in all phases of treatment, including long-term prevention of future episodes after symptom remission.
- Divalproex (Depakote) alone is preferred as an initial treatment for patients with either depression or mania with rapid cycling. It is the preferred first-line mood stabilizer for mixed states, and it may be better than lithium for patients with extensive histories of previous manic episodes (Swann, Bowden, Calabrese, Dilsaver, & Morris, 1999).
- For patients with hypomania, the use of a single mood stabilizer alone is reasonable.
- If either lithium or divalproex alone does not work, it is appropriate to use them in combination as the next trial.
- Carbamazepine (Tegretol) is the leading alternative mood stabilizer. Other commonly used anticonvulsant mood stabilizers include lamotrigine (Lamictal) and topiramate (Topomax).
- In cases of mild bipolar depression, the use of a single mood stabilizer is reasonable.
- For patients with severe depression, a standard antidepressant should be combined with lithium or divalproex and should be tapered within a few months after remission.
- Regarding the above, selective serotonin reuptake inhibitors are preferred; so is bupropion (Wellbutrin) or venlafaxine (Effexor).
- Atypical antipsychotic medications such as olanzapine (Zyprexa) and risperidone (Risperdal) are recommended as additional medications when psychotic symptoms are present, and can be used as adjuncts in treating patients with nonpsychotic episodes. Other atypical antipsychotic medications include clozapine (Clozaril) and quetiapine (Seroquel).
- Electroconvulsive therapy is a viable early treatment option in cases of severe or psychotic depression and when medications may be contraindicated.
- For short-term relief from the insomnia and agitation that sometimes accompany mania, sedatives can be prescribed until the mood stabilizer takes proper effect. Such sedatives, including benzodiazepines such as lorazepam (Ativan), clonazepam (Klonopin), and others, should be carefully monitored or avoided in patients with substance abuse histories.
- Prescribing more than three medications can become problematic, because such polypharmacy goes beyond available practice guidelines. This approach would need to be well defined and well justified (Staab, 2000).

Note. See also Sachs et al. (2000). This Exhibit provides a simple, general summary of basic practices in the pharmacotherapy of bipolar disorder. It should not be taken as a comprehensive statement, nor as a reflection of a uniform approach for all patients. For example, there are some second-line and third-line medications—some researched more than others—that are not listed above. Also, we have not attempted to discuss the issues pertinent to dosing, blood levels, or washing out. Further, side-effects can differ from patient to patient. See Sachs et al. (2000) for a more exhaustive review of this important topic.

1990). Interestingly, Bauer et al. (1999) have still maintained that lithium should be the first-line treatment for rapid-cycling bipolar disorder, although the benefits of lithium for this population take a long time (perhaps 6 months or more) to accrue, and patients should be monitored for the emergence of hypothyroidism (Dunner, 1999). Bauer et al. (1999) recommended that it is also typical for rapid cyclers to benefit from the discontinuation of any antidepressant medication they may be taking and from the addition of either a mood stabilizer to complement the lithium or "alternative therapies," including high-dose levothyroxine.

Dunner (1999) made a point that is particularly germane to this book, namely, that a psychosocial treatment such as cognitive therapy is highly desirable when patients experience depression but cannot safely take antidepression medication without risking exacerbating the cycling. However, cognitive therapists—a group that eschews "all-or-none" thinking—would argue that antidepressants should not be ruled out altogether if it can be shown that there is a "middle ground" alternative, which there appears to be in the form of sertraline (Zoloft) and paroxetine (Paxil). These antidepressants possess a short half-life, allowing clinicians the opportunity for prompt discontinuation at the first prodromal signs of hypomania or mania (Dunner, 1999). Nevertheless, this is a high-risk strategy and is best used when all conservative means of pharmacotherapy have failed and after a trial of cognitive therapy has been given sufficient time to teach patients an array of self-help skills.

Electroconvulsant treatment (ECT) has also been proposed as an option for treatment-resistant rapid cycling. However, this poses some complications, and lithium must be discontinued prior to ECT to prevent neurotoxicity (Small, Kellams, Milstein, & Small, 1980). Again, where specific medication options are ruled out, secondary drugs (e.g., other mood stabilizers) can be used, and cognitive therapy can emerge as a particularly important part of the treatment package. It should be noted that ECT is a somatic treatment option when medications as a whole are ill advised, such as when a bipolar sufferer is in the first trimester of pregnancy and decides to eliminate all pharmacotherapy as a precaution against possible teratogenicity (Schou, 1990). As Chor et al. (1988) illustrated, cognitive therapy can play a central role in the treatment of such patients.

Response to Subsyndromal Mood Fluctuations

Substantial numbers of actively treated bipolar patients experience interepisode symptoms (Solomon et al., 1995). This is part and parcel of the disorder, where treatment-induced improvements in functioning are common, but long periods of symptom-free living can be frustratingly elusive. This is another area in which cognitive therapy makes a significant contribution, by helping patients to cope with residual symptoms; recognize a worsening of prodromes before they become full-blown; and maintain a structured, moderated, goal-directed lifestyle that restricts the exacerbation of symptoms and improves overall quality of life.

Cognitive therapy is also extremely important in the management of subsyndromal mood fluctuations, based on the data indicating that inter-episode symptoms predict poorer outcome to pharmacological treatment (Tohen et al., 1990). For example, significant affective morbidity exists even in adequately treated bipolar patients, and this morbidity is predictive of relapse with full affective episodes (Gitlin et al., 1995). Anecdotally, we have witnessed that a ramping up of the frequency of cognitive therapy sessions and homework assignments at such times helps stave off such relapses. In other words, affective symptoms that occur between full-blown episodes serve as an excellent, natural testing ground for the prophylactic benefits of cognitive therapy.

Ubiquity of Side-Effects

Side-effects can occur at any serum level of the medication in question, including those in the therapeutic range (Bauer & McBride, 1996). However, serious side-effects and toxicity are most likely to occur when dosages go above the ceiling of the therapeutic range. At first blush, it may seem that this situation should be fairly easy to avoid; however, that would be an overly simplistic view. For example, different medications have different half-lives, thus making the timing of successive doses quite important and sometimes easy to confuse (such as when a patient cannot remember whether he has taken his lithium and so mistakenly takes it again too soon). Also, medication interactions can pose a problem, such as when a typically harmless diuretic causes a patient's typical lithium dose to result in too high a concentration in the bloodstream. Environmental conditions can also play tricks with a patient's blood level, such as when a patient experiences unexpected problems as a result of traveling to high altitudes. A patient's age is also a factor, with the elderly being more susceptible to side-effects, even within the standard ranges of many medications (Bauer & McBride, 1996).

Some patients will react adversely to the side-effects they experience when they are on dosages that their doctors are confident will be effective and safe. At times, a slight downward adjustment or the addition of another medication can ease the situation. Unfortunately, such action can just as likely cause further problems, such as a diminishing of therapeutic effectiveness (in the case of the decreasing of a dose) or the introduction of further side-effects (e.g., when an additional agent is added, presumably to counteract the problems associated with the first medication). At times, the patients must be taken (carefully) off an otherwise helpful medication altogether, thus causing both the patients and their therapists considerable consternation. Yet another problem associated with some of the medications for bipolar disorder is "switching" from depression to mania. This type of iatrogenic result can be minimized with painstaking attention paid to a gradual titration phase, but this is an inexact science. Therefore, as mentioned earlier, some medications should be avoided altogether, such as antidepressants in isolation.

Because side-effects are a prime cause of medication discontinuation, therapists must be very alert and sensitive to their bipolar patients' responses to the medications in all respects, not just with regard to the target symptoms. Practitioners must be very respectful and empathic when helping their patients make important decisions about their treatment while they are in the midst of anger, dismay, fear, pain, and mistrust associated with their side-effects.

Additional special considerations in bipolar patients' pharmacotherapy appear in Exhibit 5.2. As we have stated previously, these are intended

EXHIBIT 5.2
Special Considerations in the Pharmacotherapy of
Patients With Bipolar Disorder

- For patients with heart disease, kidney dysfunction, or stroke or head injury resulting in mania, divalproex (Depakote) is the preferred, first-line medication.
- For patients with liver disease, lithium is the preferred, first-line medication.
- For patients who are wary of taking medications that lead to weight gain, carbamazepine (Tegretol) and lamotrigine (Lamictal) represent very high second-line agents.
- For female bipolar patients who are trying to get pregnant or who are in their first trimester of pregnancy, conventional antipsychotic medications such as haloperidol (Haldol) provide the preferred cost–benefit ratio. Lithium, divalproex (Depakote), and carbamazepine (Tegretol) all carry some fetal teratogenic risk in early pregnancy. Gradual discontinuation of these medications in advance of pregnancy lowers the risk of bipolar symptom relapse in comparison to abrupt discontinuation (Viguera et al., 2000).
- Electroconvulsant Treatment (ECT) is a somatic treatment option when the risk of medical complications from (and possible teratogenicity of) pharmacotherapy is deemed unacceptably high.
- In cases where a pregnant bipolar patient in her first trimester is at high risk of self-harm, the pros and cons of medication must be carefully weighed (in terms of fetal risk vs. risk to the mother). If it is determined that medication is needed to reduce the risk of catastrophic result for the mother, lithium is the preferred choice.
- For female bipolar patients in their second or third trimesters of pregnancy, conventional or atypical antipsychotics are preferred.
- There is uncertain consensus about what constitutes the best course of pharmacotherapy for postpartum, breast-feeding bipolar patients. This is a high-risk time for bipolar symptom relapse in women who remain off medication (Viguera et al., 2000).
- Conventional antipsychotics generally are not recommended for children or adolescents with bipolar disorder.
- For elderly patients with dementia, divalproex (Depakote) is the preferred, first-line medication.

Note. See also Sachs et al. (2000). As we have stated, these points represent general caveats. To make the best informed decision, the psychiatrist should assess each patient individually.

to be a nonexhaustive set of helpful guidelines. However, they are no substitute for an individualized medical assessment of risks and benefits.

MAKING PEACE WITH MEDICATIONS

Even when pharmacotherapy seems to be working, it is fairly common for bipolar patients to wish to be rid of their medications. In many instances, they stop taking their medications, believing that they are "fine" and therefore no longer need to subject themselves to this yoke (Goodwin & Jamison, 1990). As a result, many bipolar patients unwittingly increase the risk of symptom relapse (Silverstone & Romans-Clarkson, 1989; Strober, Morrell, Lampert, & Burroughs, 1990), hastening the onset of a new round of negative consequences for their lives, and perhaps reducing the efficacy of future trials of pharmacotherapy (Post, 1993).

Some patients have difficulties in taking their medications in the precise manner in which they were prescribed because of the complexities of their regimens. Simply put, the more medications—and dosages thereof—that one has to take, the more likely it is that mistakes are made. Even "minor" episodes of forgetfulness and benign neglect can have serious consequences, the likes of which can further reduce patients' motivation to take medications.

Even when medication schedules are straightforward and side-effects are mild, some patients are loath to be on medications for a variety of personal reasons. These patients maintain certain "antimedication beliefs" that turn them off to the idea of pharmacotherapy. In some cases, this occurs only when the patients are in their euphoric moods; however, in other instances patients have negative attitudes about medications regardless of their mood states. Still other patients may be neutral or ambivalent about taking therapeutic drugs, only to be swayed from compliance by friends or relatives who themselves harbor misgivings and misconceptions about the medications (Rush, 1988).

In addition to providing a technology of coping that can help bipolar patients modulate their affect and behavior, cognitive therapy can be immensely helpful when patients are having difficulties with their medications. For example, Cochran (1984) demonstrated the effectiveness of cognitive therapy in improving patients' fidelity in taking their prescribed dosages of lithium, both during adjunctive cognitive therapy and at a 6-month follow-up. She noted that a thorough assessment of patients' beliefs about their illness and toward medication can predict risk for their going off lithium, and these beliefs can be modified by cognitive therapy so that adherence to pharmacotherapy is enhanced. These observations of the efficacy of cognitive therapy in facilitating the proper and faithful use of necessary medication have been corroborated by the findings of several clinics (see Newman & Beck, 1992; Rush, 1988; Scott, 1996a, 1996b, in press; Scott et al., in press).

Beliefs That Discourage Patients From Taking Medication

Many patients who are engaged in active treatment understand the threat their bipolar illness poses and are receptive to pharmacotherapy to regain their mental health. However, when patients begin to feel well, they sometimes experience a strong motivation to discontinue their medications. This sentiment is especially strong when they are feeling hypomanic.

Hypomanic and Manic Phases

Patients who are feeling elated and powerful often do not believe that they are troubled individuals. They believe that their euphoric, energized feelings are quite desirable, and they may take offense at the suggestion that they are likely demonstrating a mood abnormality. This sentiment may be particularly strong if patients feel more creative and productive when in their "up" phase and believe that they must hurry up and accomplish as many things as possible before they slip back into a darker mood. Even when bipolar patients buy into the idea that something is wrong with their states of mind, they may still resist the plan to intervene to change such seemingly wonderful feelings. Common beliefs include the following:

1. "Medication will make me lose my happiness."
2. "Medication is only for people who feel sick. I feel perfectly fine, so there is no reason for me to take the medication."
3. "If I take the medication, I will lose all my good ideas."
4. "If I take the medication, I will lose all my energy."
5. "If I take the medication, I will become depressed again."
6. "Medication will turn me into a dull conformist."
7. "Medication will do more harm than good."

Additionally, some people who are in hypomanic or manic states object to medications more on the basis of their need to feel strong and in control of their lives than on the basis of their desire to remain euphoric per se. Because they highly value their sense of autonomy, freedom, and power, patients on a high are prone to maintain viewpoints that suggest the medications are a threat to these personal goals. Examples of such beliefs include the following:

1. "The therapist's telling me to take my medication infringes on my freedom."
2. "The therapist's telling me to take my medication implies that I am not in my right mind, and I take offense at this implication."

3. "If I take my medication I will be publicly admitting that something is seriously wrong with me."
4. "Being told to take my medication is patronizing and insulting."
5. "Taking medication puts me at risk for loss of privacy and social stigma."
6. "If my therapist instructs me to take medication, it means that he or she doesn't trust me or have faith in me the way I am."
7. "People won't take me seriously anymore if they know I am taking medication."
8. "I hate being told what to do; therefore if my therapist tells me to take my medication I will resist."

Beliefs such as these rarely are articulated without the therapist's prompting. Patients typically either thwart the therapists' attempts to enlist their cooperation without explaining why, or they divulge their negative beliefs as a result of skillful therapist questioning and other techniques (to be reviewed later in this chapter). In any case, it is helpful for therapists to be aware of these autonomy-protecting beliefs in advance, so that they give accurate empathy to their bipolar patients who are looking to bolster their sense of confidence and control under trying circumstances. Furthermore, by being closely attuned to the bipolar patient's viewpoints about medication, control, and freedom, therapists are more likely to conceptualize the patient's difficulties within a case formulation, rather than simply become exasperated and give up on treatment.

Depressed Phase

In general, our clinical observation is that bipolar patients who are experiencing depressive symptoms maintain somewhat less antagonistic views toward psychotropic medication than they do when they are hypomanic or manic. One may hypothesize that depressed patients are acutely aware of their suffering and therefore are a bit more willing to try medication that may alleviate their emotional pain.

Nevertheless, we do see patients who oppose pharmacological interventions while in their depressive states, even when these phases go on for months at a time. The complaints that such patients offer are similar to the objections put forth by unipolar depressed patients who wish to solve their problems without the use of chemicals. Perhaps the most common of these involve negative reactions to side-effects. In other instances, the patients' hopelessness gets in the way of their understanding the potential benefits of the medications. Instead, they simply see the sacrifices and hardships, to no avail. When patients are faithful to their pharmacotherapy regimens, yet still experience ongoing depressive symptoms, they may openly challenge the usefulness of putting themselves through a difficult treatment when they feel little or no benefit. Therapists must empathize with this position, even as they support the need for medications, perhaps while increasing the frequency or intensity of concurrent psychosocial interventions.

It is interesting—and perhaps most relevant from a psycho–educational standpoint—that some depressed patients entertain certain beliefs about medications that are borne of lack of knowledge and unsubstantiated fears:

1. "I will become addicted to my medications."
2. "The medications, taken as prescribed, could kill me."
3. "If my therapist tells me to take medication, it means that psychotherapy cannot help me."
4. "I will forget how much medication I already took, and I will wind up overdosing."
5. "Once I get into a long-term routine of taking medications, my life will never be the same again."
6. "If I take medications I will never be able to have children without worrying that they will be deformed."
7. "If I take medications I am agreeing to be a guinea pig for all these doctors' experiments."

If we evaluate beliefs such as these, it is possible to detect a kernel of truth in some of them. For example, on rare occasions medications that are properly prescribed and faithfully taken can indeed precipitate serious medical conditions. It is also sometimes true that patients become confused and take too much of their medications, thus putting themselves at risk of overdose. It is also entirely understandable how women patients may fear the effects of long-term medications on the health of their planned, future children. Additionally it is plausible that patients are right when they say that their lives will never be the same again. However, in this instance, the meaning patients attach to this belief is most salient. If they maintain that their lives necessarily will be miserable, then they will be less inclined to accept medications as a way of life. On the other hand, if patients view their use of pharmacotherapy as a sensible adjustment they must make as they make a transition to a new phase of life, they may not hold prejudices against their medications.

What we are saying is that although most of the antimedication beliefs we review are not backed up by the preponderance of data and are unlikely to be borne out in a statistical sense, they still pose a tangible threat to some patients. Therefore, we must make every effort to try to understand these fears with as much compassion and as little patronization as possible. On balance, the advantages of most well-tested medications for bipolar disorder outweigh their drawbacks, and we should highlight this to our patients. Nevertheless, we cannot dismiss the concerns of our patients. We must address them head on, validate the patients' feelings, yet still examine the evidence for and against the use of such medications as lithium, divalproex, carbamazepine, olanzapine, risperidone, lamotrigine, topiramate, and others.

Even when depressed bipolar patients do not hold fearful or antagonistic beliefs about their medications, they still may be disinclined to take them if they believe their situation is hopeless (e.g., "I am never going to recover from this horrible illness anyway, so what's the point of going to the trouble of taking medications?"). In such instances, therapists must demonstrate a great deal of sensitivity by focusing sympathetically on the patient's negative views of the future as an important therapeutic issue. This is especially true in light of the data suggesting that hopelessness is a conspicuous risk factor for suicide (A. T. Beck, Steer, et al. 1993). Although it certainly is important for therapists to assist their patients in modifying their negatively slanted beliefs about medication to facilitate their pharmacotherapy, the more basic and primary concern should be to focus on the patients' giving up on treatment and perhaps on life itself.

Yet another obstacle to patients' properly taking their medications is their inattentiveness and low concentration, which are symptoms of both mania and depression (American Psychiatric Association, 1994). Therapists must bear in mind that bipolar patients may be remiss in taking their medications as prescribed not out of fear, suspiciousness, hopelessness, or aversion to side-effects, but simply because of difficulties in attending to their doctor's instructions. Therapists must monitor their patients' train of thought during sessions to determine whether their negative ruminations and cognitive disorganization are getting in the way of understanding key points raised in session, including medication issues.

Strategies for Maximizing Proper Usage of Medications

To help bipolar patients take optimal advantage of the benefits that can accrue through the proper taking of medication, therapists can use two broad, "nonspecific" areas of interventions. These include providing patients with an education about the medications they are taking and building and maintaining a strong, trusting, therapeutic relationship. Following elaboration of these ideas, we review the application of a number of specific, standard cognitive therapy techniques (see J. S. Beck, 1995) in the service of increasing adherence to the medication regimen.

Education

When fear-producing beliefs are at the root of bipolar patients' neglect in taking their medications, a powerful remedy is to educate patients about the various drugs in question. (It is good practice to give patients information about their disorders and treatment as a general rule, whether the patients are fearful or not.) The psychiatrist should be willing to discuss the indications, risks, and benefits of each drug that has been prescribed (or that is being proposed). If the therapist is not the prescribing psychiatrist, he or she can consult with the latter to gain and clarify this information. When addressing pharmacotherapeutic issues with patients, nonpsychiatric therapists should take care to explain to patients that the psychiatrist should be viewed as the person who is best positioned and most responsible to provide information and directions about medications. Nevertheless, this should not prevent patients and their nonpsychiatric cognitive therapists from becoming informed participants in the process.

The nonpsychiatric therapist may refer to sources such as the Expert Consensus Guidelines on the Medication Treatment of Bipolar Disorder (Sachs, Printz, Kahn, Carpenter, & Docherty, 2000) as the basis for an informed discussion with patients about their medications. Many patients search the Internet for information about their illness, where peer review may be absent and the risk of misinformation is too high for comfort. Therefore, therapists should review and discuss the information that their patients print out from various web sites, reiterating that the psychiatrist should be consulted as well. Additionally, many patients consult with the Physician's Desk Reference (PDR; e.g., PDR, 2000). Although the PDR arguably is the single most authoritative text on medications on an annual basis, it is ill suited for patients to use, because it extensively lists "every side-effect that has ever been recorded [and] may lead to unfounded fears about the dangers of pharmacotherapy" (Wright & Schrodt, 1989, p. 273).

Therapists may educate their bipolar patient about their disorder and their medications through the following methods: (a) presenting the facts verbally, (b) answering patient's questions, (c) writing down instructions, (d) providing pamphlets and books, (e) checking for feedback and understanding, and (f) repeating the above steps (Wright & Schrodt, 1989).

The following example illustrates the manner in which a psychiatrist may explain the expected benefits and common side-effects of lithium to a patient. The informed, nonpsychiatric cognitive therapist can provide the same explanation to provide a powerful professional consensus for the patient:

> "Mr. G., I would like to give you some information about your Lithobid prescription, and afterward I would be happy to answer any questions you might have about what I have said. Lithobid is one of the brand names for lithium, which has been shown to be effective in moderating the extreme mood swings that otherwise cause bipolar patients so much suffering. This medication, taken in the proper dosage, will not make your mood bland or flat. In fact, you will still be able to experience joy, and you may occasionally feel blue, just like anybody

else. However—and this is the major benefit—your moods will not seem way out of proportion or out of control.

Like any other medication, lithium has side-effects, and there are times when patients who have pre-existing medical conditions should not take this medication. For example, persons who are early in pregnancy or who have kidney disease generally should not take lithium. However, for most people, lithium is safe as long as the prescribing doctor regularly measures the level of the drug in the patient's bloodstream to make sure that it is within safe and effective limits. This means that you will need to have blood drawn from time to time.

Here are some of the side-effects you may experience, especially early on: slight hand tremors, upset stomach, moderate weight gain (averaging about 10 pounds), and possibly more skin blemishes than usual. However, not everyone gets these side-effects, and most of them become milder on their own after a few weeks anyway. In summary, the benefits to your mood and thinking usually far outweigh the physical drawbacks. You will be the judge as to whether or not you are pleased with the overall results of taking this medication—and there are other types of medication you can try instead if the need arises—but research and clinical experience indicate that most people see positive results from this treatment. Lithium is one of the true miracle drugs in psychiatry [from Gorman, 1990], as about 80% of patients respond very well, and the risk of suicide is decreased [from Tondo et al., 1997]. Furthermore, it is safe and effective when used and supervised properly.

Speaking of proper use, it is very important that you take the lithobid as prescribed to get the maximum benefits. For example, you will need to take it regularly and faithfully, because missed dosages can diminish its effectiveness. On the other hand, you should never try to 'catch up' after a missed dose by taking more than you should at one time. Therefore, we'll work together to devise a routine for you that will enable you to use the medication like clockwork, with minimal inconvenience.

Now, if you have any questions about what I have just said, I would be happy to answer them for you. In fact, why don't you write down the main points of what I've just told you, for your personal reference? If there are any questions that I cannot answer, I would be happy to consult with (or direct you to) someone who can."

As alluded to in the above monologue, it is often important to give patients a written instruction sheet to make certain that they understand and remember what the therapist has said. This can circumvent the non-adherence that occurs as a result of patient confusion and lack of retention. An overview of selected, published materials geared toward patient education regarding pharmacotherapy appears in Exhibit 5.3.

The psychoeducational process continues throughout therapy. It is important for therapists to check regularly for the patients' understanding of their prescriptions and their responsibilities thereof. Similarly, therapists

Gorman, J. (1995). *The essential guide to psychiatric drugs* (2nd ed.). New York: St. Martin's Press.
Provides a broad review of psychiatric drugs, their side-effects, and their therapeutic effects in understandable language.

Schou, M. (1989). *Lithium treatment of manic-depressive illness; A practical guide.* Basel, Switzerland: Karger.
Offers straightforward advice about lithium.

Lithium Information Center/Stanley Center for the Innovative Treatment of Bipolar Disorder, Madison Institute of Medicine, 7617 Mineral Point Rd., Suite 300, Madison, WI 53717; (608) 827-2470. This center provides a number of pamphlets on lithium and other pharmacological agents, including the following:

Bohn, J., & Jefferson, J. (1992). *Lithium and manic depression.* Madison: University of Wisconsin, Lithium Information Center.
Guidebook about lithium in question-and-answer format.

Lithium Information Center. (1993). *Carbamazepine and manic depression: A guide.* Madison: University of Wisconsin, Author.
Discussion of the anticonvulsant carbamazepine (Tegretol) and its use for the treatment of bipolar disorder.

Jefferson, J. W., & Greist, J. H. (1996). *Divalproex and manic depression: A guide.* Madison: University of Wisconsin, Lithium Information Center, Dean Foundation.
Essential facts about valproate and valproic acid (Depakote, Depakene), and their use in treatment of bipolar disorder.

Dries, D. C., & Barklage, N. E. (1989). *Electro-convulsive therapy: A guide.* Madison: University of Wisconsin, Lithium Information Center.
Addresses the most frequently asked questions about electroconvulsive therapy and its use in treating depression.

See www.healthtechsys.com/mim.html for some of the above information and more (Madison Institute of Medicine).

---

must keep an open ear and an open mind to patients' concerns and complaints about their medications. As Wright and Schrodt (1989) noted, "Regular questioning about medications can also help to identify new issues (e.g., additional side-effects, conflicting information from other sources, questions from family members) that may require further psychoeducational efforts" (p. 273).

Establishing a Pharmacotherapeutic Alliance

A good therapeutic alliance between clinician and patient is necessary for pharmacotherapy to proceed with the fewest complications. As noted, the therapist facilitates the patient's developing trust by educating him or her about the specifics of both cognitive therapy and pharmacotherapy. With regard to medication, the therapists (e.g., the psychiatrist and the nonpsychiatric provider who works in tandem with the psychiatrist) engender a positive working alliance by explaining the various properties of the prescribed agent, including clinical action, side-effects, appropriate dosages, length of time before therapeutic effects are to be expected, and cost (Bassuk, Schoonover, & Gelenberg, 1983). This is especially pertinent to bipolar patients; they may feel that medication is useless when they are depressed and is superfluous when they feel euphoric. The therapist must provide an understandable rationale and emotional support if patients are going to have the best chance of using medication optimally.

The following points, adapted from a text on managing medication within the context of maintaining a therapeutic relationship with those who have borderline personality disorder (Layden et al., 1993), serve as useful guidelines in bipolar disorder as well:

1. Keep a positive attitude toward medication, without implying that it is a panacea or a magic substitute for responsible living.
2. Explain that medication is a vital part of the treatment program. At the same time, make sure that patients understand the importance of being invested in cognitive therapy as well. The combination of the two treatments may provide the most powerful effect.
3. Be prepared to tolerate the patient's angry, critical reactions to any monitoring of medication intake and to deal rationally and promptly with medication refusal or adverse symptom responses by examining the patient's automatic thoughts, beliefs, emotions, actions, physiological symptoms, and intentions. The risk of improper medication usage increases to the extent that you are unable to appreciate the patient's apprehensions, lack of understanding, and personal views.
4. Elicit the patient's thoughts and beliefs about medication. For example, a patient may believe erroneously that therapists prescribe medication only when they have given up on helping patients through psychosocial modalities. Be willing to take the patient's concerns seriously and to explore them thoughtfully while distinguishing the realistic from the unrealistic.
5. Combat your own pessimistic thoughts (as a therapist) by examining the patient's negative reactions to pharmacotherapy as a useful, rich source of hot cognitions (emotion-laden thoughts).

6. Calmly and respectfully clarify the roles and responsibilities of both therapist and patients (and the psychiatric consultant, if a third party is involved in the process). Discuss and institute safety controls (e.g., the patient should not make adjustments in the dosages without first consulting the psychiatrist).

7. Give high priority to teaching bipolar patients self-monitoring and self-instruction skills. Continue to work on these areas until it is clear that they are able to follow the prescription faithfully. As a corollary to this point, build on these skills as a way of increasing the patients' capacity for concentrating and attending to details. In addition to facilitating safe, effective use of the prescribed medications, this approach may teach patients to control social, academic, and vocational behaviors more successfully.

8. Maintain vigilance in monitoring patients' daily medication use. Be alert to inappropriate use, "forgetfulness," and stockpiling of drugs for possible suicide attempts. Keep close tabs on blood levels, such as is required for lithium and anticonvulsants.

Establishing a pharmacotherapeutic alliance requires a combination of knowledge, practice, positive attitude, humility, and persistence (Bassuk et al., 1983). Clearly, meeting these lofty goals requires that the pharmacotherapist possess excellent psychotherapeutic skills. This reemphasizes the importance of an integration between pharmacotherapy and cognitive therapy, as well as active cooperation between the two professionals who may be working with the same patient (as we describe later in this chapter).

Cognitive–Behavioral Strategies

Four basic, powerful cognitive therapy techniques may be used to modify bipolar patients' negative attitudes toward taking their medications and to help them stay organized and up to the task of adhering to their schedules and dosages: (a) Daily Thought Records (DTR), (b) guided discovery questioning techniques, (c) analysis of the advantages and disadvantages of taking psychotropic medication, and (d) stimulus control methods.

Daily Thought Records

DTRs (see J. S. Beck, 1995) help patients elucidate their thoughts and beliefs that discourage them from taking medication and also guide them in finding new ways of looking at their medication regimen.

For example, Ms. J. often "skipped" taking her Eskalith yet professed not to know why she was so inconsistent. When she completed her DTR (Exhibit 5.4), she made two interesting discoveries. First, until she had pondered her automatic thoughts at times when she was supposed to be taking her medication, she was convinced that her sporadic adherence was simply due to carelessness. Following completion of the DTR, Ms. J. realized that she was making some rather cavalier rationalizations (e.g., "Oh well. It isn't going to kill me if I miss a few times," and "I probably don't need lithium anyway").

Second, as Ms. J. pondered the situation further, it became apparent to her that her laissez-faire attitude toward her medication actually masked a more active reluctance to engage in pharmacotherapy. Specifically, she worried that "people [will] think I'm a freak or psychotic or something. I want to be regarded as a normal person!" When she realized that she viewed the taking of lithium as tantamount to wearing a scarlet letter, she was able to address this concern with her therapist directly.

As can be seen by her responses under the "rational response" column, Ms. J. successfully destigmatized her medication (and by extension, her bipolar disorder) and gave herself some compelling reasons for taking her lithium as prescribed. A further benefit accrued from the use of the DTR in that Ms. J. was able to modify her thoughts and behaviors while still saving face. In other words, by monitoring and changing her own thinking about the medication, she maintained her sense of autonomy and control. She did not have to construe her collaboration with the therapist as an act of sheer obedience, dependency, and helplessness. Thus, her working alliance with the therapist strengthened. Not surprisingly, the DTR indicates that the patient's outcome ratings show a diminishing of her feelings of annoyance and apathy.

Guided Discovery Questioning Techniques

Therapists can help bipolar patients begin the active process of assessing and modifying their negatively slanted beliefs about medication by engaging in Socratic questioning and dialogue about the issue in session. This is the essence of what is called "guided discovery" in cognitive therapy (A. T. Beck et al., 1979).

The first step involves the therapist inquiring about the patient's present medication status—for example, is the patient taking the medication regularly, as prescribed? Is the patient keeping his or her appointments with the prescribing physician (if there is another professional handling the medications)? Is the patient experiencing any noticeable benefits, or conversely, any untoward side-effects? Is the patient getting any negative feedback from others about being on medication for bipolar disorder? Does the patient have the next appointment arranged with the prescribing physician? These are but a few of the questions (asked at a relaxed pace) that start the process of guided discovery.

EXHIBIT 5.4
Ms. J.'s Daily Thought Record on Lithium

Date/Time	Situation	Automatic Thought(s)	Emotion(s)	Alternative Response	Outcome
Sunday	It's early Sunday morning and I realize I forgot to take my midday and nightly dosage of lithium the day before.	Oh well. It isn't going to kill me if I miss a few times. (100%)	Annoyed (85%)	Well, should you suddenly plummet into a depression you might very well feel suicidal again. So it might actually kill me if I skip a few times. (90%)	Annoyed (20%)
		I probably don't need lithium anyway. (90%)	Apathetic (50%)	Most signs show that you do need lithium. It's to your benefit to take the lithium. It isn't painful, and you have little side-effects. It isn't worth going off the meds and taking the risk of going through all that pain and craziness again. (90%)	Apathetic (0%)
		I don't want people to think I'm a freak or psychotic or something. I want to be regarded as a normal person!		I'm not crazy. I have a treatable disorder that many successful and creative and important people have had. If someone does, by chance, regard you as abnormal, it's not worth your time to have them as friends. People who really care about you won't stop being your friend because you take lithium. (100%)	

Patients' answers to these questions, along with their concomitant nonverbal reactions, serve as the therapist's initial cues about the existence of problematic behaviors and beliefs that may hinder their adherence to pharmacotherapy. For example, if a patient states that he is following the medication regimen but sounds less than convincing, the therapist may note that the patient seems a bit unsure and may ask him,

> "You seem to be a little uncertain. Are there some days when you're having difficulty in following through with all of your dosages? What is happening at those times when you intend to take your medication but then change your mind for some reason? What goes through your mind at those times?"

Questions such as these, asked in a friendly, interested, nonaccusatory manner, pave the way for an exploration of the patient's antimedication beliefs.

Another example is the patient who seems overtly angry when asked about her vigilance in taking her medication. Again, the therapist responds by asking questions, such as

> "Hmmm. I'm sorry if my questions struck you the wrong way. What was going through your mind when I began to ask you about your medications? Is there something about these particular medications that you don't like? Is there something about medications in general that you're not happy about? Is there something about being checked up on that rubs you the wrong way? Is there anything else on your mind that I should be more aware of? I will be more than happy to listen to your concerns and complaints and to answer your questions."

Then, follow through and show your willingness to do just that, with professionalism, composure, and grace.

The following dialogue illustrates how a therapist may use guided discovery questioning to assess and begin to modify the patient's excessively negative attitudes toward her medication:

Therapist: Colleen, do you have an appointment scheduled in the near future to have your blood lithium level checked?

Colleen: (Exasperated tone) No, not yet. I can't do everything at once, you know.

Therapist: (Recognizing a potential therapeutic alliance strain) I'm sorry. I didn't mean to imply that you had to do it right this minute. I know that you're under a lot of pressure in your life right now, and I certainly don't want to add to that pressure. How did my question strike you?

Colleen: It just gets to be a bit much sometimes. I have to come see you. I have to go see the psychiatrist. I have to get blood drawn. It's like my whole life revolves around my being a patient. It's all just a bit much.

Therapist:	Are you saying that your treatment is more trouble than it's worth sometimes?
Colleen:	Well, not exactly. But it would be a lot easier if I had only one appointment to worry about, instead of all these other appointments and all these daily medications to keep track of.
Therapist:	So, in some ways, the medication adds additional complications to your life?
Colleen:	(Nods yes, emphatically).
Therapist:	Is there anything else about taking lithium that you find troublesome? I'd like to try to help if there's a problem.
Colleen:	Well, I don't think there's anything you can do, actually.
Therapist:	Try me.
Colleen:	Well, I don't like the fact that everyone checks up on me all the time.
Therapist:	Everyone?
Colleen:	Yes. You, and Dr. G., and my husband. Everyone.
Therapist:	Hmmm. So, if I've got this straight, you view our attention to the medication as a form of looking over your shoulder?
Colleen:	Absolutely.
Therapist:	What does that signify to you?
Colleen:	That you all don't trust me, and you all think I'm a child or something. [At this point, the therapist makes a summary statement. She points out that the patient is annoyed in part because of some beliefs she has surrounding the lithium. For example, Colleen believes that taking medications for bipolar disorder unnecessarily complicates her life and that it sets her up to be monitored by people on a regular basis. Therefore, she feels like she is being treated like a child. The therapist then proceeds to ask questions that are geared to help Colleen reconstrue some of these negative beliefs more benignly.]
Therapist:	I know that taking lithium twice a day can be bothersome, and I know that you don't appreciate all the various appointments. Is there some other plausible way that you can look at this situation, other than thinking that it simply complicates your life and patronizes you?
Colleen:	I don't think so.

Therapist: Well, let me ask you this—how complicated is your life today, while you're getting cognitive therapy and lithium, compared to how complicated your life was when you had no treatment and no appointments?

Colleen: Well, you know that when I first came here to see you my life was in shambles. I was all over the place. It was sheer chaos.

Therapist: Sounds pretty complicated to me.

Colleen: Well, yeah . . . I guess so.

Therapist: How do things seem now by comparison?

Colleen: When you put it that way, I guess things aren't nearly as complicated now.

Therapist: Even with all the appointments, and dosages, and checking up on you, and everything?

Colleen: Yes.

Therapist: Are you willing to take a chance on going back to the way things were before you sought treatment?

Colleen: No way.

Therapist: What do you think might happen if you stop taking the lithium?

Colleen: I'd be taking a risk. (Pauses and frowns) But are you saying that cognitive therapy alone wouldn't make me well? That it wouldn't help me at all? If that's the case, I'll keep taking my medication, and I'll stop seeing *you*.

Therapist: What I'm saying is that the combination of lithium and cognitive therapy seems to be helping you a great deal. One treatment by itself may not be as powerful and may not cover all the bases. So, I'm asking if you're willing to take a gamble by breaking up a winning combination, in hopes that a simpler formula of treatment will work just as well?

Colleen: No, I'm not. But I've got to tell you that I don't appreciate being monitored all the time.

Therapist: Who does the monitoring?

Colleen: I already told you. What are you driving at?

Therapist: Well, when you figure in all the dosages you take, and the appointments that you keep, who actually does most of the checking up?

Colleen: When you put it that way, I would have to say that *I* do most of the checking up myself.

Therapist:	That's right. Is there someone looking over your shoulder 14 times a week telling you to take your medication?
Colleen:	Just my conscience.
Therapist:	You said you felt that you were being treated like a child. Are children generally placed in charge of taking their medications?
Colleen:	No.
Therapist:	In fact, with a medication as powerful as lithium, it is imperative that a mature, competent person is in charge of taking his or her own dosages. What does it tell you that you are in charge of the most important day-to-day monitoring of this potent drug?
Colleen:	I guess it means that you trust me and see me as an adult. (Pauses, pensively) Okay. If that's so, then why do you have to ask all these questions about the lithium? Why can't you just stick to the cognitive therapy and leave the medications off our agenda?
Therapist:	I'll give you my answer, but first I want to hear your own beliefs about the matter.
Colleen:	I usually think it's because you don't trust me to handle it on my own.
Therapist:	Do you still believe that?
Colleen:	Not as much as before, I guess.
Therapist:	What other reason could I have for asking you about your medications and blood levels?
Colleen:	Maybe you want to give me the chance to express some of my concerns about the medication.
Therapist:	Right, what else?
Colleen:	Maybe you want to find out if there are any side-effects that the psychiatrist should know about.
Therapist:	Right, why else?
Colleen:	I don't know. Why else?
Therapist:	Well, everything you have said so far has been accurate. In addition, I ask you about your lithium to stimulate the sort of discussion we're having right now, where we highlight some of your negative beliefs, and then begin to re-evaluate them in a more positive light. This is precisely what cognitive therapy is all about.
Colleen:	Ah-ha! So you're deliberately provoking me! (Chuckles)

Therapist:	That sounds terrible, doesn't it? (Chuckles) I just want to be privy to your thoughts and feelings about the medication, in addition to your thoughts and feelings about all the other things on our therapy agenda.
Colleen:	(In a playful tone) You're probably asking about the medications to cover your own behind as well.
Therapist:	Now that you mention it, it *is* good professional practice to keep abreast of all the aspects of a patient's treatment. Whenever I work with someone such as yourself—who is also seeing a psychiatrist—it is common sense for me to be up to snuff on the pharmacotherapy that's going on. So, in sum, you're right—I'm covering my behind! But I hope you see that it's in your best interest, too.
Colleen:	I do. I'm just giving you a hard time. See how it feels? [Therapist and patient share a hearty laugh.]

This dialogue is but one of many ways that therapists can use guided discovery in the service of testing and modifying patients' negative beliefs and feelings about their pharmacotherapy.

Weighing the Advantages and Disadvantages of Taking Psychotropic Medication

While patients are experiencing inconvenience, bothersome side-effects, fears of stigmatization, or other negative reactions pertaining to taking psychotropic medication, they may be apt to ignore the obvious benefits. Similarly, they may selectively forget the problems associated with having not been on medication and wax nostalgic about the days when they did not have medications to think about taking on a daily basis. In these instances, it is very instructive to examine systematically the pros and cons of both taking and not taking their prescribed pharmacotherapeutic agents.

To facilitate this process, therapists may use a format that has been applied successfully in the treatment of substance abuse patients (A. T. Beck, Wright, et al., 1993). Here, they use a 2 × 2 grid, within which patients write down the advantages and disadvantages of taking medication and of not taking medication. With substance-abusing patients, therapists try to help patients realize that abstention from drugs is the wisest choice. By contrast, therapists of bipolar patients endeavor to demonstrate that continued use of medication is the preferred course of action.

Exhibit 5.5 highlights the thinking of "Lanny," the college student discussed in chapter 3 who wanted to spend all of his time talking to the other residents of his dormitory about the meaning of life, rather than studying and completing class assignments. Although he typically took all of his med-

EXHIBIT 5.5
Lanny's Analysis of the Pros and Cons of Medication

NAME: _____Lanny_____ DATE: _May 15_____

AXIS I: _Bipolar I: Most recent depressed_____ AGE: _____21_____

MEDICATIONS: ___Lithium, Zoloft, Zyprexa_____

Advantages of Taking Medications	Advantages of Not Taking Medications
1. Keeps me out of the hospital.	1. Freedom!
2. Makes my mother worry less.	2. Save out-of-pocket expenses.
3. Helps me to feel that I'm doing all I can to help myself with my problems.	3. Nobody will ask me what I'm taking and why I'm taking it.
4. Gets my doctors off my back.	4. It's easier to deny that I have a serious problem.
5. Helps keep me in school so I eventually graduate.	5. Less stuff I have to carry with me.

Disadvantages of Taking Medications	Disadvantages of Not Taking Medications
1. I hate blood tests!	1. I might flip out again.
2. I feel like a zombie half the time.	2. I might try suicide again.
3. I'm sick and tired of damn side-effects!	3. I might have to go back into the hospital again.
4. It reminds me that I have a mental disorder.	4. My mother will scream bloody murder, and my father will say, "I told you so."
	5. My doctors will read me the riot act.
	6. I'll have messed up again.
	7. I'll have nobody to blame but myself if I get sick.

ications in a consistent fashion, he frequently complained that they slowed him down too much, and he often threatened to discontinue their use.

As demonstrated by his responses on the advantages–disadvantages grid, he gained a more balanced view of the situation as a result of this exercise. Therefore, instead of abandoning the use of medications, he decided to ask his psychiatrist if there was a way he could gradually diminish one of the medications (with sedative properties) on a trial basis. This middle-ground approach helped Lanny feel that he and his psychiatrist were collaborating in his best interest overall, because both parties had an active say in the direction that treatment would take.

Another patient used the advantages–disadvantages technique to conclude that her first priority was to have a "clear head." Therefore, she was willing to deal with troublesome physical side-effects as long as she believed her mental faculties were at optimal level. By the same token, she was not willing to tolerate medications that made her feel sick or feel badly about her body image, if her thinking and moods were not sufficiently aided in the process. Her psychiatrist understood this as a common sense reaction to her treatment, and as a result there was no power struggle between the therapist and patient.

Sometimes patients arrive at rather dramatic realizations about the advantages of taking medications. When patients come to their own conclusions, it is usually more powerful, personally credible, and durable in their memories than when they hear it from the therapist (complete with wagging finger, at least in patients' view). One of our patients, "Susan," wrote the following tribute to the advantages of taking her lithium, something she had not previously articulated until she did the advantages–disadvantages 2 × 2 grid for homework:

> Actually, being diagnosed as manic–depressive and being given a bottle of pills to help my condition has been a big relief. Before, I just thought I was a bad, self-centered, weak person who had few redeeming qualities. Now, I realize that I have an illness that can be treated. It took 13 weeks of careful monitoring and nasty side-effects, but I persevered and now swallow five capsules a day and have normalized behavior. I have no vicious mood swings, no holes in my memory, no outlandish shopping sprees, no heavy drinking, no desire to die, and no belief that I am a fundamentally bad person anymore. I donated a blood sample for research and it seems I inherited genetic markers for the disorder. After graphing my family tree, this is not surprising because my mother exhibits extreme moodiness and recklessness, my great-uncle committed suicide, and my great-grandmother was reported to have had a number of nervous breakdowns (which probably means she got so depressed she needed to be in the hospital). I also found out that I was one-eighth Navajo Indian, which is just really neat and has nothing to do with manic depression. Anyway, thanks to my diagnosis, my doctors, and my medication, I have a happier and healthier life. When I wasn't on lithium, my manic depression created sheer havoc in my life. Now it's not really a big deal.

The advantages–disadvantages grid is also a useful technique in that it may call to the therapist's attention some actual hazardous reactions that patients are having to a given medication. Patients may have their medications adjusted, thus improving the management of their care, increasing their sense of control over the course of treatment, and demonstrating that an adverse reaction to medications does not necessitate the cessation of pharmacotherapy altogether.

Stimulus Control Methods

Sometimes bipolar patients maintain fairly positive attitudes toward their medications but still do not adhere to the regimen because of lack of concentration or organization. In such cases, a number of stimulus control techniques can be used to maximize the likelihood that patients remember to take their medications in the prescribed fashion.

First, patients are instructed to keep activity schedules that highlight their daily patterns of behavior. Second, they note the activities in which they typically engage during those times of the day when they are supposed to take their medication. Third, they pair the activity with the medication on a regular basis, leading to the formation of a routine. Finally, therapists help patients generate a system of reminders to help them stick to their plan even if their concentration levels are not at their best. The following instructions illustrate the above; we have noticed better results when patients write down the instructions:

1. First dose of lithium. 7:00 A.M. Take first thing when entering the bathroom to brush teeth and shower. Tape a typed note under the medicine cabinet with the message "Li before brushing teeth" as a reminder.
2. Second dose of lithium. Noon. Take with lunch. Always start the meal by taking the medication along with a beverage.
3. Third dose of lithium. Take with supper. Always start the meal by taking the medication along with a beverage.
4. Fourth dose of lithium. At bedtime. Take medication in bathroom before brushing teeth. Record a check-mark in dated log book kept on night-stand (when setting the alarm) to signify "mission accomplished" for the day.

Daily calibrated pillboxes, which can be obtained easily at most pharmacies, serve as simple and effective organization tools, especially if the patient has to take more than one type of medication. Some patients benefit from using two pillboxes, one that they use exclusively for their doses upon awakening and at bedtime (kept in the bathroom or on an end table), and the other that they carry with them (in purses, briefcases, athletic bags) for the doses they take at work, at meals, or on the road.

When patients have exceptional difficulty in remembering to take their medications, therapists may also use telephone prompts, at least on a temporary basis until patients settle into a routine on their own. Although this technique sounds as if patients would find it intrusive on the one hand, or dependency-fostering on the other hand, there is anecdotal evidence that it can enhance adherence without complication. For example, when Colleen returned for a booster session 2 years after completing cognitive therapy, she reflected back on the telephone prompts as having been a positive turning point in treatment. She stated that the therapist's gentle persistence and vigilance in sticking to this plan inspired her to do the same and helped her feel that she was an important person who was "worth the effort."

WHEN PATIENTS ARE ROUTINELY FOLLOWING THE TREATMENT PLAN

It is very easy for therapists to take for granted those patients who steadfastly adhere to their medication. The former may not take notice that this is a rather extraordinary accomplishment on the part of the patient and therefore may not say anything about it. In other words, therapists may take a "no news is good news" approach to treatment.

We strongly advise practitioners who treat patients with bipolar disorder to take active notice of those patients who stick to the program through thick and thin and to express admiration, respect, and even gratitude (because the patients are making the job of treating them a lot easier!). This may seem like a "given" to some therapists, but if it is unspoken, patients may not realize what they are accomplishing. In the same way that we espouse that family members give each other positive, verbal reinforcement, we must do the same for bipolar patients who are bravely answering the call. The following are actual examples of therapist responses to patients and should serve as exemplars for showing support for patients who are faithfully following through with the demands of their treatment:

- "It occurred to me as I was reviewing your chart this week that you have been on [whichever medication] for over a year, and I have never once heard you utter a complaint about it. You just take it like a trooper, and I have to say that I attribute a great deal of your progress in therapy to your willingness to go along with the program, whereas many others do not. You are to be commended."
- "I'm so pleased that you have had such a reduction in your symptoms, and yet you are not looking for the first opportunity to get off your medication. You really understand the importance of continuing the treatment, even when you feel relatively well. That is a very sophisticated viewpoint, and it's the right one. Your long-term outlook is so much better because you have shown the wisdom—and accepted the responsibility—of making your medications a way of life. This is exactly what needed to happen, but few have mastered the art. You should be proud and very hopeful."

- "I have to tell you how much I admire the way that you have been bearing up despite the side-effects. We have been able to make some important changes in your medications because you were willing to continue with treatment even though you felt so sick and even before you had reason to believe that the medications would help your bipolar illness. It would have been so easy to stop taking the medication, what with all the discomfort you have had to endure. It would have been so simple for you just to conclude that nothing was going to help you and that you should discontinue treatment. Instead, you took the more difficult, but far better route. You kept trying. You kept me apprised of your symptoms and side-effects, and you followed instructions when we tried to make adjustments. Your collaboration with treatment is making it possible for us to zero in on what could be most helpful for you. You're helping your own cause tremendously, and I want to let you know how much I appreciate your efforts."

This kind of verbal support and encouragement is warranted for patients who are succeeding in their quest to "make peace" with their drug therapy. It is also an important way for the therapists and patients to reaffirm their common bond and their working alliance.

THE COGNITIVE MODEL AND COLLABORATION WITH OTHER PROFESSIONALS

Bipolar patients often hire the services of a psychiatrist who prescribes the medications and at least one other mental health practitioner who provides psychosocial counseling and interventions. One of the benefits to this arrangement is that patients receive multidisciplinary care (and the increased frequency of clinical contact that goes along with this). However, one of the drawbacks is that the two or more professionals may not communicate with each other, leading to suboptimally coordinated care. In addition, this arrangement complicates the therapeutic relationship (Wright & Thase, 1992). These are problems that need to be averted through a method of planned collaboration between all parties (Scott, 1996a).

It is interesting that despite the high prevalence of the practice pattern of combining a psychiatrist and another nonphysician therapist in the care of bipolar patients, there has been almost no systematic research on case consultation strategies for such conjointly delivered treatment (for a rare exception, see Hansen-Grant & Riba, 1995). Fortunately, a promising, exciting study at the University of Pennsylvania is investigating this issue with a population of depressed patients who require combined cognitive therapy and medication (Moras & DeMartinis, 1999). The research aims to test the effectiveness of a new, rigorous consultation model for psychiatric outpatient treatment that involves two providers for one patient. The purpose of the model is to facilitate the coordination and integration of the practitioners' interventions and to stimulate more thorough communication about the patients involved.

The ultimate goal, of course, is to enhance patient's adherence with each component of the treatment and to maximize the potential efficacy of each component of treatment. As Moras and DeMartinis (1999) stated, "It is crucial to coordinate providers' interventions so that a consistent 'message' and intervention strategy [are] being given to a patient at all times" (p. 5). This prevents inadvertent (and intentional!) comments from one practitioner undermining the credibility or methods of the other. Instead, if practitioners have a concern or disagreement, they have ample opportunity and sufficient guidelines to hash out the issues among themselves—and come to a shared conclusion—rather than give the patients conflicting information about the direction of treatment. Most intriguing is the component of this consultation model that helps the two practitioners overtly support each other's work, such as when the cognitive therapist assists the patients with their fears about medication and the psychiatrist emphasizes that medications are vital but that "pills don't teach skills." Not only does this mutually reinforce the respective treatment plans, it also diminishes the likelihood of scenarios where some patients attempt to form an alliance with one health care provider against another (Basco & Rush, 1996).

Another advantage of the Moras and DeMartinis model is that it makes use of a new assessment instrument, the Depression Beliefs Questionnaire, Version I (Moras, Newman, & Schweizer, 2000), which examines patients' views about their mood disorder, including their beliefs about causality, prognosis, the role of medications, the role of talking to a therapist, and stigma, among other issues. The psychiatrists and nonphysician therapists taking part in this study have access to individual patients' data and therefore are able to spot patients' problematic beliefs that may impede one or both modalities of treatment. The practitioners then are able to form a joint plan to address these beliefs, so that patients have a clearer picture of what an optimal treatment entails and so their misconceptions can be addressed from two therapeutic fronts simultaneously. Given that the psychiatrists and nonphysician therapists in this study work out of offices in the same building, face-to-face communication is facilitated in a way that may not be the norm in everyday practice. However, the consultation model being tested allows for all manner of communication (telephone calls, letters, e-mails that identify patients by code number) that are likely to be used when the practitioners are located at different facilities.

We do not expect that cognitive therapy would be given to bipolar patients in isolation except in the rarest, most extraordinary clinical situations. Therefore, an understanding of the efficacy of cognitive therapy in the treatment of bipolar disorder will need to take into account its role in facilitating pharmacotherapy. The model being tested by Moras and DeMartinis (1999) promises to go a long way toward empirically spelling out what needs to be done.

CONCLUSION

It is one of the basic facts in the field of mental health that patients who have bipolar disorder require some sort of somatic treatment, generally medication. Lithium and Depakote generally are considered to be the first-line medications of choice for bipolar disorder. Faithful use of lithium has been associated with markedly decreased rates of suicide. Anticonvulsants such as Tegretol typically are used as second-line medications, often in conjunction with lithium or Depakote. Antidepressants—most preferably selective serotonin reuptake inhibitors, Wellbutrin, and Effexor—are sometimes used in conjunction with mood stabilizers in the treatment of bipolar depression. Great care must be taken in their delivery so as to minimize the risk of patients' "switching" to mania. The new generation of neuroleptic medications, such as Risperdal and Zyprexa, which pose less of a risk of inducing tardive dyskinesia than their earlier counterpart medications (such as Haldol), are being used with some success when bipolar patients exhibit marked agitation or psychotic symptoms. A host of pharmacological agents have been recently developed and used, including Lamictal and Topomax, as well as thyroid medications, providing hope for patients who have not been optimally responsive to first-line and second-line medications.

Effective pharmacotherapy provides patients with more than chemicals; it involves respecting their desire to minimize side-effects, giving empathy for their frustration and uncertainty, and expressing realistic hope for therapeutic effects. Unfortunately, many individuals with bipolar disorder choose to go off their prescribed medications at some point during the course of their illness, typically leading to highly negative consequences. To encourage maximum collaboration from patients regarding their pharmacotherapy, therapists must assess, conceptualize, address, and try to modify the patients' magnified, negative beliefs about their medications. Therapists have to educate their bipolar patients about their treatment, including the advantages and disadvantages of various medications. They must also be willing to listen to their patients' complaints without summarily dismissing them. Therapists can use a variety of cognitive–behavioral techniques to maximize the patients' adherence to medications, including DTRs to modify negative beliefs, stimulus control and daily routines to reduce carelessness and forgetfulness, flashcards for instructive reminders, family assistance, and other strategies.

A new consultation model being developed at the University of Pennsylvania by Moras and DeMartinis (1999) promises to improve the degree of support that multiple practitioners with the same bipolar patient give each other, thus improving the coordination of care for bipolar patients receiving both medications and cognitive therapy.

6

BIPOLAR DISORDER AND THE FAMILY

Bipolar disorder and its treatment frequently are family affairs. The extreme, cyclical symptoms that people with bipolar disorder exhibit can have a profound effect on those who are closest to them, altering their lives in unwelcome and disturbing ways. Similarly, the process of treatment for bipolar disorder can be affected, for better or worse, by the actions of those with whom they live. Along these same lines, episodes of relapse and recovery can be influenced by the manner in which patients and the people who are most important to them relate to one another over time.

This chapter will address the role that significant others and immediate family members play in the course of patients' bipolar disorder (see Miklowitz & Goldstein, 1997). We examine the concept of negative expressed emotion (EE) as an important variable in anticipating between-sessions risk of symptom exacerbation in patients, and address the use of couples or family therapy sessions in making family interactions more of an asset to the patient's therapeutic progress, rather than an unfortunate and inadvertent hindrance. This is done within an approach that is mindful of the high degree of distress that bipolar patients and their loved ones typically endure, and thus we offer interventions from a standpoint of empathy and problem-solving, not from blame or shame.

The siblings, parents, children, spouses, and lovers of people exhibiting bipolar symptoms suffer consequences of the disorder as well. This effect is heightened if they reside full-time with the patients or otherwise depend on them for running a secure, effective household. For example, such people often have to contend with such trials and tribulations as monetary loss, infidelity, deceit, neglect, safety hazards, excessive responsibilities, legal troubles, abusive behavior, and general worries about the well-being and future of the bipolar patients, to name a few.

By the same token, bipolar patients may experience stress, stigma, anger, guilt, demoralization, and related increased risk for exacerbation of the disorder as a result of the overcontrolling behaviors and critical attitudes (or the perceptions of such) expressed toward them at home. Vicious cycles of aversive and coercive behavior between patients and their stressed-out families are all too common and pose a significant drag on therapists' attempts to promote treatment adherence and efficacy. Therefore, thorough treatment for patients with bipolar disorder must include assessment of the patient's family situation, structure, living arrangements, strengths, and weaknesses. With the patient's permission, couples or family sessions are usually advisable during the course of treatment.

CASE EXAMPLES

The following are representative examples of the important interplay between bipolar patients and their immediate families or significant others. Later, when we discuss family interventions, we refer to these case examples (the details have been altered sufficiently to safeguard the patients' identities).

Case 1: Edgar

Edgar, age 40, sells insurance, has been married for 7 years, and is the father of a 4-year-old son. Although he had a few moderate depressive episodes dating back to adolescence and only one clearly identifiable hypomanic period during the honeymoon phase of his marriage, Edgar did not experience a full-blown manic episode until his son was born, which constituted an unusually late onset. Weeks of sleep deprivation were followed by Edgar's becoming highly irritable, verbally abusive toward his wife, and hypersexual. This resulted in his having an affair with a co-worker, a marked increase in secret expenditures, disappearances from home without warning or explanation, and a litany of lies to his wife. When he lapsed into a depression, Edgar confessed his affair, and his wife filed for divorce.

However, things soon became much more complicated. Edgar responded to the threat of losing his marriage by making a suicidal gesture. His wife decided to stay in the marriage and to help him through his psychiatric treatment. Unfortunately, Edgar did not take his medications as prescribed and missed several therapy sessions. Before long, his mania returned, along with his adulterous behavior. Edgar's wife was livid, and she left the house with their son to take up residence with her parents. Edgar returned to therapy, begging the therapist to help him get his wife and son back.

Case 2: Roxanne

Roxanne, age 32, is single and works in advertising. Although she had lived on her own since she graduated from college 10 years ago, she was living with her retired parents at the time of treatment. This followed the loss of her job and the suspension of her driver's license for repeated moving violations, as well as a solicitation charge (Roxanne explained that she was just trying to flirt her way out of a traffic ticket).

Roxanne was diagnosed with bipolar disorder and on the surface seemed to be willing to invest in both her cognitive therapy and pharmacotherapy. However, Roxanne spent most of her therapy sessions angrily recounting interactions with her parents, in which she accused them of mistreating her in numerous ways. For example, she railed against her father for confiscating her credit cards and checkbook and fought against her mother's attempts to monitor her whereabouts and associates. Roxanne threatened to abandon all treatment and to escape from the household if this "infantilizing" behavior did not stop. When the therapist suggested a family session to address these concerns, Roxanne snapped back that she had nothing to say to her parents and that any therapist who would work with her parents was unwelcome in her life. After carefully, sensitively discussing the issue with Roxanne, the therapist succeeded in convincing her to invite her parents to attend one session. Unfortunately, Roxanne's father turned down the offer and could be overheard over the telephone (in the background) yelling that "doctors don't know [anything]" about this disorder.

Case 3: Conrad

Conrad, age 25, is a graduate student who is engaged to be married. He entered therapy in a deeply depressed state and noted that his paternal grandfather had "manic depression" and killed himself 15 years ago. Conrad was concerned that he would be unable to finish his degree, because he could not face his coursework or thesis and could not envision a future in which he could cope with stress. Conrad also worried that his fiancée was becoming "another mother" to him and that this was going to be trouble.

Two months into treatment, Conrad became manic and related to the therapist that he no longer needed therapy. The therapist tried to convince him to continue with his cognitive therapy, to chart his progress toward his degree, and to consult the psychiatrist to "update" his medications in light of his mood shift. Conrad verbally agreed but did not show up for his next appointment, which had been scheduled for 2 days later. Instead, the therapist received a telephone message from Conrad's distraught fiancée, saying that he now wanted to quit school because he thought he was the "second coming of Bill Gates." She implored the therapist to return the call, to advise her on what she should do, and to try to get Conrad hospitalized.

Case 4: Mathilde

Mathilde, age 62, is a married homemaker with three adult sons. She entered cognitive therapy at the advice of her long-standing psychiatrist. He believed that although her most extreme mood swings were now controlled by her medications (including divalproex, which is known to be useful in the treatment of geriatric mania; cf. R. C. Young, 1997), she was still suffering from irritability, "bitterness," excessive self-isolation, and family discord.

Mathilde's husband accompanied her to her first cognitive therapy session and answered many of the questions that had been asked of her. The therapist asked to see Mathilde alone, whereupon she stated that although she knew her husband was a good man, she felt only anger toward him. She added that her sons were very worried about her but that their poor choices of wives had only made her life worse, and therefore she was disinclined to interact with them anymore. Mathilde further noted that she felt extremely guilty and "bad" for having such feelings about her husband and sons. Nevertheless, she said that her motto in life was, "No people, no problems." In other words, she wanted to be left alone, but her family would not comply.

What do these four patients have in common? Although diverse in demographics and symptom manifestations, each patient was experiencing significant problems with loved ones, and each situation suggested the possibility of couples or family interventions at some point. Although many of the family relationship problems may have had roots that predated the onset of the patients' bipolar disorder, it is clear that the bipolar disorder was highly associated with an exacerbation of the interpersonal strife noted in each example above. Therapy with these four patients would have to address the couples and family problems so as not to miss the central, maintaining factors in their clinical presentation, responsivity to treatment, and prognosis.

EXPRESSED EMOTION IN FAMILIES

As with families of people with schizophrenia (Kavanagh, 1992; Miklowitz, 1994), high EE in the families of people with bipolar disorder is associated with a more problematic course of the disorder (Miklowitz et al., 1988; Miklowitz, Simoneau, Sachs-Ericsson, Warner, & Suddath, 1996; O'Connell, Mayo, Flatow, Cuthbertson, & O'Brien, 1991; Priebe et al., 1989). This refers to high levels of negativity and criticism, although not necessarily an absence of positive verbalizations (Simoneau, Miklowitz, & Saleem, 1998). The bipolar patients themselves are part of this interactional system and have been observed to evoke hostile reactions from their relatives (Miklowitz, Wendel, & Simoneau, 1998). A typical high-EE interchange is characterized by an escalating volley of angry comments, in which the patient and the family members express negative affect, do not define and confront their problems constructively, and do not acknowledge the other party's points of view.

Low-EE families do have arguments, but their exchanges are not nearly as likely to escalate into a vicious cycle of attacks and counterattacks as are those that take place in high-EE families. Simoneau et al. (1998) noted a low-EE pattern in which either the bipolar patient or the loved one derailed the argument by changing the subject or maintaining a neutral tone. Based on these findings, the authors hypothesized that it would be highly beneficial for patients and their families to learn and practice effective communication skills and to use them in the service of active problem-solving.

Wendel and Miklowitz (1997) examined the transcripts of high- and low-EE families in their interactions with their bipolar relatives and found that there seemed to be a difference in attributional style. Specifically, the high-EE families were more apt to assume that the bipolar patients could control their symptoms (including their impulsive and destructive behaviors) if they were to "try" harder. Therefore, if patients were to engage in what family members regarded as obnoxious behavior, the latter would be prone to assume that the patients had acted with wanton disregard and deliberate malice toward the rest of the family. This creates more ill will between the parties than when the patients' behavior is construed as a manifestation of an illness. It is interesting that when it comes to ascribing controllability to patients' positive behaviors, no such difference is found between high- and low-EE families.

The clinical implications of the above findings are clear. The issues of blame and shame need to be addressed. If families believe that the bipolar patient is deliberately and maliciously causing problems, they are going to point fingers at him or her, which sets up a highly adversarial interpersonal situation. Family members must learn to express their concerns, fears, and even anger in constructive rather than stigmatizing ways.

However, they may first need to see that the problematic behavior of the patient cannot simply be attributed to bad intentions and character defects. Rather, the extreme mood states make it very difficult for the patient to control behavior. Inhibiting manic behavior and counteracting depressive withdrawal require caring assistance from surrounding parties, not vilification.

It must be remembered, however, that it is not always easy to offer such sympathetic assistance to someone who may have been behaving erratically, recklessly, and angrily, and causing negative repercussions for others. A striking reminder of this consideration comes from the work of Chakrabati, Kulhara, and Verma (1992), who investigated the extent of the burden on the families of patients with major affective disorders. Of the 29 relatives indicating that they felt "severe burden," 27 of these were relatives of patients with bipolar disorder. Lam et al. (1999) cited clinical instances in which spouses of bipolar patients at first tried to offer nurturance and understanding and were motivated to work things out. Unfortunately, the compromises and arrangements that the healthy spouses made with their manic–depressive spouses were broken as soon as an extreme affective episode occurred. The symptomatic spouses more readily would behave in ways that reflected the mood disorder than in ways that reflected the previous spousal agreements. This pattern would typically lead to disillusionment in the healthy spouses and outright anger if they believed that their ill spouses were acting with cavalier disregard. Over time, the healthy spouses tended to feel hopeless about things ever changing and at times regretted having entered into the marriage.

The phenomenon described above probably is at least partly responsible for the high rate of marital separation and divorce among bipolar patients (Brodie & Leff, 1971; Coryell, Endicott, Andreasen, & Keller, 1985). In a study of bipolar patients and their nonbipolar spouses, Targum, Dibble, Davenport, and Gershon (1981) found that 10 out of 19 nonbipolar spouses reported that they would not have married their spouses had they known about the bipolar disorder prior to the marriage, and 8 out of the 19 indicated that they would not have had children with their bipolar spouses. These are dramatic data, indicating the serious emotional impact that bipolar disorder has on a marriage and highlighting the potential for marital dissolution. Therefore, therapists need to assess the potential for discord in the marriages of patients and be prepared to provide conjoint interventions (or at least to make an appropriate referral for such treatment). At the very least, therapists can help the nonbipolar spouses to modify their more negative interpretations of their partners' behaviors. As the couple begins to work more as a team, the well spouse can assist in other ways, such as by being a "look-out" for the spouse's prodromes.

Another couples issue is the bipolar patient's sexual drive. In a nondiscordant relationship, a hypomanic increase in libido actually can enhance marital satisfaction, at least in the short run (cf. Jamison, Gerner, & Goodwin, 1979). However, hypomanic sexual desire and confidence in a marriage can sometimes start the patient on a slippery slope toward manic acts of infidelity, which can be problematic. This puts the therapist in the awkward position of deciding whether to tell a seemingly sexually content couple to watch out for this sort of trouble. It may be best to bring up this cautionary message to bipolar patients in their individual sessions. Nevertheless, if the nonbipolar spouse asks directly about the risk of infidelity (or expresses suspicions) in session, the therapist should not skirt the issue. This is just one of many problems that therapists must handle with the utmost respect and delicacy.

Whether couples and family sessions are held or not, the family is likely to affect the treatment, and clinicians need to do what they can to understand this influence. For example, patients often spontaneously discuss their interactions with the people with whom they live. Therapists can seize on this as an opportunity to ask questions that assess the nature of these relationships, including the patients' perceptions of them. Examples taken from the four cases previously described include the following:

- To Edgar: "When your wife asked that you not look after your son alone and insisted on being there with you, what ran through your mind? How did you feel?"
- To Roxanne: "When your parents keep asking if you've taken your medication, how much does it actually influence you? Does it make you more apt to take your medication when you're supposed to? Does it make you want to defy them by not taking your medication? Does it roll right off your back and have no influence at all? How would you characterize the situation?"
- To Conrad: "What goes through your mind when your mother makes reference to your grandfather who killed himself? What are your thoughts about your fiancée having called me about your symptoms?"
- To Mathilde: "What happens to your mood when your sons try to get you out of the house and when they invite you to family events? What do you think they're trying to accomplish? What message are you trying to give to them, and how do they take it?"

Naturally, the answers to these questions are subject to the biases of the bipolar patients' memories and attributions. Nevertheless, they shed light on the patients' information-processing style and provide a window into the patients' views of their significant others. To obtain additional points of view that may assist in gaining some objectivity, it may be beneficial for therapists to communicate directly with family members. Depending on the circumstances, and provided that the patient gives consent, this additional communication may take place over the telephone, by mail, or (preferably) in session.

FAMILY AND COUPLES SESSIONS

There is much to be achieved by seeing bipolar patients together with their immediate family members or other loved ones in session. First, clinicians have an opportunity to observe how the couple or family interact, which sheds light on some of the communication patterns that may be aggravating the patient's (and everyone's) condition. Although it is true that family exchanges in session may not accurately reflect the sorts of communications that go on at home, they are still likely to provide useful data. Second, therapists have the valuable chance to provide psychoeducation to both the patients and their family. This may involve a straight imparting of information about bipolar disorder, its treatment, and its course; giving feedback to correct misconceptions; or helping all parties to have reasonable and similar expectations about prognosis. Third, therapists can provide in-vivo interventions to break chains of aversive communications and to model more benevolent, effective ways of addressing one another.

Observing Patients and Their Family Members

Family sessions involving bipolar patients are similar in some respects to standard family therapy when there is no single identified patient. Clinicians must be highly skilled observers to keep track of many people, their reactions to the therapist, and their reactions to one another. Furthermore, therapists have to be "empathy jugglers," in that they need to be able to express concern and support to each member of the family, without unduly aggravating the others in the process. This alone represents excellent role-modeling, because therapists demonstrate how to listen, reflect, and show some respect and caring, yet make suggestions for change.

Regardless of how much conflict patients and their families are experiencing on a variety of issues, they are likely to agree wholeheartedly about at least one issue—namely, that they would prefer that they had never heard of bipolar disorder or experienced its ravages. The therapist can point out that nobody in the family asked for this problem and that everyone would be glad to see it go away, if that were easily accomplished. Therefore, patients and their families have a central, common interest. Even in cases in which a hypomanic or manic patient is minimizing the severity of the disorder, the therapist can still note that everyone in the family can benefit from a reduction in conflicts and worries. This requires cooperation and collaboration. The therapist can begin by asserting that he or she is determined to help the patient and the family as a whole.

Psycho-Educational Interventions

Education—for the patients, the family, and the therapists—is central to the initiation of couples or family therapy for bipolar disorder. Therapists can demonstrate respect for distressed patients and their families by asking them to "educate" the therapists about their experiences in dealing with bipolar disorder in the family. Especially when more than one person in the family has a severe affective disorder, the family may have a great deal to relate to the therapists.

For example, Edgar's wife taught the therapist that Edgar was most likely to engage in destructive, impulsive behavior in the aftermath of being sleepless or irritable. She alerted the therapist that when Edgar looked haggard or spoke in a caustic manner, this presaged a manic episode. Such information was invaluable in that it allowed the therapist to recognize when it was necessary to have an increase in the frequency of therapeutic contact and when to contact the prescribing psychiatrist for prompt pharmacotherapeutic intervention. Similarly, Roxanne's parents informed the therapist that their daughter's telephone habits were a tip-off about impending mania, in that she would telephone her friends indiscriminately, regardless of the hour of the night. In Conrad's case, the fiancée warned the therapist that Conrad favored taking antidepressants along with his lithium but that she had seen him experience breakthrough mania each time he had taken Zoloft in the past (perhaps because of missing his lithium doses). Mathilde's sons told her therapist that their mother often isolated herself when she was going into a mixed state of agitation and depression and that she was likely to stop taking her medications at such times. When therapists show respect for the education that families can provide about the individual patients, it stands to reasons that they are more receptive to the therapist's attempts to educate them in turn about the disorder and its interventions in general.

What can therapists tell patients and their families that they have not already learned the hard way? The following are some points that therapists can emphasize, toward the goal of addressing and modifying misconceptions and misattributions:

- Nobody deliberately causes his or her own bipolar disorder, as far as we know. Nobody asks to get this disorder, and nobody welcomes its devastating effects. (Some therapists may need to be apprised of this fact. One of Roxanne's most painful memories was of an allegation by a previous therapist that she produced her bipolar symptoms because she "wanted to be sick.")

- Stress can bring on an episode or worsen one. Therefore, it is important for the patients to learn stress management techniques and for the family as a whole to learn and practice interpersonal conflict resolution. Medication alone will not reduce environmental stressors; they must be dealt with directly.

- Although some form of pharmacotherapy (or other somatic treatment, such as electroconvulsive therapy) is almost always indicated in bipolar disorder, the question of which medications is far more unclear and problematic. Therefore, when patients complain about their medications, families should neither ignore this plea nor overreact as if the patients were being gratuitously oppositional. Instead, families should take these complaints seriously and encourage the patients to contact their prescribing psychiatrists, while supporting the necessity of medications as a general treatment strategy. Power struggles over medications should not be allowed to escalate. Communication with the mental health professionals providing care is a far better alternative. To handle thorny confidentiality issues, we suggest that therapists solicit an agreement from the patients and their families that families can report any perceived problems (e.g., difficulties regarding medications) to the therapist. The therapist in turn will report this information to the patients. No information should be shared "behind the patient's back."

- Bipolar patients are at risk for suicide. Suicidal threats or gestures must be taken seriously and reported to the therapist. When families feel as if they are being manipulated by the patients' suicidal comments or behaviors, their concerns become a high-priority topic in session. It is usually a sign that mutual empathy has broken down and that communication methods have become faulty. (We refer family members to the Appendix of Ellis and Newman's 1996 volume, which serves as a guidebook for loved ones of those who are threatening to commit suicide.)

- Hospitalization is sometimes necessary to save a suicidal patient's life or to make an important change in treatment that requires continuous professional supervision. However, it is not a panacea, in that it is a short-term solution to a long-term problem. Hospitalization should never be used as a "punishment" for the patient, and if the patient mistakenly interprets an inpatient commitment as such it will need to be addressed in session. At the same time, families sometimes need a respite from the rigors and stresses of caring for their symptomatic bipolar relative. Therefore, they should not feel guilty if they sometimes wish their patient could get inpatient care, just so they could get a rest. The best outcome, if it can be achieved, is for patients never to take the sort of action that would require emergency hospitalization. This goal can be spelled out explicitly.

Clearly, there is much more information that therapists can provide for bipolar patients and their families. They can discuss what is known about the course of the disorder and about the factors that influence prognosis for better or worse. For example, the chances of favorable response to treatment are enhanced by (a) steady, uninterrupted use of prescribed medications; (b) positive, available social supports; (c) good premorbid history; (d) an atmosphere of cooperation and good will in the patient's household; and (e) early intervention, to name a few. Treatment outcome is hindered by (a) episodes of straying from pharmacotherapy, (b) concomitant substance abuse, (c) high levels of interpersonal conflict in the patient's household, (d) social isolation, (e) poor premorbid history, and (f) failure to seek treatment until multiple episodes have occurred. This review is intended neither to promise a cure nor to demoralize patients and their families. Rather, it is an attempt to let them know where they stand regarding the course of treatment and to provide them with information that will allow them to do what is necessary to maximize the probability of more favorable outcomes.

Additionally, the family can be instructed to engage in bibliotherapy (see Exhibits 6.1 and 6.2) and to contact organizations that can give them useful information on mental health issues (see Exhibit 6.3). Therapists should encourage patients and their families to ask questions, and therapists should answer in good faith or at least seek the information if it is not immediately available.

Cognitive Therapy Strategies With Families

The methods we present here comprise standard, general methods of cognitive therapy as applied to couples and families (Baucom & Epstein, 1990; Dattilio & Padesky, 1990; Epstein, Schlesinger, & Dryden, 1988), with a focus on the treatment of bipolar disorder in a family system (cf. Miklowitz & Goldstein, 1997). The focus is present oriented, so that the family may make prompt changes in their interactions to reduce the levels of stress for the patient and family members. A review of the family history is important in terms of ascertaining the degree of genetic loading and family schemas that may be driving some of the conflict and turmoil (e.g., "If you leave school, you are a failure in this family"). However, in the interest of time, relatively greater emphasis is placed on making proactive changes in attitude and behavior, without necessitating the pursuit of deeper insights.

Accurate Empathy and Realistic Hope

From the outset, therapists need to be mindful of their power in treating vulnerable families—their power to assign responsibility for problems, their power to dictate treatment, and their power to set expectations for prognosis. It can be enormously helpful for patients and their families if the therapist starts by expressing empathy for all of them and a desire to help all of them. This is an important ingredient in standard family therapy, and it is certainly so in working with bipolar patients and their families.

One of the most respectful, reassuring things that therapists can do is to do a "strengths assessment" of the family. In other words, instead of focusing entirely on the patient's mood cycles, cognitive distortions, and behavioral extremes, the therapist can talk about the patient's talents, positive personal qualities, and future goals. Likewise, rather than exclusively pointing out family problems such as high EE, power struggles, and behaviors that "sabotage" treatment, therapists can review how family members show concern, extend themselves to help, and present the patient with positive resources for the present and future. Essentially, the therapist asks

EXHIBIT 6.2
Educational Brochures on Bipolar Disorder for
Patients and Their Families

Patients and their families can call 1-800-826-3632 to obtain these brochures from the National Depressive and Manic–Depressive Association (NDMDA) bookstore. Many of the resources listed below are available from NDMDA free of charge.

- "A Guide to Depressive and Manic–Depressive Illness: Diagnosis, Treatment and Support." 23 pp., 1998. National Depressive and Manic–Depressive Association.
- "Dark Glasses and Kaleidoscopes: Living with Manic Depression." This educational, 33-minute video features interviews with people who have manic depression. Doctors outline symptoms of the illness and coping strategies. 1997.
- "Depressive Illness: The Medical Facts, The Human Challenge." This booklet discusses symptoms of depression and manic depression, medications, doctor selection, and the possible impact of mood disorders on careers. Provides a mood chart for tracking mood fluctuations. 9 pp., 1998.
- "Expert Consensus Treatment Guidelines for Bipolar Disorder: A Guide for Patients and Families." This pamphlet provides answers to frequently asked questions about bipolar disorder. 8 pp., 1997.
- "Finding Peace of Mind: Medication Strategies for Bipolar Disorder." This brochure addresses issues related to manic depression and medications used to treat the illness. 22 pp., 1998.
- "If You Suspect Someone You Care About is Considering Suicide." This brochure was prepared in consultation with members of the NDMDA Scientific Advisory Board, including Robert M. A. Hirschfeld, MD; Jan Fawcett, MD; David Clark, PhD; Margaret Duthie; and Nancy Sheff. 6 pp., 1992.
- "Bipolar Illness: Rapid Cycling and Its Treatment." This brochure was prepared in consultation with members of the NDMDA Scientific Advisory Board, including Robert M. A. Hirschfeld, MD; Mark Bauer, MD; Joseph Calabrese, MD; and David Dunner, MD. 6 pp., 1991.
- "Living with Manic–Depressive Illness: A Guidebook for Patients, Families and Friends." This guidebook offers information about symptoms, diagnosis, and treatments of manic–depressive illness. 35 pp.
- "Manic–Depressive Illness, A Guide for Patients and Families" (Rev. ed.). Ruth Thompson et al. Excellent introduction for new patients and their families. 24 pp., 1987, Clarke Institute of Psychiatry.

implicitly or perhaps explicitly, "What can all of you do to help one another and to make an atmosphere of good will prevail in your family relationships? What can all of you do to support one another and to diminish one another's worries and pain?"

The skilled, empathic therapist is able to understand the frustration that a patient such as Roxanne feels when her access to money and mobility is denied by her father. At the same time, the father's view of the situation must be appreciated as well. He may be wary that Roxanne will

EXHIBIT 6.3
Organizations and Information Relating to Depression, Bipolar Disorder, and Suicide Prevention

1. National Institute of Mental Health, Public Inquiries, 6001 Executive Boulevard, Room 8184, MSC 9663, Bethesda, MD 20892-9663; www.nimh.nih.gov/public (general web site): www.nimh.nih.gov/publicat/bipolar.htm (bipolar Web site).
2. Stanley Foundation Bipolar Network, 5430 Grosvenor Lane, Suite 200, Bethesda, MD 20814; (800) 518-SFBN; Fax: (301) 571-0768; E-mail: info@bipolarnetwork.org; www.bipolarnetwork.org.
3. National Foundation for Depressive Illness, Post Office Box 2257, New York, NY 10116; (212) 268-4260, 1-800-248-4344; Fax: (212) 268-4434.
4. National Mental Health Association, 1021 Prince Street, Alexandria, VA 22314-2971; (703) 684-7722, 1-800-969-NMHA (6642); Fax: (703) 684-5968; www.nmha.org.
5. American Association of Suicidology, 4201 Connecticut Avenue, NW, Suite 408, Washington, DC 20008; (202) 237-2280; Fax: (202) 237-2282; www.suicidology.org.
6. American Foundation for Suicide Prevention, 120 Wall Street, 22nd Floor, New York, NY 10005; (888) 333-2377; Fax: (212) 363-6237.

spend herself—and the family—into financial ruin. All parties are hurting, and the therapist needs to appreciate and express this understanding. Similarly, therapists should be able to relate to why Edgar may feel suicidal in the aftermath of losing his wife and having limited access to his son. However, the therapist should be able to imagine how frightened, betrayed, and helpless the wife feels in response to Edgar's infidelity, lying, and erratic behavior. It would be ill advised for the therapist to agree blindly to Edgar's therapeutic agenda of restoring his marriage as it was. In summary, therapists have to be able to comprehend and express accurate empathy for the members of the family unit, yet still establish an agenda for change. This is the foundation for the interventions that follow.

Communication Skills

For patients and families to interact with less conflict and stress, they need to be able to talk and listen to each other with respect, thoughtfulness, and a collaborative mindset. Unfortunately, this requires exceptional skills and cooperation even under favorable circumstances. When patients are feeling irritable and agitated or when the families are especially worried, worn out, or exasperated, communication often deteriorates. At such times, the rate and intensity of criticisms, threats, and other forms of aversive comments often increase between the patients and their families. Under such conditions, problems do not typically get solved; on the contrary, they often become exacerbated, and the patient's condition may worsen. This is the general scenario that is emblematic of high EE, and it is associated with a less favorable symptomatic course and therapeutic outcome. Therefore, it is a major target for therapeutic intervention (Miklowitz & Goldstein, 1997).

In the spirit of examining the family's strengths and resources, therapists help families by focusing on shared goals. Yes, they may disagree about how much supervision patients need, or how much they should be willing to tolerate the side-effects of their medications, or how much they should use credit cards, but most families agree on some things, and these should be explicated. For example, patients and their families may agree that (a) it would be preferable if patients could lead a life free of serious, frequent negative consequences; (b) life would be easier if there was less anger and resentment between the parties; (c) the patients' successes in their work or academic life and personal life would be a success for the whole family; and (d) mutual understanding and cooperation are better than rampant mistrust and criticisms.

A minimum requirement for effective, constructive communication in the marriage and family is that the parties must improve their ability to listen and reflect. Unfortunately, interactions between patients and families often are marked by interruptions, quick counterpoints, and the mental filtering and stereotyping of what the other party is trying to say. Consider the following dialogue between Roxanne and her retired parents.

Roxanne: I need to stop at the mall on my way back from my therapy session. I'm going to need my credit card.

Father: (Sharply) You don't need a credit card! I'll give you 20 bucks. Bring me back the receipt.

Roxanne: (Angrily) I don't need or want your stinking money! Keep your (expletive) money! I just want my credit card. Why are you being so impossible?

Father: You can't be trusted with a credit card! But since you don't want my money, then fine! Suit yourself. Forget it! Have fun.

Roxanne: (Shouting) You're the biggest (expletive) cheapskate in the world. I hate you!

Mother: She's been like this all day. Call the doctor. She's out of control.

Roxanne: Shut up! Stay out of it!

Father: Just go to your therapy session and leave us in peace.

Roxanne: Screw that! I'm not taking this (expletive) anymore. *You're the problem, not me!*

The above dialogue is characteristic of families who are prone to exhibit high EE. The original problem (negotiating Roxanne's access to money) is abandoned, and the situation worsens through cross-complaining. The tone of the conversation also grows more contentious and hurtful for all parties (cf. Miklowitz et al., 1988). As a result of the unfortunate interchange between Roxanne and her parents, the family's problems were exacerbated, not resolved, and their relationships were damaged in the process. Roxanne felt deprived of respect, freedom, money, and support. The father felt manipulated, maligned, and disrespected. The mother felt helpless. Later, when the therapist was informed about the above scenario, he called for a family session in which communication problems were placed at the top of the agenda.

Rather than get into a "he said, she said" rehashing of the events, the therapist tried to model how each family member could have interpreted each other's comments and how they would have profited from reflecting in a respectful manner. For example, the therapist reviewed how the situation broke down:

> *Therapist:* Roxanne, you wanted to make a stop at the mall. It seemed like a reasonable thing to ask for your credit card that your father is holding for you. Mr. X (Roxanne's father), you wanted to give her $20 instead, because you were worried about Roxanne's history of excessive spending with credit cards. Roxanne, when you heard that your father wanted a receipt, you felt mistrusted and overcontrolled, and you got angry. However, instead of saying that you wanted to spend your own money, and not your father's—which could have been construed as a very responsible gesture—you instead told him in strong language to keep his money. Mr. X, instead of looking for the merit in what Roxanne was saying, and instead of explaining calmly why you saw things differently, you withdrew your offer and told Roxanne she could not be trusted. Roxanne, you then attacked your father's character, telling him he was a cheapskate. By the time that Mrs. X got into the conversation, you had all stereotyped each other in the worst possible way and resorted only to mutual recrimination. This was most unfortunate. Disagreements are going to happen in your family, but they need to be handled with much greater thought and care if you want to see an improvement in your family situation.

At this point, the therapist checks in with Roxanne and her family, to discover how they are interpreting these comments. Do they feel criticized further? Do they think that the therapist is minimizing their difficulties, implying that it would be easy to change their communications if they only acted "smarter?" Do they feel a lack of respect and empathy from the therapist? Patients and families who feel emotionally beaten up and depleted are apt to feel this way, and therapists must therefore be sensitive to this condition. The therapist must emphasize that the intent is to demonstrate the chain of events that comprise ineffective communication in the family, not to scold or blame the parties involved. With the patient's and family's forbearance, the therapist can then demonstrate how the conversation could have gone. For example,

> *Therapist:* Roxanne, you wanted to be able to spend your own money. You didn't ask your father for his money. Mr. X, you could have said, "Roxanne, I'm not comfortable with you having free rein over your credit cards yet. I would prefer if I just loaned you the money, so that you won't be tempted to overspend. I'm sorry if this seems overly restrictive, but I feel strongly that we shouldn't take any undue "risks." Roxanne, you could have replied, "But Dad, that makes me dependent on you, and I'm not comfortable with that situation. I would rather just be responsible for myself and use my own money." Mr. X, you could have said, "I agree with you in principle, but I think it makes more sense for you to limit your spending and to itemize what you buy. It's very important that you stick to a set budget, which is not what you do when you're hypomanic." Roxanne, you then could have come back with, "I don't like being denied access to my own credit card, but I'll go along with your suggestion if it will help show you that I'm composed, trustworthy, and in control of myself. I would also like to start talking about what I am going to have to do to regain some basic adult privileges again. As things stand now, I feel very powerless in this family, and that upsets me." Mr. X, a good response from you at that point might have been, "I appreciate your willingness to go along with my suggestion, and I think your request for a discussion about your future with money is reasonable to pursue. When shall we have this conversation, and should it be in your therapy session?"

The above represents a high standard of communication. At first blush, it looks as though the therapist not only is asking too much of a beleaguered patient and her family, but is also acting presumptuously, as if to read Roxanne's and her father's minds. However, this is a minor drawback compared to the potential benefits that may be derived from learning how constructive communication could be possible in their household. Therapists must remember to check with the patient and family for more feedback. For example, has the therapist ascertained each party's intentions accurately? Are the therapist's suggested comments realistic? Would the proposed, positive course of the conversation actually represent an acceptable outcome for each party? If so, the family can be asked to "reenact" the conversation, with the new, improved specifications. If not, the therapist should elicit further ideas for productive communication.

This process may have to be repeated many times over several sessions. Old communication habits die hard, especially when patients and their families hold negative attributions about the meanings of each others' comments. Such destructive interpretations not only lead to problematic miscommunication, they also inspire upset feelings, which further discolor attributions in a vicious cycle. For example, Roxanne believed that her father enjoyed being able to control her. In actuality, he expressed fatigue at playing the role of the financial gatekeeper. His fatigue led him to be curt, rather than take the time to explain his position. Roxanne then escalated her negative tone, denounced her father's idea, and insulted him by calling him "impossible." This further angered her father, who then withdrew his offer of money and spoke to her in a snide manner. This reinforced Roxanne's stereotyped view of her father as being a heartless dictator who loves money more than his own daughter, leading her to scream out that he is "the worst cheapskate in the world." The mother, hearing the commotion, started thinking that Roxanne's problems were beyond repair, and in her helplessness suggested that they "call the doctor." Roxanne took this to mean that the problems were all the result of her bipolar disorder. She felt blamed and stigmatized and lashed back by taking the extreme opposite position—that the parents were the ones with the problems, not her. Of course, this ignores the obvious interactional nature of the family's difficulties.

At times, the therapist may be taken to task by one or more members of the family. The essence of their critique might be, "If you had to live with this situation, you would not be so quick to demand all this thoughtful, respectful, calm dialogue. You would realize that this is not possible to do most of the time." Therapists would do well to validate this point: It is enormously difficult to keep one's cool and solve problems under adverse conditions. However, therapists should emphasize that by improving the family's communication style, the baseline level of stress that the family experiences can be lessened, making it more probable that improved communication skills can be used. In other words, a positive feedback loop can be established where a vicious cycle once existed. This is an important goal for all persons involved.

The principles of effective communication for bipolar patients and their families are highly similar to those taught to married couples in cognitive–behavioral therapy. They include the following:

1. *Use "I" statements rather than "you" statements.* Each member of the family is taught to start a sentence by expressing how he or she feels, instead of blaming or accusing another party. For example, Mathilde often made hostile comments to her

husband and sons such as, "You all make me sick." The therapist taught her to start by expressing her emotional state by saying something like, "I really don't feel like talking right now. Please leave me be." The therapist emphasized that this should become the prevailing method of initiating what might otherwise be an unpleasant dialogue.

2. *Turn complaints into requests.* When people stop to think before they speak, they find that it is possible to convert almost any aversive complaint into a moderately reasonable request. This method of communication enables someone to maintain his or her assertive stance without seeming unduly oppositional. For example, instead of telling her father that he is the world's worst cheapskate, Roxanne could ask her father to please take a calculated risk and allow her the freedom of making one or two planned expenditures. At the same time, Roxanne's mother could avoid saying things such as "[Roxanne] is out of control," in favor of asking Roxanne if she could please lower her voice and sit down to discuss the matter at hand in a calm fashion.

3. *Eschew the use of derogatory labels and profanity.* When family members deride and curse one another, they are eroding their relationships, not solving their problems. Edgar wanted to convince his wife to return to him, but when she refused he responded with vulgar language. This served only to reaffirm his wife's decision to go ahead with the divorce. Edgar's therapist made it clear that the therapeutic agenda had to be about getting well, not about persuading his wife to change her mind. Clearly, to demonstrate his fitness as a parent and to secure visitation privileges with his child, Edgar would have to demonstrate that he could control his temper. One of the best ways to achieve this was to aim at eliminating the use of all profanity in the presence of loved ones. Edgar was challenged by his therapist to state his opinions in a forthright, dignified, factual way.

4. *Make statements that express empathy, or provide new information; otherwise remain quiet!* This rule is reminiscent of the adage, "If you can't say something constructive, don't say anything at all." One of the more subtle aspects of high EE is a tendency for bipolar patients and their family members to repeat themselves and to "rub it in." Sometimes they believe they need to "drive home a point." At other times, they simply forget what they have said before. Whatever the case, excessive repetition is likely to be perceived as an irritant. Conrad had a tendency to repeat his "insights" to his fiancée,

which only served to convince her that he was high. This in turn led her to shun him, which incited Conrad to pursue her more vigorously. The therapist taught Conrad to monitor his urges to verbalize. When he felt compelled to talk at great length to his fiancée, he was instructed to ask himself the following questions before proceeding: "Will this tell her something that she hasn't already heard before?" and "Will this give her support and understanding?" To follow through, the answer to at least one of these questions had to be "yes," otherwise he pledged to restrain himself.

5. *Observe standard etiquette.* Patients and their family members are instructed to communicate in ways that do not reflect frustration and would not be seen by an outside party as being rude or inappropriate. For example, the patient should not telephone family members after a certain hour. Family members should not deliberately embarrass the patient by making belittling comments in public. Patients and family members alike should not make melodramatic threats (e.g., "I'm going to throw all your clothes out the window!" or "If you don't shut up I'm going to make you get out of the car, and you can hitch a ride home for all I care!").

Throughout this process, therapists must be acutely aware of how difficult it is to observe these high standards of communication even under routine familial circumstances. Therapists need to explain that the above guidelines are ideals to be pursued, not absolute edicts whose violation will bring the wrath of the therapist. All the while, therapists need to model these principles themselves by being graceful when they must intervene during heated family arguments in session.

Problem-Solving and Conflict Resolution

The behavioral manifestations of bipolar disorder often produce an increase in life problems. These range from the mundane, everyday sequelae of being moody, distractible, and argumentative to the more severe problems that stem from financial recklessness, social improprieties, sexual disinhibition, and suicidality. To make matters worse, bipolar patients often find themselves in emotional states that limit their ability to pull themselves together to address the difficulties their disorder has wrought (Jamison, 1995). The frequent result is a spreading of the problem, in terms of both the circle of people who are affected (e.g., loved ones) and the vicious cycle that is perpetuated.

The first step of effective problem-solving is to define the problem (Nezu et al., 1989). This seems straightforward enough until the therapist realizes that the patients and their families have radically different definitions of the problem. For example, Mathilde stated that her problem was that her husband and sons would not respect her privacy. She felt they had no right to insist that she leave her room and act sociably with visitors (including her daughters-in-law and grandchildren) when she was feeling "out of sorts." Mathilde believed that her family members were selfish men who just wanted her to be available to cater to their needs (e.g., prepare a snack for everyone). In stark contrast, Mathilde's husband and adult sons defined the problem as consisting of Mathilde's self-imposed isolation, her descent into depression, and her neglect of her loving grandchildren. On hearing this disparity in viewpoints, the therapist recognized that the first order of business in a family session would be to find a common ground in defining the problem.

One of the most fruitful ways to reach a compromise position in problem definition is to use the communication skills described above. Blame must be reduced, and thoughtful requests must be increased. Each party must be willing to try to summarize the other person's perceptions of the problem. Each party must be prepared to examine his or her own idiosyncratic interpretations of the situation and of the behavior of their family members. Toward this end, each member of the family who attends sessions should be introduced to the Daily Thought Record (DTR), so that they may be able to generate more benign attributions for one another's behavior. The seeds of compromise are sown by each person's use of such techniques. To shape their behavior and to increase the rate of learning, the therapist can give each family member a DTR for directed, organized use in session.

Exhibits 6.4, 6.5, and 6.6 represent DTRs written for homework by Mathilde, her husband, and her oldest son. The forms reference a single incident and thus shed light on the parties' respective personal interpretations and individual attempts to cope with the situation. Specifically, one of Mathilde's sons liked to come over to his parents' house with his wife after church on Sundays. He believed that this was a nice way for his wife to spend some time with his family, and he admitted liking the routine of watching Sunday afternoon football with his father. Mathilde was not as enthusiastic about these visits, as the DTRs demonstrate.

When the parties are able at least verbally to reflect each other's views of the problems they face, they are ready to brainstorm some solutions. For example, when Edgar and his wife decided that they needed to work together (even in the midst of their marital separation) for the benefit of their young son, they came to a conjoint session. At first, Edgar defined the problem as being his wife's overly harsh restrictions on visits with his son. By contrast, Edgar's wife viewed the problem as her husband's untrustworthiness and secretiveness. As far as she was concerned, she could no longer be sure of Edgar's whereabouts, but she was adamant that she wanted to know her son's whereabouts at all times, even if that necessitated

EXHIBIT 6.4
Mathilde's Daily Thought Record

Date/Time	Situation	Automatic Thought(s)	Emotion(s)	Alternative Response	Outcome
Sunday around lunch	My son and that woman are here again.	They expect me to wait on them. They have no compassion for an old woman who's not well. They're so selfish. I'm not budging from this room. I'm getting tired of my husband always inviting them. Why does he always do this to me?	Angry (100%)	I almost never leave this room when they're here, but they always come on Sundays anyway. Maybe they don't need me to cook for them after all. Maybe I'm just being stubborn. My husband goes about his business in the way he sees fit. He's not trying to make life difficult for me. I don't mind seeing my son, and I don't really have to talk to his wife if I don't want to.	Angry (50%) Ashamed (10%)

EXHIBIT 6.5
Daily Thought Record of Mathilde's Husband

Date/Time	Situation	Automatic Thought(s)	Emotion(s)	Alternative Response	Outcome
Sunday lunch	B. and his wife stopped by after church. The plan was to have lunch and then watch the Eagles game. Mathilde wouldn't open her door.	Here she goes again. Her kids are going to disown her. She's so stubborn. Nobody can figure her out. Does she hate everybody? Is she getting senile?	Exasperated (60%) Embarrassed (80%) Ticked (40%) Afraid (40%)	I'll just talk to B. and his wife, and we'll have some deli and watch the football game. I can't control Mathilde. She's ill, and it's not my fault or my responsibility.	Embarrassed (40%) Ticked (20%)

EXHIBIT 6.6
Daily Thought Record of Bobby, Mathilde's Son

Date/Time	Situation	Automatic Thought(s)	Emotion(s)	Alternative Response	Outcome
Sunday after church	Went to see Mom and Dad with Collette. Kind of a habit on Sundays in the fall when the Eagles are on. Mom snubbed us again.	My own mother can't stand me and my wife. She's making everything so difficult for nothing. Collette's going to stop wanting to come here, and that will hurt my Dad.	Hurt (90%) Guilty (30%)	Dad's cool. We'll just hang out with him, and Mom can do as she pleases. Collette understands that Mom's got manic depression, and it doesn't flip her out, and she likes my Dad anyway.	Relieved (90%)

supervised visitations between father and son. Furthermore, she feared that Edgar's reckless suicidality posed a potential threat to their son's safety and well-being, a position that the therapist validated.

However, Edgar and his wife were able to redefine the problem in a way they could both accept, namely, that their son needed some time with his father and that Edgar needed to commit to the concept of "safety for all." They then had to brainstorm the specifics of the arrangements. Edgar suggested visiting his son in the home, but Edgar's wife was not prepared to have Edgar spend time in the home at this time. Edgar then offered that he would see his son for unsupervised visits but that he would call his estranged wife to check in. Edgar's wife preferred that he visit his son in a neutral setting, such as the park, or the mall, in her presence. This did not sit well with Edgar, in part because of his cognitive interpretation that he was being treated like a child himself. This struck a nerve, as he often felt that his own parents continued to belittle and control him.

As can be gleaned from the above, the brainstorming session had not yet produced a solution. However, the next step, entailing a review of the pros and cons of each choice, led to a more fruitful outcome. In summary, Edgar and his wife saw advantages in his coming to the house. Edgar would feel at home instead of feeling like *persona non grata*, and his wife would know where her son was at all times. What needed to be solved was the wife's sense of discomfort at having Edgar come to the home. She believed he would initiate contentious discussions with her, which she hoped to avoid. To address this, Edgar and his wife decided that she would have guests at the house when Edgar would come for a visit. The best choices were members of the wife's family and neighbors. This would allow Edgar to interact with his son while she was occupied with other adults.

The final stages in problem-solving involve testing the suggested solution in practice, evaluating its merits, and making adjustments if necessary. Interestingly, the arrangement worked so well that Edgar and his wife decided to try once more to reconcile. They informed the therapist that in addition to attending therapy together, they would join a church group as well. The therapist supported this approach but added that bringing religiosity into Edgar's life should not be seen as a substitute for ongoing pharmacotherapy.

It is a fact of life that problem-solving is an ongoing process. Bipolar patients and their families are likely to have to deal on a regular basis with such problems as (a) arguments over the patient's medications; (b) the fallout of academic and occupational difficulties; (c) struggles over control, autonomy, and personal space (especially if the patient is an adult living at home with the parents); and (d) the aftermath of destructive, impulsive acts (Miklowitz et al., 1988). These major issues test the mettle of any family's collective coping skills.

Given the above, therapists can impress on the patients and families the utility of regularly engaging in "problem prevention." This ties into such ongoing therapeutic tasks as (a) anticipating high-risk, high-stress situations (e.g., moving to a new residence, starting a new semester of classes, taking on a new job, trying a new medication) and planning how they view and deal with such situations; (b) ongoing self-monitoring, so that patients and family members do not slip back to old, aversive communication patterns; (c) setting goals toward improving the self-efficacy of the patient and improving hope for all; and (d) preparing for the possibility of symptom relapse, so that nobody overreacts with rage, hopelessness, or the abandonment of the treatment plan.

In the case of Conrad, no cognitive therapy family sessions were ever held, although the parents did fly in to see him when he was hospitalized following his manic episode and subsequent depressive crash. However, with Conrad's permission, telephone contacts were used to facilitate communication between patient, family, and therapist. In the end, it was decided that the solution to Conrad's academic difficulties would require more parental supervision of his health and study habits. They ultimately decided that Conrad would transfer to a local university and live at home. The therapist gave them a referral to see a psychiatrist in their city who was trained in cognitive therapy. At that time, unfortunately, Conrad's fiancée called off their plans to marry. Conrad's family came to play an important role in supporting their son through this painful loss.

SPECIAL ISSUES WITH FAMILIES

When therapists recognize the importance of the family in treating patients with bipolar disorder, they increase the chances of facilitating positive systemic change in the patient's life. The research currently being done on focused family therapy (FFT; Miklowitz & Goldstein, 1997) may shed light on whether this leads to better outcomes, better maintenance of psychological skills, and reduced symptomatic relapse when compared to treatments that do not address the impact and influence of (and on) families.

However, there is no "free lunch." Therapists who involve loved ones in treatment have to deal with greater degrees of difficulty in executing treatment. They are likely to invest more of their professional time between sessions (e.g., telephone calls), take on greater responsibilities (e.g., the psychological well-being of more than one patient in one family), and work harder in session (e.g., mediating disputes). The following touches on some of these issues.

Confidentiality

Involving spouses, parents, children, and other loved ones in treatment raises the question: "Who is the patient?" Is each person a patient, or is there one patient (diagnosed with bipolar disorder), accompanied by relatives who are facilitators in treatment? Along these lines, should the therapist hold therapy sessions when the diagnosed patient is not present (e.g., just with the patient's parents)? If so, is the therapist ethically bound to keep this information confidential, so that the identified patient should not be informed of what transpired in this session? Should the therapist accept telephone calls from one member of the family when the implicit message is not to tell the others?

Without clear, open communication among the therapist, the patient, and the family at the outset of therapy, the answers to the above questions are likely to differ from person to person. This is a hazardous situation, putting the entire treatment at risk. Clearly, these questions need to be addressed openly among all parties from the start. There simply is no substitute for good, honest communication in preventing misunderstandings.

Perhaps the most typical way to handle the confidentiality issue is as follows:

- The person diagnosed with bipolar disorder is the identified "patient." Even if the therapist is not the prescriber of the medication, the therapist knows about the patient's pharmacotherapy and communicates with the psychiatrist about this.
- One-on-one sessions are always with the identified patient.
- Unless otherwise agreed on by all parties, or unless an emergency exists that would warrant the breaking of confidentiality, communications between therapist and the identified patient are kept between the two of them (or perhaps shared with other concurrent treatment providers with the knowledge of the patient).
- Sessions involving loved ones are the exception, not the rule.
- If any other member of the patient's family is in his or her own individual therapy or is taking psychotropic medication, the patient's therapist has no official responsibility for that person (see below for the complications that arise when family members have diagnosable psychiatric disorders of their own) and does not need to monitor this.
- If family members wish to communicate with the therapist in session, by telephone, or in writing, the identified patient is informed of this. However, communications between the identified patient and the therapist are not revealed to the

other family members (except as required by law or when explicitly endorsed by the patient).

If this arrangement is agreed on from the start, unfortunate misunderstandings can be minimized. However, this is but one way to handle the confidentiality dilemma. Bipolar patients and their loved ones can craft other agreements with therapists, provided that all parties accept the terms. For example, they may hold family sessions exclusively, especially if another professional—perhaps the prescribing psychiatrist—is serving as the individual therapist for the patient. In such an arrangement, it may make the most sense if nobody monopolizes the right of confidentiality. Rather, anything said between a family member and the therapist, whether in person, by telephone, or in writing, is allowed to be shared with all the other members of the family.

Another permutation of the above is the rare case in which the therapist agrees to treat more than one person in the family on an individual basis. Couples or family sessions may also be held as well. This situation may create increased complications in confidentiality, which may require written releases from each patient so that their common therapist can use his or her clinical judgment to decide whether to share clinical information with other family members.

What all of the above situations have in common is the following: The ground rules for confidentiality need to be set at the start, and they must be clearly spelled out for all parties. If there are any doubts or disputes about these issues, the more restrictive interpretations of the rules of confidentiality should prevail, and perhaps the therapist should recommend that family members seek individual counselors of their own to air their concerns and grievances in private.

Psychiatric Problems of Family Members

As bipolar disorder, related mood disorders, and suicide run in families, the chances increase that bipolar patients have parents, siblings, or children who also have similar psychiatric conditions and risks (Brent, Bridge, Johnson, & Connolly, 1996; Coryell et al., 1985). If they live together, the interaction can be noxious and harmful to all parties. Even if they do not live in the same residence, psychiatric difficulties in one's immediate family are a source of concern and stress for many people and can trigger relapse episodes in family members who would otherwise be in remission. Therapists need to be aware of this source of stress and strain on patients.

Bipolar patients can benefit greatly from supportive family members. However, this presupposes that family members are capable of providing a stable, caring environment. If patients provide evidence that family members are so troubled themselves as to be relatively incapable of providing such support, it may be in the patients' best interest to gain some distance.

Unfortunately, the situation is rarely simple or clear-cut. For example, bipolar patients may indeed benefit from some emotional and physical distance from family members, but they may be in no position—financially or otherwise—to live in residences of their own. Alternatively, the untreated or symptomatic family member who is so troublesome for the patient's health at one time may be extremely helpful when treated or in remission. Another complication occurs when the therapist believes that one or more family members are detrimental to the well-being of the patient, but the patient is too dependent to change the system. Not to be overlooked is the situation in which family members begin to clamor for the therapist's attention, as if to make the therapist their own individual counselor on an on-call or as-needed basis. These are significant problems that need to be addressed and resolved as soon as they are ascertained, because they do not go away on their own.

Remedies for the above include the following:

- When appropriate, recommend that family members seek individual therapy of their own. Be willing to provide referrals to facilitate this process.
- Do not disparage the patient's family members. Today's "problematic, critical father" may become tomorrow's "caring, concerned benefactor."
- Help the patient to brainstorm ideas for living arrangements, should a change become necessary. Take an inventory of resources, both public (e.g., programs, boarding houses, low-cost apartments) and personal (e.g., friends with whom the patient may be able to stay temporarily).
- Validate for the patient that rarely is the patient the only source of trouble in the family. The key is to look at interactions and vicious cycles, not to place blame or scapegoat anyone.
- Keep the lines of communication open, but make sure that everyone understands the parameters of confidentiality and treatment. Whenever possible, facilitate dialogue between the patients and their family members rather than fall into the role of go-between. Obtain signed releases to discuss clinical issues with other professionals who may be treating the patient's family members.

Grief and Estrangement

As mentioned above, bipolar disorder and related affective disorders can be prevalent within families. This means that the level of morbidity and mortality in the family of bipolar patients is higher than the norm, thus subjecting patients to higher rates of grief situations than the norm. Aside from being a relevant clinical issue in its own right, grief is a major stressor and must be regarded as a risk factor for the patient.

In assessing the patients' life situation and history, therapists should pay special attention to the interpersonal losses that bipolar patients have experienced. In particular, therapists ought to be aware of suicides and other premature deaths of people who were near and dear to the patient. Similarly, it is advisable for therapists to be aware of the patient's history of voluntary separation from loved ones, including divorce and familial estrangement. Bipolar patients often feel the pain of these losses deeply, contributing to their sense of vulnerability, emptiness, self-reproach, hopelessness, and anxiety.

Therapists who neglect grief and loss issues risk missing important data. For example, a therapist may be unaware that the anniversary of the suicide of the patient's father is coming up. As a result, the therapist does not put the issue on the agenda, and the patient soon experiences a suicidal crisis of his own. It seems to come "out of the blue," but actually its likelihood could have been predicted and discussed in session. Likewise, a divorced patient's wedding anniversary may be a flashpoint for grief, despair, and perhaps suicidality, especially if the patient has a sense of guilt about the loss.

Even in instances in which bipolar patients have not experienced irretrievable interpersonal losses, they may be quite worried about the well-being of loved ones who have emotional disorders. For example, a patient's condition may be affected by her sister's depressive state, or her mother's drinking, or her son's behavioral problems. These represent areas of vulnerability that are best addressed as part of therapy. This is not to be confused with cases in which patients characteristically deflect attention away from themselves in session to complain about others. We are talking about points of major stress for bipolar patients—legitimate topics of discussion for patients who are trying to cope with myriad problems, both in themselves and in those for whom they care.

When therapists make it a point to assess and address issues of grief and loss, they succeed on at least three important counts. First, they facilitate and strengthen the therapeutic relationship by being attuned to highly personal issues such as the anniversary of an important death in the patient's family. Second, they help patients prepare for the emotional upheavals that may accompany painful reminders of the past or personal losses that seem imminent. Third, as noted earlier, therapists may be in a position to facilitate the treatment of the patients' loved ones who are at risk, perhaps through referrals or by family sessions. This preventive step is clinically useful in its own right and also models for the patient the importance of being proactive in solving problems.

CONCLUSION

Bipolar disorder and its treatment often occur in a family context, with an increased incidence of affective disorders in the families of bipolar patients and a frequent interpersonal cycle of patients and their families acting in ways that increase one another's stress. A familial communication style known as negative, high EE has been shown to be related to increased family dysfunction and impeded therapeutic progress in bipolar patients. When therapists help patients and their families improve their mutual problem-solving and communication skills, the patient's progress is facilitated and the entire family may benefit. A key cognitive component in improving the interpersonal relationships among bipolar patients and their family members is the modification of their negative, global attributional styles regarding their behavior. Therapists must be mindful of the stressors that both patients and their families face in dealing with each other, especially during symptomatic periods. Therapists must model giving empathy to all parties, with the intention of demonstrating how they can do this for one another.

Therapists can help bipolar patients and their spouses or families by providing education about bipolar disorder and its treatment, while humbly receiving information from patients and their spouses and families about what they have learned through personal experience. Working with families necessitates that therapists establish ground rules for such issues as confidentiality, proportion of individual to family (or couples) sessions, identification of one or more patients, and teamwork toward common goals. Conducting couples and family sessions is strenuous work, but many gains can be made by helping bipolar patients and their spouses and families. As with many things in life, facing the difficult tasks head on often leads to greater efficacy.

7

STIGMA, LOSS, AND ACCEPTANCE

Cognitive therapists, who are accustomed to helping a wide range of patients to reduce their tendency to catastrophize, must be able to adjust their methods to deal with problems that are very well grounded in an all-too-painful reality. Bipolar patients often express sentiments such as "I have ruined my marriage," or "I've damaged my professional reputation," or "My life feels so much out of my control." A typical cognitive therapy question at this point might be, "What is the evidence for these beliefs?" With bipolar patients, this may be an especially poor choice of inquiry, as the supporting evidence often is compelling and stark. This may be disconcerting to therapists who are trying to find a way to purvey hope to patients. It is infinitely more distressing to the patients themselves, and the compassionate therapist does not lose sight of this fact.

Cognitive therapists must ask a different set of Socratic questions with bipolar patients than they ask with many other patients. Examples include "What can I still do with my life so that my suffering would not have been in vain?" or "What constructive lessons can I learn from my painful past mistakes?" or "How can I present myself to others so that I maintain both my honesty and my privacy?" and "How can I rebuild my life so that I have things to look forward to in the future?" Along the way, therapists serve patients best by recognizing the enormous difficulties that the patients must confront, the significant losses they have had to endure, and the effects of social stigma they are likely to face. This empathic stance provides the foundation for addressing issues of loss, grief, and stigma—topics that are easy to shy from but vital to address. Out of this apparently negative focus comes the basis for discussing the constructive building of a patient's future.

LOVE AND LABOR LOST

Building a life, including academic progress, vocational success, and secure, long-term interpersonal attachments, requires as much steadiness, stability, commitment, and well-directed energy as a person can muster. The problems generated by the extreme symptoms of bipolar disorder repeatedly interrupt this process. Bipolar patients often face the prospect of "starting over"—going back to school after a year of hospitalization, looking for a new job after a career was damaged beyond repair, and finding friendship and love following rifts and break-ups, to name a few examples. Like the victims of repeated natural disasters who lack the means to move from their unfavorable geographic location, patients become demoralized by their repeated batterings. With each harmful mood episode, whether mania or crushing depression, it becomes more and more difficult to rebuild, and the prospect of continuing episodes becomes ever more frightening. If therapists are to provide accurate empathy, they must understand these aspects of the patient's reality.

We mention these problems not to cast a pall over the therapeutic work we describe and advocate herein but rather because we recognize the importance of providing bipolar patients with the best treatment possible. The cognitive approach (in combination with new developments in pharmacotherapy) provides a promising new direction. However, without an appreciation of the sense of loss, utter frustration, and stigma that many bipolar patients feel as a result of living with their disorder, therapists risk portraying their interventions as rote exercises that sound good in theory but are insufficient in reality. Both the therapeutic alliance and the patient's commitment to treatment are likely to wane under such circumstances.

With this in mind, it is important to give patients the opportunity to express their anger and grief. It is a necessary act of caring and kindness for therapists to acknowledge patients' struggles in trying to come to terms with their involuntarily altered lives. A review of their personal histories often reveals a series of relationship rifts; lost employment; interrupted academic progress; downward economic and residential mobility; repeated episodes in hospitals; times when the world moved forward while they lay in bed, immobilized; and other traumatic events. It requires great sensitivity and artfulness for therapists to acknowledge on the one hand that many of these consequences were at least substantially out of the patients' control, and on the other hand to convey that there are therapeutic steps they can take to reclaim some measure of control over their lives. This is the balance between validation and change that is characteristic of therapy with clinical populations where symptoms are so problematic and complex (see Layden et al., 1993; Linehan, 1993).

"Lester" ("Les") was a 45-year-old divorced man, temporarily living in a boarding home when he entered cognitive therapy. He had recently been hospitalized for the third time in his life following an impulsive suicide attempt (he had overdosed on his lithium, causing a hypertensive crisis). Now he was trying to regroup and begin again.

When Les started cognitive therapy, he found it very important to tell the therapist who he "really" was. He did not want to be viewed as a pathetic character whose life was going nowhere and whose treatment would entail mere maintenance of the status quo, namely, a stable mood but an impoverished life situation. Les recounted the story of his life, from popular high-school sports jock to college scholarship winner. He had a loving, supportive family, many loyal friends, and a future that seemed promising and almost without limit. His first manic episode occurred when he was a junior in college, leading to a hospitalization following an ill-fated attempt to run a marathon without proper preparation (and without sleep as well). Les collapsed from dehydration, and his medical treatment turned to psychiatric care when the story of his behavior in the weeks prior to the race came to light.

This was the beginning of a long and frustrating period where Les would apparently recover from bipolar symptoms and would begin to forge a new, productive direction in his life, only to be stopped dead in his tracks by a recurrence of the disorder. Over time, this would be more and more likely to entail a vegetative depression that would prevent him from taking an active part in the world. As Les reported the story, the therapist learned that he had been married for 3 years but then got divorced when his wife felt betrayed by his failure to disclose his illness to her until a total collapse occurred. Les added that he had a successful career as a cable news network reporter. He brought in videos of his work on the air, and copy from his best stories, in a poignant attempt to prove his mettle and to present himself as more than just another patient who was going nowhere fast.

Additional episodes of mood crises and suicidality led to the collapse of his career, a humiliating return to his parents' house, a series of brief affairs that left him feeling empty, and finally the necessity of going on disability, which he reported dealt the final blow to his self-esteem. Now, following his most recent suicide attempt, Les wondered aloud what was left of his life and whether it was worth playing out. He wanted his therapist to know what he had won and lost in his life and how he felt that he was but a shell of what he used to be. It was extremely important to Les that his therapist understand this. The therapist realized this, temporarily suspended his usual directive, problem-focused approach, and gave Les the support, attention, and validation he needed. In the treatment of someone such as Les, this would be a necessary prerequisite to the standard procedures of cognitive therapy. Therapy would entail not only the usual tasks of building hope, solving problems, and maximizing the benefits of his somatic treatments, but would also involve a process of "grieving the lost healthy self" (Miklowitz & Frank, 1999, p. 74). Along the way, Les educated his therapist in a dramatic way about the issues that we discuss below.

SELF-BLAME, STIGMA, AND THE DILEMMA OF DISCLOSURE

When many bipolar patients look back at the course their lives have taken, they often experience shame and regret. They understand that they have done things that resulted in severe, negative consequences and wish desperately that they could go back and undo these events. Sometimes these patients remember all too well the episodes of recklessness, interpersonal turmoil, and academic and vocational failure (and sometimes others remind them). At other times the patients can only infer what has happened by observing the aftermath of the trouble that has occurred—friends who won't speak to them, bills that pile up, work projects abandoned or eliminated, and the like. Additionally, as Jamison (1995) explained, the person in a manic state may scarcely remember what he or she has done that was so dysfunctional, but the inevitable depression carries with it a merciless ability to comprehend the consequences. This, of course, just deepens the sense of despair and self-reproach.

In a related vein, Susan described the stigma, self-doubt, and solitude involved in having extraordinary experiences discounted by others as fantasy, psychotic perceptions, or confabulations. She referred to a movie to drive home her point and to give her therapist a frame of reference. Referring to a recent film, *Contact* (Robert Zemeckis, Producer/Director, 1997), based on a book by the late Carl Sagan, Susan said,

> In the movie *Contact*, there is a scene where the main character—an astronomer played by Jodie Foster—plummets through intergalactic "worm holes" of bright, racing colors with no peripheral vision. At the other end, she meets an alien disguised as her late, beloved father and proceeds to converse with him. When she "returns" to Earth, her account of these events is not believed by the scientific establishment, the government, or by the public. She is shown a video that indicates that her spacecraft simply fell through a shaft in the launching pad and landed in the ocean without ever leaving the planet. She is accused of defrauding the government for the cost of her project. If I were Jodie Foster, this would have been a manic episode.
>
> I wouldn't remember much of the space ordeal except the bright,

fast colors and maybe some parts of the conversation with my father, but I do know that I would have said something, done something, or encouraged something completely out of character during the mania. In fact, there is a moment when you "return to Earth," so to speak, and find that, generally, everybody is pissed off at you because of what you have done while manic.

As an untreated, rapid-cycling manic–depressive, I was probably out of touch with reality two or three times a week. There are approximately 7 months in 1996 that I barely remember during which I bought $55,000 in diamonds. This is all a blur to me, but it is burned into my husband's memory forever. I'm much better now, but these events will always be associated with me and with the trouble I caused. You can move on with life, but you can't erase the past.

Self-Blame

The self-reproach seen in Susan's comments above is a common part of the stigma experienced by bipolar patients. During his course of cognitive therapy, Les sometimes would ask his therapist the following question, "Do you think this disorder was my fault? Did I make this happen? Did I bring this misery on myself?" These questions were never asked in a dry, intellectual manner. Les invariably was tearful and feeling extremely guilty and remorseful for the course his life had taken. Again and again, his therapist emphatically affirmed that his disorder was decidedly not his fault, that nobody would ever volunteer to suffer in such a way, and that his guilt reflected a depressive thinking style much more than it represented reality. Les found these reassurances comforting, much to the surprise of his therapist, who believed he was simply responding with the obvious. Les reminded the therapist each time that the stigma of bipolar disorder was such that a reprieve from blame from an outside party, no matter how redundant, was a welcome message in contrast to the implicit attitude of the world at large.

The stigma that patients with bipolar disorder experience is manifested in ways that have profound impact on their attempts to recover. For example, patients face discrimination on a number of fronts. Corrigan (1998) noted that members of society who misunderstand or fear mental illness withhold opportunities related to housing, work, and income. Lundin (1998) described the financial problems stemming from his having difficulty in obtaining health insurance as a result of his bipolar diagnosis. Along these same lines, Jamison (1995) recounted the time her physician matter-of-factly told her that she should never have children, a pronouncement that delivered a devastating emotional blow. Bipolar patients also are left to wonder whether adoption agencies would take the same view. These are just some of the overt problems that result from the stigma of bipolar disorder. There are covert ones as well.

Writers such as Lundin (1998) and Jamison (1995) have emphasized that it is a blessing to find friends, family, and colleagues who are supportive even after ascertaining their bipolar diagnosis. They also noted that it is far from common and point out that even in relatively benign social and vocational circles there is still an awareness that people may be judging bipolar patients behind their back. Lundin (1998) commented, "While in my work there are many friends and colleagues who are comfortable with my having a mental illness, there are still many encounters with individuals who carry attitudes I find at best uninformed, at worst . . . threatening" (p. 224). There is even some evidence that simply perceiving a sense of stigma, regardless of the level of acceptance in the environment, can lead to lower moods and poorer employment (Lam et al., 1999). For example, bipolar patients may avoid pursuing a high-level job for which they are qualified, owing to fears that they will be rejected outright for admitting their psychiatric history (such as occurs when one explains gaps in one's resumé) or will perpetually sense the sword of Damocles hanging over them if they hide their disorder and obtain the job. This is an added element of stress that nobody needs, least of all people for whom stress is an additive risk factor for the recurrence of symptoms.

Even when people with bipolar disorder succeed in getting hired for a good job, or find an affordable but comfortable place to live, or enter a promising new relationship, they may worry that a return of the acute symptoms will take this all away. They may ruminate about what would happen if they have to be hospitalized. They wonder how they would explain their absence, or take care of their personal business, or keep their jobs.

Those who have recently left the hospital and have been able to maintain their jobs or relationships may assume that others are looking at them in a far different way than before, and they would generally be correct in making such assumptions (although it is possible that some people may be more concerned than judgmental, contrary to what patients fear). Although hospitalization may be necessary at times for bipolar patients, especially when they are acutely suicidal or are having great difficulties achieving a stabilization of their medications, the very fact of being "committed" (whether voluntarily or not) can have iatrogenic effects on their morale and hopefulness. For many people, hospitalization is equivalent to stigma, pure and simple; for a more benign viewpoint of hospitalization, see Jamison's (1999) account of William Styron's recollections of the benefits of having a safe haven away from the stressors of everyday life.

Most fundamental of all is the sense of stigma that those with bipolar disorder may feel about themselves. It is not unusual for people with bipolar disorder, a population that often demonstrates insight and sensitivity, to carry great self-doubt with them wherever they go and whatever they do. The defectiveness schema can be particularly intense and harsh for such people, causing them to feel unworthy and undeserving of the truly good things they earn for themselves and bring to the lives of others around them (Lam et al., 1999).

Yet there are aspects of bipolar disorder that arguably make a person more attractive to others, at least in its milder form. People with manic depression may be extremely personable, engaging, and contagiously enthusiastic in a group. Several studies have indicated that, on average, bipolar patients may be more creative and intellectually astute than the population at large (e.g., Coryell, Endicott, et al., 1989; Woodruff, Robins, Winokur, & Reich, 1971). Similarly, there is evidence that those who possess high levels of emotional and intellectual sensitivity and creativity are more at risk for affective disorders (including bipolar disorder) and suicide than the general population (Andreasen, 1987; Jamison, 1993; Ludwig, 1995; Schildkraut, Hirschfeld, & Murphy, 1994). Patients must be made aware of these facts, if for no other reason than to offset some of their negatively biased views of themselves.

Countering the Effect of Stigma

What is one to do about the phenomenon of stigma? What can the cognitive therapist do to assist patients in dealing with this significant problem? Practical strategies have been put forth by Link, Mirotznik, and Cullen (1991), Hayward and Bright (1997), and Holmes and River (1998), among others. Perhaps the least optimistic views are those of Link et al. (1991), who posit that patients who hope to deal with stigma have to choose among three main strategies: secrecy, withdrawal, or forthrightly trying to educate others about their illness. Unfortunately, the most important source of change—social attitudes—is beyond the patients' control, and this leaves patients in a relatively powerless position to deal effectively with stigma.

A somewhat more empowering and hopeful view is explicated by Hayward and Bright (1997) and Holmes and River (1998). First, the therapist must be willing to acknowledge the existence of stigma. It does patients little good to pretend that the positive regard they experience in therapeutic relationships represents the norm in society. It is better to validate the patients' experiences with stigma in the real world and to focus instead on changing their self-image and improving their problem-solving skills.

Therapists can help bipolar patients by addressing their self-stigmatizing beliefs. These take a number of forms and can be ascertained when patients express them spontaneously during the course of treatment. One such manifestation has to do with the cause of the illness. Earlier, we noted that Les at times believed that he was to blame for his illness. This view, sometimes expressed by bipolar patients, is a faulty, internal attribution that therapists must refute at every opportunity. Instead, therapists can help patients replace this view with the far more functional view that patients bear some responsibility for taking care of their health to the best of their ability. This is not a simple matter. Bipolar patients, who must contend with noxious side-effects from medications as well as the symptoms of the bipolar disorder itself, face the burden of having to be more vigilant about their health than people who are free of such corporeal and spiritual yokes. Therapists can explain that when patients commit themselves to a regimen of pro-health behaviors and attitudes, they are acting above and beyond the call of duty and are to be commended for whatever degrees of recovery they are able to gain and maintain. On the flip side, therapists must not shame patients for their slip-ups in taking their medications, keeping their appointments, keeping their daily schedules constant, eating and sleeping well, and using the skills learned in cognitive therapy. Shame does not teach anything productive. Caring, corrective feedback is what is called for in such instances.

Therapists also should be alert to bipolar patients who express self-stigmatizing beliefs about their identity. Comments such as "I'm a nutcase," "I'm hopeless and useless," or "I'm just a burden to everyone" need to be addressed on the spot. Not only are these beliefs harmful to the patients' self-esteem, they induce hopelessness, which may not only impede therapeutic progress but may even exacerbate the patients' suicidality. When Les would call himself a "misfit and mental cripple," the therapist would urge him to redefine himself in terms of his personal interests, his political views, his interpersonal qualities, and his aspirations; for example, a "jazz aficionado and a left-wing, benevolent, friendly dreamer who loves the outdoors and wants to write and help society." Otherwise, as the therapist put it, Les would be "unjustly casting himself in the least flattering, one-dimensional term possible." Instead, the therapist reasoned, Les needed to see himself as the multidimensional person that he was—someone who was battling a dreadful illness and who was capable of giving himself the same benefit of the doubt that he routinely gave to others in unfortunate circumstances.

As Lam et al. (1999) explained, cognitive therapy itself presents a destigmatizing approach that bipolar patients can adopt over the course of their treatment. For example, cognitive therapy focuses on goals, tasks, hypotheses, and objective assessments rather than on labels, absolutes, and judgments. By learning and applying the concepts and skills of cognitive therapy, patients can see that their illness has multiple etiologic and maintaining factors that cannot be boiled down to a simple assessment of blame. By tackling their problems in a step-by-step fashion, they can see that their treatment and recovery efforts are not measurable by a success–failure dichotomy. Patients work on a program of self-help skills that build self-efficacy as well as an appreciation for their own efforts in tackling a major illness.

(See Exhibit 7.1 for a brief listing of books geared to teach patients the skills of cognitive therapy in general and managing bipolar disorder in particular.)

In summary, cognitive therapy works to destigmatize from the inside out. Social change would be highly desirable as well, and although accomplishing this goes well beyond the scope of individual cognitive therapy, it is more likely that a self-accepting patient models a more sympathetic and respectful approach for others to emulate, even if only one at a time.

It is extremely important for therapists to assess the variety and extent of patients' coping skills, personal talents, social support networks, and other strengths. By doing this, therapists gain useful ideas about how to pace the therapy and how to use the patients' ceiling of functioning to get the most out of the process of learning new skills. At the same time, patients feel more respected and valued and become more active partners in the process of change.

For example, patients who believe they are experienced and knowledgeable about the process of therapy, who are secure in the idea that they understand themselves well, and who perhaps heavily endorse autonomy

EXHIBIT 7.1
Reading for Patients

Burns, D. (1989). *The feeling good handbook.* New York: Plume.
A self-help workbook for cognitive therapy.

Copeland, M. E. (1992). *The depression workbook: A guide for living with depression and manic depression.* Oakland, CA: New Harbinger.
Self-help guidance for charting moods, coping with symptoms of mania and depression, and developing a support system.

Copeland, M. E. (1994). *Living without depression and manic depression: A workbook for maintaining mood stability.* Oakland, CA: New Harbinger.
Self-help workbook for management of bipolar symptoms and relapse prevention.

Court, B. L., & Nelson, G. E. (1996). *Bipolar puzzle solution: A mental health client's perspective.* Washington, DC: Accelerated Development.
Provides 187 questions and answers typically heard in a bipolar support group.

Ellis, T. E., & Newman, C. F. (1996). *Choosing to live: How to defeat suicide through cognitive therapy.* Oakland, CA: New Harbinger.
Provides empathy for those who feel suicidal, along with self-help strategies and inspirational points of view to help prevent suicide and to improve the quality of life for patients and their families.

Greenberger, D., & Padesky, C. (1995). *Mind over mood: A cognitive therapy treatment manual for clients.* New York: Guilford Press.
A "take-home" guide to cognitive therapy, chock-full of the best techniques for personal practice and mastery.

---

items on the Sociotropy–Autonomy Scale (A. T. Beck et al., 1983) and Dysfunctional Attitudes Scale (Weissman & Beck, 1978) can be asked to generate their own homework assignments or do extra self-help work. If patients are proud of their writing or artistic skills, therapists can encourage them to use these creative media to keep a detailed journal of their cognitive and emotional experiences and to express themselves through music or the fine arts (which they may share in session, if appropriate). As an example, Salzman (1998) encouraged his patients to harness their hypomanic ideas and energy in the service of creative purposes only, thus compartmentalizing symptoms in a way that maximizes self-esteem while minimizing undue risk. Patients who have special expertise in their career or hobby can be encouraged to use their fund of knowledge and logical problem-solving skills to curb their own manic ideation or spur themselves toward action in the midst of depression. Patients who have "emotional intelligence" (Goleman, 1995) and who have an extensive support network as a result of their interpersonal acumen can be urged to take the counsel of the people in their spheres of concern and influence—the very people they may have supported and advised many times in the past. This is reciprocity at its best, with the "helpers" accepting the assistance of those they have helped before. Viewed this way, bipolar disorder does not have to put patients in a "one-down" position. Instead, patients can construe their most important relationships as involving a measure of mutual interdependence. Such an approach counters shame and stigma.

Self-Disclosure

The issue of self-disclosure of the illness is extremely thorny. The first step, naturally, is for patients to acknowledge their bipolar disorder to themselves. This is not so easy, especially early in the course of the illness. It is natural for patients to seek desperately for alternative explanations for their symptoms other than the diagnosis of bipolar disorder. When experiencing a pure manic episode, especially for the first time, people subjectively feel in a glorious state, and the idea that they may be ill may be far from their mind. Here, the person with bipolar disorder may not be the first to recognize the illness, and the "disclosure" may actually come in the form of a diagnosis proffered by a professional, much to the patient's chagrin. In such instances, the people closest to the patient do not need to be told that there is a problem. The patients themselves may have to be convinced, and until they agree they may be less than willing to take necessary treatment, including lithium (Jamison, 1995), still the most commonly prescribed medication for bipolar disorder.

The scenario changes dramatically when time goes by, and the patients (perhaps begrudgingly) accept that they have bipolar disorder and encounter new people who may play significant roles in their lives—prospective employers, graduate program directors, colleagues, friends, roommates, lovers, spouses, and the like. The list below presents some of the questions that are likely to go through the minds of patients with bipolar disorder who confront the dilemma of the disclosure of their diagnosis, covering issues of professional training, employment, and personal relationships respectively:

- "Even though I'm entering a doctoral program in clinical psychology, where you would expect people to have an open mind about the need for treatment of an emotional disorder, will I be rejected or dismissed if I forthrightly explain that I'm being treated for bipolar disorder? If I do not reveal that I have bipolar disorder, am I behaving improperly and deceptively, thus showing that I am ashamed and have something to hide, and therefore deserving of expulsion at the first sign of a relapse? Am I going to be an exceptionally compassionate therapist by virtue of my own experience with a psychological illness, or will I risk endangering the well-being of my patients if my judgment becomes impaired, or both? Should I choose another profession? But why should I avoid the profession at which I may be most well suited, especially if I receive proper treatment, just out of fear of being discovered? Isn't this the height of hypocrisy? Or is it common sense and a necessary sacrifice?"

- "Should I lie on my job application when it asks about my medical and psychiatric history? Is this legal of them to ask? Dare I refuse to answer? If I omit the truth, and later have an episode that requires special understanding or medical time off, will I have forfeited my right to compassionate handling because I lied in the first place? But if I answer honestly on the application or the interview, will I be blackballed? (They can always hide the truth, saying that they hired someone who was 'better qualified.') Or will I put myself in a position to have a good job without having to look over my shoulder and worry about being 'found out'?"

- "I really value my friendship with Sal. We share so much— it's great. But I haven't mentioned my bipolar disorder yet. I won't really feel totally safe or comfortable in this friendship until I can talk about my diagnosis and treatment and know that Sal will accept me and care about me anyway. But if I say something, won't I be taking an undue risk with this friendship? If I stay true to my treatment, and I get lucky, I may never have another relapse, so why should I rock the boat and take a chance by talking about my bipolar disorder? On the other hand, if I say nothing, am I not really saying that I don't totally trust Sal? If I really want to have a close friendship, shouldn't I take a risk and open up? After all, if I can't open up to Sal, who can I talk to? I'll be consigning myself to a life of secrecy where I can't really be myself, not totally, anyway. If I say something, will I put everything on the line? How long can I put this off without Sal asking why I didn't say something sooner?"

- "I'm in love, but I'm scared, because I don't want my partner to know about my bipolar illness. This is the best relationship I've had in years, and I think it's got the potential to lead to a lifelong commitment. I'm afraid to jeopardize everything by telling him about my disorder. I haven't had an episode in months, and everything has been wonderful, so maybe I can put my illness in the past and not say anything. But wait a minute, what if we try to have children? Don't I owe it to him to say something about my illness, given the hereditary implications? If we're really meant for each other, shouldn't we be willing to be together in sickness and in health? Or is that only in fairy tales? If I say nothing, and he finds out later, will I be guilty of an egregious lie by omission? Or is this nobody's business but my own and my doctors'? Will a secret erode my relationship, even if I never have a recurrence? Can I hide my medications forever, even when we share the same bathroom, day in and day out, for years and years? Should I forget about taking the medication and take my chances? What am I saying? I'm so scared, because I have something so precious and therefore so much to lose. What should I do?"

It is very easy to see how dilemmas such as these increase the bipolar patient's stress level, the very thing they need to avert to reduce the risk of new episodes. Yet these questions cannot be ignored, especially when patients raise them with their therapists. At such times it would be easy for therapists to hide behind their supposed cloak of neutrality and impartiality, saying (in effect): "The answer to this problem is up to you." However, it is far more helpful, collaborative, and empathic for therapists to engage actively in the struggle to weigh the pros and cons of patient self-disclosure for each episode and to provide support and encouragement in the aftermath of the patients' attempt to share the details of their illness with an important other.

In general, we support the patients' right to privacy and therefore do not pressure them or judge them should they choose to keep their diagnosis to themselves. By the same token, we are also strong proponents of the model whereby patients take responsibility for their decisions and actions. Toward that end, we strongly urge patients to consider the potential consequences of their withholding information about their disorder from others and to be willing to accept responsibility if their decision has an adverse effect on their relationships with other individuals. In summary, consistent with the general problem-solving model (Nezu et al., 1989) that is part and parcel of cognitive therapy, we work with patients to weigh the advantages and disadvantages of self-disclosure and nondisclosure, across separate situations, for themselves, and for others. Along with this we provide empathy for the stress that they experience in being in this precarious position in the first place.

After showing a good response to treatment, Susan made the decision to divulge the nature of her illness and its treatment to her friends. She found that most of her friends were quite supportive, but a few appeared to distance themselves from her. At first, Susan was angry and disillusioned, and at times she regretted that she had ever said anything. However, she used her skills of rational reevaluation to disabuse herself of the idea that she had made a mistake in disclosing her psychiatric problems. She reasoned that now she had a much better idea of who her real friends were and that this knowledge was priceless.

In cases in which bipolar patients divulge their psychiatric problems to significant romantic partners or spouses who then become very concerned (or angry), we recommend holding at least one conjoint session. Here, therapists can help answer important questions that the patients' partners may have about the course of the illness, treatment options, prognosis, and their own role in helping their partners. Therapists can facilitate a dialogue between patients and their loved ones so that they understand the methods of monitoring that are effective yet not overly intrusive. Sometimes the patients and their loved ones do not wish to have the latter serve as mental health sentries. That is their prerogative. The point we are making simply is that once loved ones are made aware of the patients' condition, it is advisable that they become partners in the process of facilitating health, rather than pretending that the illness does not exist.

One of the most sensitive issues between bipolar patients and their life partners has to do with having children. They may be very anxious to know what the therapist thinks about the implications of bipolar disorder for the health and well-being of their future offspring. We recommend that therapists communicate clearly that a couple's ultimate decision whether to have children is entirely their own and should not be dictated by a third party. Having said that, therapists can help arm the patients and their partners with some of the facts, such as the following:

- The risk of a child developing bipolar disorder when only one parent has the illness is significantly less than when both parents have it.
- An expectant mother may not be able to take first-line medications for bipolar disorder in her first trimester, but she can reduce the risk of symptom relapse by gradually being weaned off her medications in advance, having more frequent cognitive therapy sessions while she is not on a standard mood stabilizer, and paying close attention to getting proper clinical care and social support in the year after giving birth.
- Parents with bipolar disorder who commit themselves to their own treatment can be excellent parents and can give their children all the advantages of a safe, loving upbringing.
- A child who develops signs of an emotional disorder is not doomed. Early detection and proper care lead to a favorable prognosis.

When these observations are spelled out, bipolar patients and their partners can make an informed, joint decision about bearing and raising children, free of the harmful effects of misinformation and catastrophizing.

Social Support and Breaking Stereotypes

Regardless of whether the patients are in significant relationships, it is important that they be apprised of opportunities to receive social support in the form of self-help groups. As mentioned in chapter 4 (Exhibit 4.3), organizations such as the National Depressive and Manic Depressive Association (NDMDA), National Alliance for the Mentally Ill (NAMI), and Depression and Related Affective Disorders Association (DRADA) are sources of information, referrals, group meetings, and general advocacy for those with bipolar disorder. For patients, attending support groups is a win–win situation. If they feel supported by the other members, believe that they have found a "home" to talk freely about their problems in an accepting environment, and come to see that they are not alone, the benefits speak for themselves. Conversely, if they feel uncomfortable, find themselves looking down on other group members, or believe that they do not belong in such a group, this stimulates necessary discussion in individual therapy about their difficulties in accepting the illness, as well as their own stigmatizing beliefs about the disorder. Because self-stigmatization can lead to lower self-esteem, higher levels of discouragement and hopelessness, increased social withdrawal, and perhaps lessened adherence to necessary treatment, the elucidation of these negative feelings (through contact with the group) can help therapists and patients prevent problems that otherwise may go undetected.

Les initially had an adverse reaction to attending a support group meeting for bipolar disorder. When the therapist asked Les if he wanted to put his experiences in the group on the session agenda, he at first demurred, stating that it was not worth talking about. His facial expression cued the therapist into the idea that Les was a bit distressed by the group meeting and therefore that it would be advisable to discuss the issue. After some tap dancing around the issue, Les acknowledged that he did not like being reminded that he was part of a "community of misfits." Then he added that he felt ashamed of himself for judging other people who obviously suffered greatly, as he did. This led to a discussion of his perceptions of the people in the group—specifically, how he had formed premature opinions about some of them based on their appearance and the way they spoke. When asked what was going through his mind at that time, Les recounted the following automatic thought; "These are not the people with whom I want to establish relationships; I want to be among healthy people who will accept me as one of them."

The therapist, caught somewhat off guard by Les's perceptions, stated, "People with bipolar disorder often are among the most witty, creative, personable, and energetic among us—the ravages of their acute symptoms notwithstanding—and so I am surprised that you found them to be so singularly without desirable qualities." The therapist followed up with this question: "Can you have it both ways, Les? Can you find community with other bipolar patients, gaining and giving validation for the struggle to overcome the effects of the disorder, while also building relationships with people who share your interests, instead of your illness?" Les immediately recognized that he had been engaging in all-or-none thinking when he told himself that the group was not worth his time. At the same time, his silent rejection of the other participants told him that he still had a long way to go in accepting his own problems. It also scared him, because it triggered the thought, "I guess this is how normal people view me." If nothing else, the group experience informed both Les and his therapist that the topic of stigma was far from resolved.

On a more mundane (but no less important) level, Les's experience in the group illustrated the heterogeneous nature of bipolar disorder (Bauer & McBride, 1996; Goodwin & Jamison, 1990; Lam et al., 1999). The symptoms associated with bipolar disorder and its many variants cover a wide spectrum. Similarly, different patients have their own levels of global, adaptive functioning, including factors related to comorbidity, social support, personal strengths (e.g., level of education, capacity for empathy), and responsivity to treatments. There is no single profile of bipolar disorder, and the diverse composition of Les's support group brought this point home to him. Nevertheless, one of the distinguishing features of stigma, like prejudice, is that it groups people into an undifferentiated mass. Stigma stereotypes people in harsh ways, caricaturizing them and robbing them of their humanity. We begin to chip away at the harmful effects of stigma when we view people as individuals. The most important place to start is with the patient's self-evaluation. This can be facilitated by a well-developed case conceptualization, taking into account the patient's unique history, personal beliefs, and individual assets.

Another important aspect of the above vignette is the therapist's support for Les's involvement with society at large: for example, by forming new ties with people who were similar to him in ways other than his diagnostic status. After all, this is a common way that people affiliate in everyday life. People with common interests and qualities tend to get along. It was important for Les to find social outlets for his knowledge of jazz and his love of books. Toward that end, he joined a book club, regularly attended readings at a local bookstore, and subscribed to a jazz concert series, with the intention of inviting a different person to accompany him to each performance. These activities were important in a number of ways. They got Les to leave the house, even on days when his dysphoria might otherwise have left him in his room all day, unbathed and unshaven. They reminded him that there were still positive things to experience and events to look forward to. Going out gave Les the opportunity to feel better about himself because of the positive halo created by "hanging out with cool people."

On a societal level, one can argue that Les's increased interactions with the general public were important as a small but significant part of educating the public that people can live and function normally even when they have a disorder whose name commonly evokes dread. If ignorance breeds misunderstanding, and misunderstanding fuels the fire of hatred and discrimination, then the normal socializing behaviors of people such as Les can be construed as a lesson for those who do not understand mental illness in general and bipolar disorder in particular.

Stigma in the Family

Patients who work hard to come to terms with the stigmatizing nature of their illness can be dealt a significant setback if they perceive that their own relatives feel stigmatized by their presence in the family. This can take a number of forms. One is simple denial, such as when someone in a household is denied access to (or discouraged from seeking) mental health care because the family does not want to admit that a mental illness exists in their midst. In such instances, the patient may go along with the denial until worsening symptoms provoke a crisis, or the patient may feel invalidated or scapegoated.

By contrast, some bipolar patients feel stigmatized at home when they perceive that their loved ones are overinterpreting their behavior as representative of pathology. For example, one patient was bemused by his wife's apparent worrying whenever he became enthused and animated about a new project at work. He found this situation terribly stigmatic but softened his anger when a couples session revealed a more complete account of his wife's anxieties, as well as her guilt for mistrusting her husband's moods.

However, in another case the situation was not as amenable to conciliation. Here, a woman who was diagnosed with bipolar II disorder was distressed that her husband, whom she felt was extremely obsessive–compulsive, controlling, and critical, would say: "You're getting manic again!" whenever she justifiably asserted herself against his many idiosyncratic rules and regulations in their household. She told her therapist that she really did not buy into what her husband was saying, but it nonetheless wore her down, made her feel self-conscious about her behavior, discouraged her about the future of her marriage, and sometimes made her doubt her own sense of reality. It did not help matters when her husband added, "I like you better when you're depressed." The husband never came to a session, although he was invited repeatedly. The patient sadly concluded that she had three choices: (a) continue to be assertive but unjustly stigmatized in her own home, (b) stay "compliant and depressed" to keep the peace, or (c) consider a marital split. These were not pleasant choices, and the situation placed a great deal of stress on a patient who certainly did not need it.

Yet another form of stigmatization from the family happens when the patient is "hidden" from the outside world, lest others discover the family "secret." Les often became quite angry when he perceived that his father was ashamed of him and did not wish to be associated with him. When Les's mood would become somewhat hypomanic, his father would not go out with him in public. Les added that his father did not want him answering the telephone either and became visibly agitated if he found Les chatting with the neighbors. Les stated that he did not take kindly to being made a pariah by his own father. When the father came to a family session, he said that he did not like being part of a spectacle when Les would "act up."

The therapist faced the challenge of providing both empathy and education to a harried father, while maintaining an alliance with a patient who felt stigmatized in his own home. A breakthrough was achieved when Les's father stated that he felt responsible for his son's illness, in that he must have passed on the "demon gene" (see Miklowitz & Goldstein, 1997, on the family phenomenon of "gene guilt"). As a by-product of this guilt, the father would think, "People will think I am a bad father," when he witnessed Les acting expansively among others. Les had never realized his father felt this way. Les had always assumed that his father's belief was, "I have a weak, crazy son who shouldn't be allowed to interact with anybody, because he'll give the family a bad name." This was a major, cognitive reframe for Les; it helped him to feel less stigmatized and more sympathetic toward his father. Conceptualizing the father's behavior in cognitive terms helped define a family problem in a way that was more sympathetic to all.

Blame and Shame

Unfortunately, blame and shame are still prominent features of mental illness. Given this societal state of affairs, it behooves clinicians to find a way to educate the public that psychological illnesses such as manic depression are no-fault disorders. We say *no fault* not in the sense that patients are absolved of taking some responsibility for their care. To the contrary, helping bipolar patients to become active participants in their treatment and maintenance of gains is one of the most important tasks of the therapist. We say *no fault* in the sense that nobody asks to become manic depressive, and nobody volunteers to pass along a genetic vulnerability of this sort. It is a harsh fact of life, not a black mark on one's character.

Nevertheless, we must admit that this is a hard sell for many people. Clinicians can make headway in taking some of the stigma out of bipolar disorder for patients and their families by emphasizing its close analogy with chronic medical illness. For example, Miklowitz and Goldstein (1997), in the context of their family-focused treatment for bipolar disorder, explained that bipolar disorder is similar to diabetes. Both involve chronic, biochemical imbalances; both typically necessitate regular pharmacological intervention; and both put great stress, strain, and worry into the lives of patients and families. At the same time, patients with both bipolar disorder and diabetes can learn to adopt top-flight self-care as a way of life and can learn to live with the disorders while still actively engaged in an otherwise normal life. As elegant as this analogy may seem, it is still the case that society is more apt to offer sympathy to the diabetic individual than the manic–depressive individual, and this state of affairs should be acknowledged to some degree if the therapist is to remain credible.

Therapists can help patients reduce their self-stigmatization and become participants in the world at large who communicate self-respect, optimism, and good will. Therapists serve as consultants, helping patients weigh the merits and drawbacks of strategic self-disclosures to specified, trusted individuals in their lives. Therapists ask patients questions that guide them toward the discovery of new ways of looking at their illness. For example,

- "Have you ever known and admired someone who later revealed that he or she had a mental illness? What do you think about that person? What does it tell you that you found that person admirable? What does that say about the ability to be liked and respected, even with an illness such as bipolar disorder?"

- "Are you aware of famous people who have bipolar disorder as you have? What are some of their accomplishments? What does this tell you about the ability of people with manic depression to achieve great things?"
- "What are some of the life problems that plague everyone, regardless of whether they have a psychiatric diagnosis? How do you deal with these problems? Is that much different from anybody else?"

These are the sorts of questions that help patients see themselves not solely as patients, but as members of an imperfect species who are nobly doing their best to get along in a stressful world. It goes without saying that therapists are among these numbers, too, a topic that is discussed in the section that follows.

Bipolar Disorder in the Practicing Clinician

Jamison's personal memoir (*An Unquiet Mind*, 1995), in addition to being a compelling, courageous account of her personal struggles with bipolar disorder in the context of a scholarly understanding of the illness, implicitly raises the question, "Should people who have bipolar disorder be treating patients in psychotherapy?" This question often results in spirited debate. It is undeniable that Jamison herself has had a very fruitful career and that her clinical work has been effective and appreciated. Furthermore, she discontinued her clinical practice not because of the stigma of "coming out" with her psychiatric history, but rather because of the utter loss of privacy necessary for an appropriate therapeutic relationship (as a result of the personal accounts in her book).

We have said earlier that bipolar disorder is quite heterogeneous. This applies to the population of therapists (and therapists-in-training) who have the illness. We believe that it would be a terrible mistake to make a blanket statement about the fitness of therapists to practice if they have bipolar disorder. All therapists, irrespective of their life situations, medical conditions, and states of emotional health, are responsible for practicing their trade competently, ethically, and with the patients' well-being as their priority. There are therapists who do *not* have a stigmatic diagnosis who have mistreated or neglected patients, just as there are therapists who personally battle with illnesses but who have been models of what a mental health professional should be.

Within the profession of psychotherapy, it seems that there is a push–pull relationship between stigma and fraternal trust when it comes to the regulation of mental health care providers who are at risk for being impaired. This is true for therapists who have bipolar disorder, as it is for those who have had problems with substance abuse, schizophrenia, and other clinical problems. On the one hand, there is general discomfort involved in "policing" one's esteemed colleagues, and yet therapists have a fiduciary responsibility to patients and to the field as a whole to monitor the activities of professional compatriots who may be at suboptimal functioning. In settings where some therapists have administrative responsibility for subordinate therapists, there is also the risk of legal liability if junior colleagues and individuals who are being trained and supervised are not performing up to the required standards of care. At the same time, it is potentially discriminatory and demoralizing to judge (and perhaps exclude from practice) therapists who are executing their duties well, simply because they are "at risk" by virtue of requiring therapy and medications of their own. The lack of clarity and certainty in resolving this issue points to the need for more open dialogue on the subject.

Most fundamentally, therapists need to monitor themselves in the manner that they would have their patients self-monitor. There is no room for hypocrisy in such circumstances, giving tangible meaning to the phrase, "Healer, heal thyself." If therapists have bipolar symptoms or a fully diagnosed bipolar disorder, they must obtain the same treatment for themselves that they would recommend to patients. Self-medication is decidedly not the way to go. The therapist with bipolar disorder can function best if he or she regularly consults with at least one other professional for therapy and medication. If therapists deny their symptoms or resist seeking treatment owing to the sense of stigma and shame, the result may be a self-fulfilling prophecy of declining functioning, additional problems and stressors, and a diminishing of their ability to perform their professional role. This sort of outcome only worsens a therapist's humiliation and self-stigmatization. It is far preferable for therapists with bipolar disorder to take a proactive stance with regard to their treatment, to take silent pride in doing the wise and prudent thing by getting help, and to use the experience as a way to deepen their sensitivity toward and effectiveness with patients. In fact, it may be argued that manic–depressive therapists who wisely engage in personal treatment (such as cognitive therapy and pharmacotherapy) may be in the best position to offer informed, insightful, compassionate care.

ACCEPTANCE

That bipolar disorder requires life-long treatment is yet another factor that makes the disorder difficult for patients to accept. The hope that one may be able to stop taking medications, throw off the bane of the illness, and move beyond the diagnosis and its effects is eminently understandable. However, this hope sometimes has a downside, in that patients who feel this way may wish to "test" themselves by going off their medications when they feel well (Goodwin & Jamison, 1990; Jamison & Akiskal, 1983). Bipolar patients want to be able to reclaim their lives and to hold their heads up high with dignity and confidence, free from stigma and dread. However, trying to put the diagnosis in the past and act as if the problem is finally over is not the way to accomplish this goal.

For patients to reach a state of acceptance of their condition, they need to find ways to empower themselves despite some limitations (McGuffin, 1998), and have to find a way to view medications (and, unfortunately, their side-effects) as a routine part of their day. Additionally, they somehow must strike a balance between taking their bipolar disorder seriously and not allowing it to become synonymous with their identity. This latter point was an ongoing issue in Les's therapy. Les would say that he felt that he and the bipolar disorder were one and the same, and he would contend that his doctors' admonition to continue taking his medications for the rest of his life was confirmation of this view. Les's cognitive therapist had to emphasize that bipolar disorder was an affliction; it did not define his personality or his values. The therapist explained that bipolar disorder is a chronic psychiatric anomaly but that it does not represent someone's capacity for love, faith, or ambition or potential contributions to humankind. At times, Les would accept this view, but then he would ask, "How can I ever accept what bipolar disorder has done to my life?" This was not a rhetorical question—Les actively worked with his therapist to find answers to this vital, existential question.

Trying to decide whether Les could accept his illness was a dead-end issue as long as it was posed in an all-or-none fashion. It was far more productive to talk about the aspects of the bipolar disorder that Les could accept and to juxtapose them against the factors that he found more difficult to incorporate into his view of his life. For example, Les stated that it would be reasonable to strive to reach a point where he could accept that he had to take medications for the long run. However, he reserved the right not to accept harsh side-effects, if it were possible to find suitable, effective medications he could tolerate better. Similarly, he noted that he was willing to accept that his life had been altered, even derailed, but he would never accept the idea that he had to relinquish all of his ambitions for all time.

Because the therapeutic relationship is of utmost importance in treatment, it is critical that therapists not make the mistake of scolding bipolar patients for having difficulties in accepting the need for treatment. To the contrary, therapists facilitate their alliance with patients best by acknowledging that life would be so much easier if the bipolar disorder would just go away. As Les's therapist put it,

> "I think we get along very well, and I think we're glad that we know
> each other and that we're working together—but I gather that in the

grand scheme of things you would just as soon never have needed to meet me in the first place, right? I guess I wish you never needed to see me either, but I would like for us to make the best of it. How about you?"

By the same token, it is legitimate for therapists to encourage patients not to accept the idea that bipolar disorder has to ruin their lives entirely and that they have no recourse. It is instructive for therapists to express the notion that bipolar disorder entails specific limitations on one's life, but these limitations are not so complete as to render one's life useless and meaningless. Then the therapist has to accept that patients do not resolve these feelings quickly or neatly. Therapists have to accompany patients on that "journey" to acceptance, without looking at the clock to check on the time of arrival.

CONCLUSION

Bipolar patients still face discrimination in important life areas such as employment, living arrangements, insurance, adoption, academic admission and reinstatements, and interpersonal relationships. Added to these problems are the self-blame and self-stigma of the patients themselves, which (when particularly acute) can exacerbate poor self-care (including avoidance of treatment) and suicidality. Therapists must be sensitive to the real obstacles that bipolar patients face in everyday life and must be mindful of treating them with a respectful, collaborative, nonpatronizing demeanor. This, in itself, is an important part of counteracting stigma. Patients face enormous practical and philosophical dilemmas regarding self-disclosure of their illness to important people in their lives. We maintain that patients have a right to privacy but that they must also be prepared to accept responsibility for the outcome of choosing not to disclose.

Practicing therapists who have bipolar disorder may very well be able to have productive careers. However, they must minimize risks to themselves and their patients by adhering to their own treatment in the manner that they would expect of their bipolar patients.

Although it is very important for bipolar patients to come to terms with their illness, and to accept the treatments and limitations that are involved in bipolar disorder, individuals with this condition can still lead meaningful, fulfilling lives.

8

COGNITIVE THERAPY FOR PATIENTS WITH BIPOLAR DISORDER: THE CASE OF "CARLOS"

The following case is representative of the treatment offered in a pilot study on the cognitive therapy of bipolar disorder run at the University of Pennsylvania in the early 1990s. The protocol involved up to a year of weekly cognitive therapy sessions, along with concurrent pharmacotherapy. The identifying features of the patient, Carlos, have been changed and combined with characteristics from other patients so that the patient's true identity remains anonymous. The details of treatment, however, are very similar to those that actually took place with Carlos and others, and one may be able to view the following as a reasonable model of a full course of cognitive therapy.

We should add that the definition of a complete course of treatment is somewhat arbitrary. Naturally, we would like to provide the quantity and quality of therapy that would be sufficient to create a remission of symptoms, an improvement in the patient's quality of life, and freedom from relapse. This is the ultimate goal. However, it is an illusive goal with a disorder such as manic depression, which tends to present patients with a lifetime need for pharmacotherapy and an ongoing risk of symptom recurrence. Therefore, research protocols aside, a naturalistic view of therapy for bipolar disorder probably involves a long-term association between patients and their health care providers.

After a period of intensive therapy (such as that portrayed in this chapter), follow-up sessions are warranted well into the future, with a renewal of more frequent sessions when episodes recur. Thus, "termination" of treatment does not mean an absolute end to the need for clinical care. Instead, it may signify an end of a period of concentrated sessions or the completion of meaningful therapeutic work between a particular practitioner and a patient. Realistically, bipolar patients would do well to follow a "dental model," whereby they get "hygiene check-ups" periodically as a routine part of their health care over the course of their lives.

When we evaluate the efficacy of a treatment model, certain constraints and limitations are expected, owing to the controls that are necessary over methods and funding in projects as large, complicated, and costly as the typical outcome study. The treatment requires some degree of standardization and manualization, along with limits on resources that are applied to any one patient. Thankfully, this does not have to translate to rigidity in the execution of the treatment. To the contrary, using an individual case conceptualization requires an inherent flexibility in use of a treatment model and its manual.

The case of Carlos highlights the unpredictable nature of therapy in general and therapy with bipolar patients in particular. When dealing with a patient population whose affect is labile, whose behavior can be impulsive, and whose treatment can involve multiple, interacting components and personnel, it is folly to believe that the course of therapy neatly follows a script. Instead, therapists will need to know how to make use of the therapy model to deal with problems that emerge in treatment, such as no-shows, risk of drop-out, suicide threats and attempts, therapeutic alliance ruptures, homework nonadherence, and other significant clinical issues. Therapists who are prepared to conceptualize these problems and to spring to action to manage such incidents promptly have the best chance of using cognitive therapy in the manner in which it was intended.

The "stages" of treatment outlined in this chapter are not official designations, although they roughly correspond to Lam et al.'s (1999) and Scott's (1996a) descriptions of the patient's progressions through a course of cognitive therapy for bipolar disorder. The subheadings listed under each stage also are not formal segments of treatment. Rather, they reflect Carlos's personal path through therapy and serve to guide the reader through the part of cognitive therapy that is being addressed and highlighted. Other patients may exhibit other pathways at different time frames. Nonetheless, the goals and methods are very similar across cases, and this will be apparent when examining the details of Carlos's treatment.

STAGE 1: BEGINNING TREATMENT

The first official session occurred following the diagnostic evaluation that served as Carlos's entry into the treatment protocol. In that intake evaluation, in which Carlos went through an open-ended interview as well as a Structured Clinical Interview for the *DSM-III-R* (SCID-I; Spitzer, Williams, Gibbon, & First, 1992), then completed Hamilton Rating Scales (e.g., Hamilton, 1960), and other self-report measures, it was determined that Carlos suffered from bipolar I disorder (currently depressed). Although many of Carlos's reported symptoms were consistent with Histrionic Personality Disorder (HPD) and Narcissistic Personality Disorder (NPD), it could not be determined whether these were artifacts of past manic episodes and mixed states. Therefore, these Axis II diagnoses were deferred, although the intake report suggested that further assessments should be done during euthymic periods to gain evidence to support or refute the diagnoses of HPD and NPD.

The intake evaluation included an overview of past treatment. It was discovered that Carlos had sought pharmacotherapy from his general practitioner when he was in college, and was prescribed tricyclic antidepressants. Carlos reported feeling "extremely good" in short order, discontinued the medication within a few months, and never received counseling. The information gleaned from the interview also served to help the therapist to gain historical and developmental information about Carlos's upbringing and important life events and milestones to formulate a preliminary case conceptualization, which is summarized below.

Demographics and Presenting Problem

Carlos, a 27-year-old, married, college graduate working as a customer relations manager in a local hotel, was born and raised in South America before moving to the United States as a high school exchange student. Carlos reported that he liked his American host family and loved the lifestyle in the United States. Therefore, he decided to stay, to apply to a college on the East Coast, and to set a goal of becoming a U.S. citizen, which he achieved. He was the youngest of four children and reported having only a "cordial" relationship with his siblings, because they were much older. Carlos stated with a wink in his eye that he had been a "surprise baby." When asked what effect this had on his relationship with his parents, Carlos stated that he was seen as a "special" child and was treated as such. However, Carlos also stated that his father had a drinking problem and a terrible temper and that he knew he would have to escape from his father if he were going to have a normal life.

Carlos was married to a woman who herself was an American citizen by choice, having been born and raised in a country in Northern Europe.

Carlos extolled the virtues of his wife ("Sabine"), describing her as "beautiful, blond, educated, and incapable of having a nervous breakdown—the exact opposite of my mother in every way." Then he added that he had been married for 4 years and was already "finished with a seventh affair." Carlos said, "I know I'm out of control, but what can I do? . . . That's why I'm here." Carlos said that he did not know if Sabine knew of his infidelities, because she let him come and go as he pleased never asked questions. Then he acknowledged that he found the marriage to be "a little distant and uninspiring."

When asked to describe more fully what he meant by saying that he was "out of control," Carlos offered that he was a "slave to [his] moods and whims"; at times he could scarcely contain his exuberance for adventure and action, and at other times his thinking was dark and morbid. Carlos admitted that he had always had a large emotional range ("just like my father") but that it had gotten more pronounced since getting married. Recently, he had come close to losing his job with the hotel, which scared him, so he was willing to seek treatment, even if it meant taking medications.

Carlos said that he wanted to learn to master his moods, to get his life "in order," and to improve his marriage. On the latter note, he was willing to state that this goal probably should entail ceasing and desisting from all affairs. However, Carlos added that he was his "father's son," meaning that monogamy was not something he had seen modeled in his parents' marriage.

Carlos scored within the normal range on every self-report mood inventory he answered, including the Beck Depression Inventory (BDI; A. T. Beck et al., 1961) and the Beck Hopelessness Scale (BHS; A. T. Beck et al., 1974). However, Carlos quickly downplayed the significance of these scales, saying that he could change at any time and that he could even become suicidal. Nevertheless, he noted for the record that he had never acted on his suicidal thoughts and did not think it would be a problem now.

Carlos recalled having been his mother's favorite child during his early years. He felt that his mother doted on him, thought he could do no wrong, and tried to protect him from his father's temper. However, it was his father who shielded him from the consequences of misbehavior at school. Carlos explained that he attended a private school for the children of aristocratic families and that his father wielded a great deal of influence with the administration by virtue of his philanthropic gifts to the school. He intimated that some of these "gifts" actually were personal bribes to school officials. He stated flatly that he never had to worry very much about obeying limits.

Carlos said to the intake evaluator, "It sounds like I had the ideal life, right?" He went on to say that he was frustrated that he could not seem to make his father proud of him and that he felt sorry for his mother when he saw her crying over his father's drinking and anger outbursts. Then, when he was 12 years old, something happened in Carlos's life that had a profound effect on him. His father abruptly left home and began to live with another woman. Carlos's mother lapsed into a suicidal depression, and Carlos became her caretaker, hero, and miniature therapist. He found this incident disturbing in many ways, including the fact that "the whole community" was gossiping about it and that his older siblings (all of whom had since moved out) were somewhat apathetic in their response to this family crisis. The father then returned to the household a year later, as if nothing had happened, apologizing for nothing and expecting life to continue as usual. Carlos's mother never confronted her wayward husband and meekly took him back. Carlos said, "By then, I had already lost respect for my father, and now I lost respect for my mother, too." When Carlos got the chance to come to the States as an exchange student, he saw it as his chance to make a clean break. His parents assumed he would return to South America after the school year. Carlos let them think this, even though he had no intention of coming home again.

The intake evaluator compiled a preliminary cognitive case conceptualization, making note of the family history, the father's probable mood disorder and alcoholism, the mother's suicidality, the public shame experienced by the family, and Carlos's possible schemas of abandonment, mistrust, and entitlement. Furthermore, it was hypothesized that Carlos was in great conflict—on the one hand craving excitement, but on the other hand being appalled at his own behavior, which must have reminded him of his own father's.

Sessions 1–3: Socialization Into the Cognitive Model and the Setting of Goals

Upon meeting Carlos for the first time, the therapist (Dr. N.) immediately set an agenda, stating that he would like to summarize what he had learned about Carlos from the intake report, describe a little bit about cognitive therapy, set some goals for the year of treatment, and answer questions that Carlos might have about the treatment program. Naturally, Dr. N. also asked Carlos for feedback about the agenda and welcomed any additional items that he wanted to add. Carlos said that he also wanted to talk about the severity of his diagnosis and his prospects for the future. The therapist agreed to broach this touchy but highly relevant subject.

After reviewing the highlights of Carlos's developmental history and current symptoms (and learning from Carlos that the information seemed accurate and "enlightening"), Dr. N. outlined the cognitive therapy approach for bipolar disorder. Essentially, he told Carlos that manic depression was a serious mood disorder that required careful, consistent clinical attention. Dr. N explained that bipolar disorder ran in families and involved significant biochemical problems that could cause symptoms such as impulsivity, anger, crushing depression, and suicidality, as well as over-exuberance, hypersexuality, and a false sense of invincibility. Therefore, bipolar disorder could do major damage to people's lives, including ruining their path to personal success, destroying their relationships, and potentially leading to premature death. Such a disorder required both medication and counseling, and there was reason to believe that this approach could lead to a much healthier outcome.

Dr. N continued by saying that Carlos would need to work with his psychiatrist to find an effective medication or combination of medications and that cognitive therapy would focus on Carlos's "mental and behavioral approach to life." In other words, by using cognitive therapy, Carlos could learn to adopt a constructive outlook on life such that he would experience less stress, feel more confident (without being overconfident), and become more adept at solving his problems, including his pressures at work, his family conflicts, and his marital troubles. By succeeding in this regard, Carlos not only would improve the quality of his life, but would learn to live with his medications as if taking them were second nature, and would be less apt to have extreme mood cycles and relapses in functioning. In summary, cognitive therapy involved learning a series of psychological skills, controlling the bipolar disorder, and reducing future vulnerability.

Carlos said that this made sense in theory, but that he didn't know if he was going to be willing or able to do everything that his treatment (both the cognitive therapy and the pharmacotherapy) would ask of him. His expressed doubt served as a red flag, and so Dr. N. addressed this first. The following is a condensed, facsimile transcript of the dialogue that followed:

> Dr. N.: I appreciate your being so direct, Carlos. So you think that you might not be willing or able to go through treatment. Is that a fair summary of what you're saying? Why do you think so?

> Carlos: I'm not saying I won't go through the whole program. I'm saying that I might not be into doing everything I'm supposed to do.

> Dr. N.: What do you anticipate that you'll be asked to do that you wouldn't want to do?

> Carlos: Like take my medications, even if they give me side-effects and take away my "edge." Like do all the homework assignments that your handouts say I'll have to do. Like change my lifestyle. All that. I don't know if I'm completely ready for that. But I know that I need help. So it's difficult.

Dr. N.: Wow, that's a lot to cover—side-effects of meds, homework, lifestyle. Pretty big issues. Let's start with the lifestyle issue. What lifestyle changes are you anticipating I'll be asking you to make?

Carlos: The life of a hotel manager. It's wonderful, and I love it, even though it's entirely crazy and bizarre. Everybody works evenings and weekends, and it's actually a little bit incestuous because nobody really has the time for a normal love life outside the hotel and restaurant so everybody's fair game for an affair, and I've had my share, and I'm not sure I want to give up *la vida loca*, if you know what I mean.

Dr. N.: Again, I commend you for being so forthright. Makes my job a lot easier.

Carlos: Don't bet on it.

Dr. N.: (raises his eyebrows, then continues) Carlos, if you have all these doubts, we'll just put them on our agenda, and work on them as we would any clinical issue. You chose to come here, so I assume that's okay with you. Or should I not assume?

Carlos: I just don't want to go so far as to screw up my whole life, and I certainly don't want to go through any more depressions. They're killers. I don't know if I could take another one like the last one.

Dr. N.: Sounds like pretty strong incentive to take part in therapy, if you ask me.

Carlos: (Blandly) I guess.

Dr. N.: That was pretty half-hearted.

Carlos: (ignoring Dr. N.'s comment) I read that manic depressives who have strange schedules and stay up until all hours can get manic, right? Well, that's my life! I can't just give that up. And since I don't want to give that up, I'll bet that means my chances of getting over manic depression aren't so good, right? That's why I need you to give me an honest opinion about my chances of recovery.

Dr. N.: That's right, your concern about your long-term prognosis is a very important agenda item for us to discuss. Well, that's a complicated question, and we may have to answer that based on some things that we can't know for sure today but that we might know better as you go through this treatment. But I can tell you this: The issues that you brought up today, about medications, homework, lifestyle changes, and so on, will all play a role in determining your chances for successful treatment and a better future. So we're off to a flying start. I'm enthused. (Pause) You don't look so enthused, though.

Carlos: I wish I could know for sure, today. I don't want to wait. I don't want to work hard in therapy, and take medications I don't want to take, and make sacrifices in my sex life, and work hard at homework, and have it all be for nothing because I don't get well anyway. At least if I knew for sure that my chances for recovery were low, I would know that I could do whatever I pleased and it wouldn't matter.

Dr. N.: *Eat, drink, and be merry, for tomorrow we die.*

Carlos: Huh?

Dr. N.: Oh, sorry. That's a reference to something that soldiers said in wartime, I believe. That they were going to die in battle the next day, so they might as well have a wild night.

Carlos: That's exactly what I mean.

Dr. N.: That kind of pessimism is something we're going to have to address, Carlos. You're telling me you are hesitant to invest in therapy if you're not sure it's going to work. But what do you think will happen if you hold back, Carlos? What's going to happen if you tiptoe through therapy and don't give it your best shot? What do you think the outcome will be?

Carlos: What you're telling me is that you think I'll stay ill and maybe get worse.

Dr. N.: Well, if I can turn it around and make it sound more hopeful, I would put it this way: If you invest in your treatment, and you bring the best of your spirit, intellect, energy, faith, and determination, you will markedly increase your chances of having a better prognosis.

Carlos: But no guarantees.

Dr. N.: No guarantees. Nobody can guarantee a cure. But you'll improve the probability of a successful treatment, and that's something you can control—probabilities.

Carlos: (pause) To be honest, I'm not totally convinced.

Dr. N.: You don't have to be. Cognitive therapy is not something you have to believe in before you even start. You have to go through it, see for yourself, and make your own judgment. My hope is that you'll give it a fair try, so that you can evaluate it on its best merits. Then you'll know whether you can truly make use of this treatment. My main concern is that you may choose to make a negative judgment before you begin, rather than exploring the treatment to its fullest.

Dr. N. and Carlos continued along this vein and agreed to meet again. Although Carlos was not keen to do any written homework, to try new behavioral strategies, or to alter his nocturnal working schedule, he was willing to buy a copy of Fieve's (1989) *Moodswing* and to begin to read it as part of his adjunctive bibliotherapy. In the collaborative spirit of cognitive therapy, Dr. N. supported Carlos's willingness to do this much (and to fill out the various weekly assessment inventories, including the daily mood log, called *Chronorecords*, designed by psychiatrists Peter Whybrow and Mark Bauer at the University of Pennsylvania; Whybrow & Bauer, 1991) and said that the issue of additional homework could be revisited later.

By the third session, it was clear that Carlos had strong ambivalence about his goals for therapy. For example, he did not want to ruin his marriage, and he professed to respect and value Sabine as a person, but he was skeptical that he could cease and desist from his serial sexual dalliances. He made it clear that he did not want his therapist to moralize about this behavior. Dr. N. replied that it was not necessary to moralize, that it was more than sufficient to look at "cause and effect," meaning that it would be useful to look at the benefits and consequences of various forms of action, including interpersonal outcomes and impact on Carlos's self-esteem. As Dr. N. said, "That should be compelling enough for our purposes."

Carlos intimated that he might want to have at least one conjoint session with Sabine. Dr. N. said that he would be in favor of this in principle, but that if Carlos were having an extramarital relationship, a couples session would not be in "good faith" and therefore would have to be postponed until Carlos had achieved a substantial period of monogamy.

Although Carlos had not yet begun to do therapy homework pertinent to the self-monitoring of his thoughts, he understood and appreciated the effects that his thinking had on his emotions and actions. In other words, Carlos accepted the cognitive model. He read the Fieve book and did the mood log, and these steps had to suffice for the moment.

STAGE 2: APPLYING THE COGNITIVE MODEL ROUTINELY

After three sessions, it seemed that Carlos was going to remain in treatment, and a modicum of rapport had been established. Carlos reported that he was taking his lithium and Depakote as prescribed, but that he was not happy about this. Nevertheless, Carlos seemed to be in a euthymic state, thus providing at least some evidence that the pharmacotherapy was doing its job. Dr. N. consulted with the psychiatrist and talked about how to respond to Carlos's misgivings in a way that would give him the most empathy, encouragement, and clear instructions. Dr. N. and the psychiatrist agreed that Carlos's views and feelings about medication put him at risk for nonadherence at any time and that this would have to be watched.

In the next stage of cognitive therapy, Dr. N. attempted to teach Carlos one of the most basic and important of all cognitive skills: cognitive self-monitoring and rational responding. In addition, both Dr. N. and Carlos made use of the preliminary case conceptualization to understand Carlos's vulnerabilities, including his schemas of abandonment, mistrust, and entitlement. This was a period of fruitful dialogue, learning, and therapeutic progress.

Sessions 4–8: Learning the Strategies and Techniques of Cognitive Therapy

One of the burning issues that Carlos wanted to address at length and in depth was his "inexplicable" dissatisfaction with his wife and his concomitant urges to seek the companionship of other women. Dr. N. agreed that these were important topics and surmised that this might be an area of discussion that would present opportunities for teaching Carlos more about the strategies and techniques of cognitive therapy. Additionally, it would open the door to a discussion about Carlos's sexual impulsivity, a topic that now would be potentially less shaming because Carlos had brought it up first.

To make sense of Carlos's marital situation, Dr. N. suggested that they examine it through three lenses: (a) as a reflection of his beliefs about relationships, formed from his view of his parents' relationship, and maintained by his views of his extramarital affairs; (b) as a function of the daily interactions between Carlos and Sabine, including all the ways they perceived and treated each other; and (c) as an overall result of his general views of himself, his world, and his future (the cognitive triad), including the schemas that were hypothesized to be relevant to Carlos in his case conceptualization. Given that Carlos was highly motivated to address this topic, Dr. N. silently reasoned that it might pose an excellent opportunity to introduce him to cognitive therapy techniques and homework while minimizing the chances of a power struggle.

Carlos explained that he met Sabine in his senior year of college and that they were the "quintessential opposites who attract." He liked her "cool, Nordic looks"; her emotional independence; and her sedate, rational intelligence. Carlos said that Sabine liked his "fire" and that he was "tall, dark, and handsome." They started living together within 6 months and were married less than a year after that.

Carlos reiterated that he was glad he had married someone who was "the opposite of [his] mother." Dr. N. seized this opportunity to respond, "Carlos, that's the second time you've made that point. Tell me what you were hoping to avoid in choosing someone like your mother, what you were hoping to get in choosing someone like Sabine, and what you think you've actually got." Something along the lines of the following dialogue ensued:

Carlos: I did not want to be with an emotionally weak woman who was going to need me to death. I've been there and done that. I was my mother's caretaker, therapist, and confidante. It was ridiculous.

Dr. N.: You hadn't put it that way before. (sympathetically and tentatively) Do you want to talk about it?

Carlos: No, let's stick to Sabine for now. I wanted a woman who could take care of herself. Someone who was beautiful and could have anyone she wanted, but who would choose me, because I was the best, not because I was all she had. I wanted somebody I could be proud of in public . . . the envy of my peers. And I got that in Sabine.

Dr. N.: (Anticipating Carlos's next phrase) But . . .

Carlos: But there were some things I didn't bargain for.

Dr. N.: Such as?

Carlos: Such as a zero tolerance for depression. I got depressed 2 years ago, just before I got my job at the hotel, and Sabine acted like it was my complete responsibility to carry on as if nothing were wrong. She had no sympathy for me. I think she thought I was being lazy or weak. It was almost like she had disdain for me. I hated that.

Dr. N.: And you felt angry and disillusioned?

Carlos: Abandoned. Emotionally abandoned. And blamed for being depressed.

Dr. N.: There's that schema. Abandonment. It felt as severe as if she had gone away and left forever.

Carlos: Pretty much, yeah.

Dr. N.: How did you make sense of that?

Carlos: I thought she stopped caring about me. But then I got the job, and I started to feel better, and . . . (stops himself).

Dr. N.: You met someone at work?

Carlos: Right. And I felt cared about again. And I had a brief, hot affair, and it was good. And I cheered up, and then Sabine liked me again, and the marriage improved, too.

Dr. N.: You weren't still angry with her? What did you do with your feelings of abandonment?

Carlos: I didn't care as much about that. Things were better.

Dr. N.: How did that change your views of her? Did you still think she didn't care about you?

Carlos: No, she still cared. She just can't deal with depression. So I guess I can't afford to get depressed . . . or I guess I find someone else who wants to take care of me.

Dr. N. designed some homework assignments, above and beyond the usual mood logs (which so far seemed within normal limits early in treatment), that would continue Carlos's work on understanding his marriage, his views of his wife, his views of himself in the context of the marriage, and the pros and cons of his various marital and extramarital behaviors.

One homework assignment was geared to combat Carlos's abandonment schema by asking him to catalogue as many memories as possible of Sabine showing him attention and affection. Another assignment took square aim at his entitlement schema, asking him to write about what he was willing to contribute to Sabine's life, apart from his swarthy good looks. Carlos was introduced to the Daily Thought Record (DTR), one of the most fundamental and important of the cognitive therapy techniques, which he was to use whenever he felt angry or hurt in response to his wife's behavior. This helped Carlos to articulate the malevolent interpretations that he was making about her reactions to him. At one point, he offered that it might be possible that she knew about his extramarital escapades, which might explain her emotional distance. He began to consider adding an important goal to his list: going back to monogamy again as a long-term commitment. Dr. N. applauded this but acknowledged that Carlos was going to face many, many temptations in the future, especially if the hotel were anywhere near as zany a place as Carlos had described.

Carlos reached an important realization when he did a homework assignment that focused on his mistrust schema. The assignment asked him to list examples of ways that he trusted or did not trust himself. He found himself at an absolute loss to write down ways that he trusted himself. Astonished, he admitted that he did not trust himself, just as he did not trust his father. Then, as if that weren't enough, Carlos realized that Sabine did have something important in common with his mother. They were both cheated on egregiously by their husbands, and they didn't say or do anything about it.

At first, Carlos found this revelation to be disturbing. When his therapist inquired about Carlos's thoughts at that critical moment, he said, "It's bad enough that I'm turning into my father, but now I find out I'm turning my wife into my mother. There's no escape." Then Dr. N. said, "That's just one way to look at it, Carlos. How can you make this important realization work for you?" This type of question is emblematic of cognitive therapy, in that the therapist does not try to deny or minimize the patient's emotionally painful experiences. Rather, the therapist asks the patient to take any given situation and try to think of it in such a way as to convert it into an opportunity. In this case, Carlos and Dr. N. hit on the following idea: If Carlos could moderate his anger toward his wife and discontinue his extramarital activities, he would succeed in creating a life for himself and Sabine that would be clearly differentiated from that of his mother and father. To Carlos, this was a goal he wanted dearly to accomplish. The therapist was also quick to seize on this opportunity, noting rather casually that such a goal would require Carlos's full engagement in the process of therapy, including collaborating with his medication regimen and doing between-sessions cognitive therapy assignments. Carlos did just that. It was a very positive development.

Sessions 9–14: Experiencing Improved Moods, Behaviors, and Hopefulness

At about 2 to 3 months into treatment, most patients with uncomplicated, unipolar depression begin to take control of the therapy process. They have become adept at setting agendas for each session; self-monitoring and conceptualizing their own thoughts, feelings, and actions; doing homework assignments as a matter of routine; feeling like active agents in their own psychological care (i.e., not feeling unduly dependent on their therapists); and preparing for the end of treatment. This is the way many of the outcome studies on cognitive therapy for depression have been designed over the years. At this point, Carlos looked like one of the ideal patients in these studies. He had shown no signs either of mania or depression, and he had settled into a steady, productive set of self-help habits. Carlos's Chrono-records showed no alarming examples of mood lability, and he professed to have had no temptations to stray from his marriage again.

However, Carlos was not a unipolar depressed patient. He had bipolar disorder, though it was easy to forget this at times. Nevertheless, continued vigilance was necessary because of the pernicious nature of recurrences and relapses in this disorder. Pharmacotherapy must be ongoing, and the cognitive therapy must be more extensive than the typical course of therapy for unipolar depression. This is because patients must learn to deal with a war against extreme moods on two fronts: They must gain experience in spotting prodromes (Lam & Wong, 1997) and in coping with periods of relapse.

In retrospect, for all of Carlos's participation in cognitive therapy, there was some evidence that he was not taking his lithium and Depakote in the manner in which it was prescribed. Soon, a stressful event would precipitate a crisis, and he would not be biochemically girded for it. Fortunately, he made a mighty effort to use the skills he had learned in cognitive therapy, and this became his lifeline through a treacherous period.

STAGE 3: USING COGNITIVE THERAPY TO MANAGE SERIOUS NEW PROBLEMS

Cognitive therapy involves a great deal of psychoeducation and skills training. It works best when patients accumulate knowledge about themselves in a thematic way from session to session, leading to a broadening of their perspectives about themselves, their world, and their future. However, clinical crises sometimes occur that interrupt this process. Crises such as schema activation, drug abuse relapse, traumatic life events, and suicidality require direct intervention, where survival is the highest priority and psychoeducation takes a back seat. Nevertheless, the cognitive model takes crisis situations into account and provides therapists with a technology to deal with these problematic and dangerous situations (Dattilio & Freeman, 1994, 2000).

Sessions 15–17: Crisis Intervention

After the 14th session, Carlos did not show up for his next scheduled appointment. Although such an event is always a red flag that something may be wrong, Dr. N. did not worry too much because Carlos's absence was the exception to the rule. However, when Carlos did not return a series of telephone messages, Dr. N. began to think that there was a problem. He called the psychiatrist and alerted her that Carlos may have abandoned treatment. The psychiatrist replied that she had a scheduled appointment with Carlos for later in the week but that she would give him a call today to try to confirm it. Later, the psychiatrist told Dr. N. that she had reached Carlos, that he sounded "shaky," but that he had agreed to come in for his medication appointment. Dr. N. promptly telephoned Carlos, got his answering machine, and offered to free up some time to see him immediately following his meeting with the psychiatrist. Carlos showed up, and filled out the BDI prior to his cognitive therapy session.

Carlos's BDI score was 43, very much in the severe range of depressed affect. He reported suicidal ideation but was adamant that he would not actually kill himself. He looked haggard, as if he had not been sleeping well, and had paid uncharacteristically little attention to his appearance. After expressing concern for Carlos and reaffirming his commitment to helping him, Dr. N. asked Carlos for a synopsis of what had happened to cause the missed session and to trigger his depressed mood.

At first, Carlos was hesitant to say anything specific about the situation. Therefore, Dr. N. asked him questions about his views about himself, his treatment, and his future. The following is a representation of that dialogue:

Carlos: I'm disgusted with myself. I'm disgusted with my father. I feel like a loathsome, horrible person. I probably deserve to lose my wife. (Pauses, collecting himself so that his voice won't crack) You did the best you could, Dr. N., but I'm not going to get better. Too much has happened. I have too many regrets and too many flaws. You can't fix that. You can only do so much. I'm not going anywhere but down.

Dr. N.:   I can always count on you to level with me, Carlos, in good times and bad. Thanks for coming in today, even though you didn't think it was going to help. I take it as a sign of respect, and I respect you in return.

Carlos: (Silent, and looking down at the floor)

Dr. N.:   You've just made some incredibly harsh comments about yourself. You nailed yourself in almost every way possible, telling me that you're disgusted with yourself and that you're so flawed that you're beyond help. Well, I'll tell you what I believe right now. I believe that something significant has happened since we last met and that you have had an extreme reaction—a reaction that does not take into account all the good work you have done in therapy and all the good plans and intentions you have for your future. If you're up to it, I would like to talk about what happened, how it affected you, and what we can do about it. Are you willing to do that?

Carlos: I don't think it will do any good.

Dr. N.:   Humor me. (Looks at Carlos eye to eye, seriously and confidently)

Carlos began to tell a rambling story, and the therapist gently brought him back to the main gist of the tale again and again. Apparently, one of Carlos's hotel co-workers was about to get married, so the gang threw him a bachelor party. They went out to a strip joint, where Carlos drank heavily and had naked women doing "private dances" for him. Then, one of the strippers offered him a little extra attention, and Carlos paid the woman for sex in a back dressing room. Carlos agitatedly explained that "everything was racing all around me" and that he got "caught up in the moment." He added that he "didn't care about anything except feeling wild and free." Later, however, he said that it seemed that his world was "crashing down."

Dr. N. nodded silently during Carlos's story, while conceptualizing in the back of his mind. Carlos described a period of impulsivity and inflated affect, perhaps induced or enhanced by an alcohol binge. His account of the evening's events could also be construed as a mixed state episode or potentially the beginning of a series of rapid cycles. Along with this, Carlos had broken his streak of extramarital abstinence, and must have felt that he had failed miserably. He probably also felt guilty and perhaps doubtful that he could control his sexual acting-out in the future. However, Dr. N. thought that there must be something more to this situation. After all, this was the first time that Dr. N. had heard anything about Carlos's involvement with prostitution. Carefully, he shared his conceptualization with Carlos and asked him if his paying for sex had made it even worse for him. The answer went far beyond what he expected.

Carlos agreed with most of the therapist's conceptualization but said that the situation with the prostitute also made him hate his father with a renewed passion. He explained that when he was 14 years old, shortly after his father returned home following his abandonment of the family for a high-profile extramarital affair, his father took him to a prostitute. The father said that it was time for Carlos to "become a man." Carlos said he never had so many mixed emotions in his life. He was curious, aroused, frightened, honored, appalled, and both hateful and grateful toward his father at the same time. Furthermore, he wanted to please his father by "being a man," that is, by going through with the sexual initiation rite.

This was emotionally confusing enough, but then the father instructed Carlos to watch while the father and the prostitute had sex in front of him. The father had said, "I want you to see how it's done right." Carlos felt tremendous remorse, "as if I was stabbing my mother in the back as bad as my father did, but I knew I would never, ever be able to tell my mother, or she would kill herself for sure." Then the father watched while Carlos had sex with the prostitute. All of these memories were accentuated in bold relief as a result of Carlos's sexual encounter at the bachelor party. Carlos hated himself, felt beyond redemption and beyond hope. This became the focus of the next few therapy sessions.

Dr. N. tried to encourage Carlos not to give up hope, as depicted in the following exchange:

Dr. N.: This is a painful turn of events. Very painful. And you're very angry at yourself and your father. I understand. But I don't believe that you have to give up your goals for yourself, your marriage, and your future. If anything, we have to try twice as hard now to get you back to where you want to be, emotionally and otherwise. You've had a setback, and now we have to regroup. Okay, so we'll regroup. I've seen your motivation and determination, and I think you can make a comeback, but we have to make sure that all the components of treatment are in place and that you're willing to re-invest in the process. I'm "in." Are you?

Carlos: (Hesitantly). Yes. Maybe you should ask if Sabine is "in."

Dr. N.: Does she know what happened?

Carlos:	(Looking at him as if he must be crazy to even ask such a question)
Dr. N.:	Well, does she at least know that you're feeling like shit?
Carlos:	Yes, and we all know how much she loves me when that happens, right?
Dr. N.:	So you feel . . . abandoned? On top of everything?
Carlos:	(Nods yes)
Dr. N.:	After we get you back on track again—and we will get you back on track again—do you want to plan on having some marital therapy sessions, provided of course that you are able to rebuild a period of monogamy? It seems like there are some issues that need to be dealt with. Am I being too presumptuous?
Carlos:	No. Let's try it. I hope she's still with me by then.
Dr. N.:	I hope so, too. For now, we really have to focus on getting you well.

Sessions 18–36: Actively Dealing With Increased Stressors and Symptom Elevations

During this middle phase of therapy, Carlos fought with a depressive episode. Because there was no evidence of rapid cycles, Carlos's psychiatrist added a low dose of a selective serotonin reuptake inhibitor to his medication regimen, but Carlos understood that his mood would have to be watched carefully to guard against a breakthrough of mania. Carlos's BDI scores ranged between 20 and 35 for much of this time, as he worried about the possibility of having contracted a sexually transmitted disease (later disconfirmed), the strained state of his marriage, and the increasing pressures of his job. At this time, Carlos endorsed beliefs such as "I am not going to be able to hold it together for long," and "I'm not even close to the man I thought I was." Carlos's self-esteem was very low, his hopelessness (as indicated by double-digit scores on the BHS) was up, and his motivation for continuing with therapy was wavering.

Dr. N. tried to rally his patient. He gave Carlos positive feedback for continuing to attend sessions and taking his medication despite his pessimism and low energy. He reminded Carlos that he was willing to conduct couples sessions after Carlos had reestablished his ability to avoid extramarital affairs for at least 2 or 3 months. He worked assiduously in session to help Carlos with a variety of self-help techniques, such as role-playing appropriate conflict-resolution skills for work, expressing positive affect at home with Sabine, and simulating dialogues with himself to work to solve problems, rather than catastrophize. Dr. N. also telephoned Carlos from time to time, just to see how he was feeling following particularly demanding and affect-laden sessions, and to gently prod him to be sure to take his medications. Of course, Dr. N. frequently asked Carlos how he interpreted these therapeutic methods, just in case Carlos was harboring resentment or unspoken negative thoughts about therapy.

It was also during this time that Carlos became a little receptive to the idea of regulating his sleep–wake cycle, even if it meant taking a more "boring" shift at work and coming directly home after his official work time was over. Carlos understood that the purpose of this strategy was not to control him or deny him his dignity, but rather to help him "hold it together." Carlos actively scheduled activities to fight anergia and low motivation, but made sure to choose mastery activities rather than hedonistic ones. For example, Carlos was a very good tennis player; he also sang and played guitar. He was encouraged to do more of these activities and to stay away from nightclubs and the race track. Similarly, he took pride in being multilingual. Therefore, Dr. N. suggested that he either serve as a college-level language tutor or take a new language course (he was sure to be a quick learner). Although marital therapy sessions had not yet been scheduled, Carlos was encouraged to be more interactive with his wife, including planning more dates. At all points along the way, Carlos worked on his DTRs, in which he tested and re-evaluated many of the pessimistic, self-denigrating thoughts he had during moments of frustration and despair.

Toward the end of the ninth month of therapy, Carlos's mood leveled off, and he felt euthymic. His BDI and BHS scored were now in the single digits, and his Chronorecords showed a reasonable range. At this point in time, two important agreements were reached. First, Sabine would be invited to attend sessions. Second, the therapeutic strategies would be shifted to include those techniques that would guard against the possible onset of hypomania and mania. Regarding the former, Dr. N. offered to telephone Sabine and invite her to come in for some conjoint sessions, which Carlos appreciated. This was because Carlos wanted to maintain a position of strength with Sabine; he feared that she disdained him for having a mood disorder. By having Dr. N. call Sabine, Carlos was able to avoid feeling as though he were "begging her" to help him. The therapist realized that this was a negative belief that probably should be tested, but decided that the benefits of assisting Carlos in this manner outweighed the necessity of testing the belief at this time. There were other, higher priorities.

Regarding the shift in techniques, Dr. N. and Carlos began to institute homework assignments such as (a) imagining and anticipating consequences of his behavior, (b) scheduling fewer activities, (c) getting feedback from two people (e.g., Sabine, his best friend, Tony, and Dr. N., among other candidates) before enacting new ideas at work or with regard to his finances, (d) delaying acting on strong emotions (e.g., anger, extramarital lust) for at least 48 hours so he could think things through, and (e) spotting the activation of his entitlement schema (called the "I can do whatever I please" belief by Carlos and Dr. N.), as well as devising alternative responses that would give him a sense of pride and self-control for following his conscience more than his appetites. Carlos began to feel good about himself again, which set the stage for a short series of conjoint sessions. He wanted to bring up some important issues with Sabine, but looked forward to doing this in a friendly environment, "in which the depressed aren't condemned," as he put it.

Sessions 37–39: Couples Sessions

On being reached by Dr. N. by telephone, Sabine rather nonchalantly agreed to come in for a few sessions with Carlos. In the session prior to Sabine's joining them, Dr. N. and Carlos talked about the planned agenda for sessions that would involve her. They hit on the following approach: Dr. N. would put Sabine at ease and facilitate her involvement in the process of therapy by asking her a question that would give her some power and authority; she would be asked to give her assessment about how her husband was doing since he began therapy.

In session, Sabine was polite, well dressed, articulate, and unemotional. She dutifully answered questions concisely, with no elaboration. She said that she was "always a little bit worried about Carlos's state of mind" but that he was a "big boy who should know how to take care of himself." Carlos shot a glance over at Dr. N., as if to say, "See what I mean?" The following is a summary of the therapeutic dialogue that ensued:

Sabine: I know that Carlos has to take his medication, but I try not to look over his shoulder or bother him. It's his responsibility.

Dr. N.: How do you think he's doing?

Sabine: Sometimes good, sometimes not. His moods go on their own timetable. I have no influence over them.

Carlos: You're wrong. You affect me a lot. Your opinion of me matters to me. How much you love me matters to me. If you think I'm not living up to what you think I should be, it's very upsetting to me.

Sabine: (Closes her eyes, giving the appearance of trying to meditate rather than lose her temper)

Dr. N.: (Wonders silently if Sabine knows about Carlos's affairs, and if his protestations about how she affects him emotionally strike her as infuriatingly hypocritical and phony) Sabine, what are your thoughts right now as you hear Carlos say that your thoughts and feelings about him matter to him?

Sabine: I've heard it all before.

Dr. N.: And when you've heard it all before, what have you *thought* about it all before?

Sabine: (Long pause)

Carlos: This is what she does to me, too. She keeps to herself, with this air of hatred. It kills me.

Dr. N.: (Holding up an index finger, to politely tell Carlos to wait) Carlos, I know how you feel about it. Let's not get off track right now before we finish this line of discussion and find out how Sabine feels about it. Sabine? Are you willing to say what you think of Carlos's comments, including this last one about how he thinks you have an air of hatred toward him?

Sabine: To be frank, I think he needs psychiatric treatment much more than he needs me. So if he's getting good psychiatric treatment, then I shouldn't have to be brought into this.

Carlos: That just makes me feel like you would rather be away from me.

Dr. N.: Carlos, have you explained to Sabine about your abandonment schema? Does she know about your father's leaving your family? Have you given her a context in which to understand your fears about her leaving you?

Carlos: No, not really. (Turning toward his wife) I didn't think you would want to hear about it. I thought you would think I was just making excuses for myself.

Sabine: And you would be right.

Dr. N.: (A little taken aback by Sabine's bluntness) Do you think I'm making excuses for him?

Sabine: That's not for me to say. I'm just here because you called me to come in, and so I'm here.

Carlos: But you're not really here . . . not in spirit. I have a problem with that.

Sabine: You have a problem with a lot of things.

Dr. N.: (Hearing the negative expressed affect, he worries that the session is going to be unproductive and perhaps damaging. He decides to regroup and find a different angle. This necessitates getting back to the basic structure of cognitive therapy, including making an agenda and setting goals) Listen, before we get too far down this adversarial track, let's take a few minutes to talk about what the goals of this session should be, and let's try to find out what you two agree on. Is that okay?

The three participants were able to agree on two goals for the session: (a) to have each party assess how Carlos was using his treatment and (b) to clarify the problems that needed to be solved. Dr. N. took the lead, stating that he felt that Carlos's moods were now stabilized (albeit somewhat dysphoric), that he was effectively using a wide range of cognitive therapy techniques, that he seemed to be doing well on his medications, and that now he was in the proper frame of mind to deal with unfinished business of his life, such as the state of his marriage. Carlos followed, saying that he agreed with Dr. N., but adding that he loved Sabine and needed her support to stay hopeful. Sabine was able to bring herself to say that she was pleasantly surprised that Carlos was actively attending treatment, adding that "I don't always know when he's really going where he says he's going." Then, before the therapist dared to ask what she was implying, Sabine said something unexpected and quite telling.

Sabine: (Turning to Carlos and saying sharply) When I married you I thought I wasn't going to have to take care of you and pick up the pieces. I thought I was getting away from that when I came to the States.

Carlos: Getting away from what?

Sabine: (Looking at Dr. N.) This is probably what you expect to hear. (Turns back to Carlos) Away from my father. My depressed, suicidal father. Away from my life as a nurse for a man who's supposed to be strong for me. Away from being in a family where my feelings aren't even considered. Away from a situation where the man is always the poor creature . . . the poor victim . . . even if he's hurting others. But that's what I have with you, and so I have to live with my lot. (Turns away, arms folded)

Carlos: (Surprisingly composed) So this is why you hate me when I'm depressed. I didn't know your father was suicidal. He seemed okay to me whenever I saw him.

Sabine: The family has to show the proper public face.

Carlos: Yes, but I'm not the public. I'm in your personal life. I want to know about what's really going on.

Sabine: (Again, a sharp glance at Carlos) So do I.

Dr. N.: (Thinking that Pandora's box has been opened and wondering what else he might have been foolishly expecting when he asked Sabine to come to sessions) You know, when I called for this meeting my intention was to get a progress report on how Carlos was doing at home. I didn't realize that some big topics were brewing. It looks like some important things are coming to a head. Carlos, if we dive in head first—assuming that Sabine agrees to do the same—we have the added responsibility of coping with the fallout and not letting it trigger any adverse symptoms or moods other than normal concern. That's a tall order. Do you want to go for it?

Carlos: (Big sigh) Man. (To Sabine) Are you talking about the women where I work?

Sabine: So it's more than one?

Carlos: (Starting to cry) I have some major problems. Major problems! I'm doing my best. I swear I haven't looked at another woman in months. I was wrong. I'm sorry. I was wrong. What do you want from me? I have serious problems, and I'm trying to get help. Did your father ever try to get help? I'm trying to get help. I'm not justifying my behavior. I'm sorry. God I'm sorry! (Sobbing)

Sabine: (Blank expression, looking away)

Dr. N.: Sabine, would you like to say what's on your mind right now?

Sabine: (Starts to tear up, but says nothing)

Dr. N.: Is it okay if I say something to both of you? (Waits for permission, then continues) I am very, very sorry if this session has become much more painful than either of you bargained for. I actually didn't think that things would come to a head like this either. I know you're both very, very stressed out right now. I don't want to make it sound like it's not a big deal. It's a big deal. (Pauses) However, I wonder if this can be the beginning of open communication, so that if there's any chance of the relationship surviving, you can manage it, because you've now broken the ice, and now you have a chance of airing your feelings and solving your problems, if both of you want to do that. (To Carlos) You and I can take this as a new beginning, too. This is a huge stressor—one that you have been worrying about for a long time. Now it's here, and it presents us with a chance to cope with it, without giving up, without sabotaging yourself, without going off your medications, and without assuming that your mood disorder is going to take over again. I'm prepared to help you—both of you—get through this time and to try to figure out what you're going to do. I know it won't be easy. I'm really sorry. But I think this can be the low point, and things can get better from this point onward, if we look at it in the most constructive way. I'll do what I can to help. What do you think about what I'm saying?

Despite the traumatic feel of the session, neither Sabine nor Carlos said they felt hopeless about the situation. They agreed to come in for one or two more sessions with Dr. N. while looking for a new therapist who would serve as their exclusive couples counselor on an ongoing basis. Carlos would continue with Dr. N. for cognitive therapy and with the psychiatrist for his medication.

Dr. N. was pleasantly surprised to see that Sabine and Carlos showed up at his office for two more sessions. They spoke openly (but calmly) about their anger toward each other and about the hurt they had inflicted on each other. They discussed everything from Sabine's father's suicide attempts to Carlos's manic episodes and extramarital affairs. At Dr. N.'s prompting, they also were willing to reminisce about the early days of their relationship and about what they had found irresistible about each other at the time. By the end of the third conjoint session, Carlos had shown no signs of relapse, and the couple indicated that they would be starting with a new couples therapist the following week. That was the last time Dr. N. saw Sabine; he continued to see Carlos for individual cognitive therapy.

Sessions 40–41: Medication Problems and Cognitive Therapy

Carlos was ebullient. He was very pleased with the couples sessions, and he stated that he felt he had a new lease on life. He was emphatic that he didn't need other women anymore and that he felt a new sense of freedom in relating to Sabine. He added that he no longer felt that she hated him, even though he had come clean with his infidelities. Carlos was also quick to point out to Dr. N. that he had survived a major, stressful life event without experiencing depression or mania. That was the good news. The bad news was that he stated rather matter-of-factly that he no longer had to take his medication. At that moment Dr. N. knew that this would have to become the top agenda item of the session but that he had to address the issue in a way that would not take the wind out of Carlos's sails just as he was feeling he had overcome a major hurdle in his recovery.

The question was this: Was Carlos on the way to becoming manic, or was he just feeling normal, hopeful, and tired of medications? Recognizing that this was not really an "either–or" question, Dr. N. started by empathizing with Carlos's desire to be free of medications. However, he also expressed empathy for Carlos's manic depression and noted that a recurrence of the disorder would involve more pathos than taking the medications would. Carlos expressed confidence that neither the mania nor the depression would recur. Given his history of mood problems, this sentiment struck Dr. N. as an example of "irrational exuberance." Nevertheless, it was imperative that he not engage Carlos in a power struggle or risk shaming him.

Instead, Dr. N. asked Carlos to explain his gripes about medications, as a prelude to talking about the pros and cons of being on and ending pharmacotherapy. The therapist expected Carlos to complain about side-effects. This was not among his chief complaints, however. Therefore, they discussed his beliefs about taking medication, based on his experiences to date and his expectations for the future. Before they did that, however, Dr. N. had something important to assess:

Dr. N.: Before we get into the nitty-gritty of the cons of medications, can I ask you something?

Carlos: (Nods)

Dr. N.: Are you *considering* going off your meds, or have you already *done* it?

Carlos: Honestly? (Pause) I stopped a few days ago.

Dr. N.: Does the psychiatrist know?

Carlos: No.

Dr. N.: She needs to know. I'd rather that it came from you, instead of from me. Would you be willing to leave her a voice mail message right now? Here's the telephone.

Carlos: I'll call her later.

Dr. N.: Now is better, but I'll take you at your word. I'm going to consult with her in a planned meeting later this afternoon anyhow. Can I count on you to let her know before then?

Carlos: (Impatiently) I'll do it. I'll do it.

Dr. N.: Thanks. We all have to be on the same page. I'm glad you're willing to tell her that you haven't taken your medications for a few days. Now, back to our regularly scheduled topic— let's get into the pros and cons of taking the medication in the first place, starting with the cons.

The therapist chose the "cons" first, to give Carlos a structured forum for airing his grievances against the pharmacotherapy, while also setting the stage for looking at the other side of the coin. Below is the gist of the discussion that followed.

Carlos: The cons are that I lose my "edge," and I have to continue to be this ill person that my wife would rather I not be. You know what I mean?

Dr. N.: I'm not sure, but let me feed it back to you and see if I'm hearing you correctly. First, you are concerned about losing your "edge." I'm not sure what that means exactly, but I'll bet it has something to do with your "fire," as you put it once. Second, you're trying to distance yourself from resembling your father-in-law, so that you can stay in Sabine's good graces. I hope that didn't sound too simplistic or irreverent.

Carlos: No, no, that's fine. That's about right. I don't think I'm as passionate a person on the medications, and I certainly don't want to remind Sabine of her father, now that I know the whole story about his problems.

Dr. N.:   (Trying desperately to be engaging) I'm getting a flood of automatic thoughts right now, Carlos. I think I need to do some DTRs.

Carlos: (Laughs nervously)

Dr. N.:   May I share my automatic thoughts with you? You can correct my faulty thinking if you like, but I want credit for my sensible thoughts too, okay? Deal?

Carlos: Deal. Fire away.

Dr. N.:   I'm thinking that you are already a passionate enough man for Sabine, but that if you let yourself get any more passionate you're going to be insatiable again, and that's going to involve other women. I don't know if you want to play with that kind of fire again. I'm also thinking that you are already succeeding in distancing yourself from your father-in-law, precisely by taking your medications and coming to cognitive therapy. He never got treatment, and his condition remains poor, according to Sabine. You've gotten better and survived a major stressor in coming clean with your wife about the affairs. I've got to think that the cognitive therapy and the medication have been a winning combination, thanks to your diligence. Do you really want to break up a winning combination, just for a symbolic gesture?

Carlos: You need a lot of rational responses.

Dr. N.:   I'm listening.

Carlos: I have no intention of cheating on my wife again. But I'm telling you, she likes me better when I've got more emotional fire.

Dr. N.:   Did she say that in your couples session with the new therapist?

Carlos: No, but I know it's true.

Dr. N.:   Ask her. Next session, ask her. Straight out. Ask her if she wants you to stop your medications and to become more passionate.

Carlos: Of course she'll say "no."

Dr. N.:   So what's the deal?

Carlos: Maybe *I* want the fire back.

Dr. N.:   That's totally believable. But who said you lost it?

Carlos: I'm a little subdued.

Dr. N.:   In other words, you're not living *la vida loca* these days.

Carlos: The people at work notice it.

Dr. N.:   (Ah-ha) "People?" Or *someone*? Perhaps a former "flame," since we're talking about fire?

Further discussion revealed that an ex-lover at work chastised Carlos for avoiding her. She taunted him, telling him he had lost his virility (in more colorful terms than that, according to Carlos) and that he probably was controlled by his wife. This woman pushed all the right buttons. Unfortunately, Carlos did not take the time to examine the flaws in this woman's reasoning, not to mention her personal agenda. Instead, Carlos came to his own conclusions. He felt that his manhood had been insulted, and the medication became his scapegoat for the problem. Then he became caught up in proving his manhood, rather than staying focused on his goals.

Dr. N. asked Carlos to look at the evidence for and against the ideas with which the ex-lover had teased him. He asked Carlos to consider what this woman was trying to accomplish (e.g., bait him into rekindling the affair with her) and how this would fit into Carlos's overall goals for his life. Then Dr. N. wondered aloud how the medication issues got mixed up in what was essentially an interpersonal battle between an ex-lover looking for mischief and a young, married man trying to build a life of trust, stability, and happiness. That's when Carlos switched over to talking about his father-in-law again.

Carlos: Every time I take my lithium and my Depakote [he had stopped taking the selective serotonin reuptake inhibitors after his mood lifted, at the instruction of the psychiatrist] it reminds me that I'm manic depressive. It's a burden. It's a stigma. I'm sick of it. I see how Sabine has lost respect for her father. I don't want that to happen to me.

Dr. N.:   Carlos, were you surprised when Sabine knew that you were playing around on her? You seemed surprised in session. I was surprised, too. She knows more than you give her credit for, Carlos. I'm sorry to say that, but that's the way I see it. If you go off your meds, and get more of the fire back, and get involved with someone else again, and Sabine picks up on it, how much do you suppose she'll respect you then?

Carlos: (Silent)

Dr. N.:   Again, I apologize for being so heavy-handed. I just want you to hang onto what you've accomplished. You confessed to your wife, and she's still with you. You were not abandoned, as you feared at first. You even tell me that things are *better* with Sabine and that you're talking more honestly and openly. Things are looking up. Have you fully considered the cons of not taking your medications?

Carlos: (Thoughtful) One of the cons from before was that I went off my meds and I wound up sleeping with a prostitute. Thank God I didn't get a disease from that. I felt like a complete failure.

Dr. N.: You don't have to risk that anymore, Carlos. You can get back on your medications and let your psychiatrist know right away that you've been off them for a few days.

Carlos: But like I said, it's such a stigma. And I miss some of the craziness, in a weird way.

Dr. N.: Those are two separate issues. Two important issues, no doubt, but they're separate.

They spoke frankly and respectfully about the topic of stigma. Dr. N. validated a lot of what Carlos said about people who don't understand manic depression, people who ridicule those who see therapists and discriminate against them. However, Dr. N. added that Carlos was discriminating against himself. By choosing to avoid medications as a way to avoid thinking about the illness, he was responding to his own discriminatory attitudes. After all, if Carlos took his medications, few if any people would know about his mental illness. It would be Carlos himself who was put off by it. If Carlos stayed on his medications, at least he could have some measure of privacy. However, if he stopped taking the medications, and the symptoms were to return full-blast, his emotional problems would become much more public. There would a greater risk for stigma.

Regarding the second issue, the therapist simply had to validate Carlos's grief about some of the "highs" that he missed so much at times. Dr. N. noted that it was actually a good sign that Carlos was waxing nostalgic about his manic episodes, because it meant he was building a substantial period of nonmanic functioning in which to forget the depth of the horrors that went along with the manias. As Dr. N. put it, "You can't be nostalgic about fresh pain." In other words, Carlos's sentimentality toward the manic periods was a natural illusion caused by the passage of time. Those really were not the good old days. When asked whether he would trade places with himself a year ago, Carlos had to acknowledge that he liked himself much better now. Still, it was appropriately empathic for the therapist to recognize Carlos's grief over the loss of his wild and crazy days and nights.

In the next session, Carlos affirmed that he had resumed his medications again, with some adjustments recommended by the psychiatrist in the aftermath of Carlos's missing a series of doses. Therapist and patient continued to explore the pros and cons of taking and not taking medications, and Carlos took notes. They also furthered their discussion about his identification with Sabine's father and how he could be a better husband if he stayed on course with his treatment. This would solidify the marriage. At the same time, Carlos revealed that as a result of the concurrent couples sessions, Sabine was working on showing more care and sympathy. Things were looking up, and Carlos seemed to be willing to reengage in his full treatment again.

STAGE 4: CONSOLIDATING GAINS AND GUARDING AGAINST RISK OF RELAPSE

Carlos was aware that he had 2 months remaining in his cognitive therapy protocol. He understood that he would continue with his medications and could be seen for up to three booster sessions of cognitive therapy during the calendar year following termination. Although he began to feel a little sense of urgency, he was pleased about his overall progress, including the state of his marriage.

Carlos and his therapist agreed that the final stage of therapy would focus on solidifying his good self-help habits, so that he could reduce the probability of future relapses. At the very least, Carlos wanted to be able to keep future symptom episodes within manageable limits. To do this, there were some lifestyle changes he still needed to make. Fortunately, he initiated these changes on his own; the changes were consistent with his growing sense of self-efficacy and with his willingness to take responsibility for his important life decisions.

Sessions 42–46: Preparing for the Future

Carlos tantalized his therapist with a pre-announced "huge agenda item" for therapy. When asked what the topic was, Carlos revealed that he had decided to look for a new job. Dr. N. was pleased to hear this, as he had always viewed Carlos's position at the hotel as a high-risk situation for everything from a disrupted sleep–wake cycle to marital infidelity, not to mention the mood problems that would accompany these situations.

It was important for the therapist to let Carlos "own" this decision, because autonomy was very important to him. It was preferable for Carlos to feel that he was directing his life in a proactive way, rather than believing that he was reacting to the feedback of his wife and his therapist. Dr. N. asked about Carlos's new plans. He asked him when he planned to resign, how he planned to manage his money during the transition, what sort of new employment he wanted to explore, and so on. He also made certain to give Carlos emotional support for making this big change. Recognizing that "life events" research suggests that a change of job might prove dangerously stressful for Carlos (but probably less hazardous in the long run than remaining at the hotel), Dr. N. gave Carlos a great deal of encouragement and moral support. Together, they did some problem-solving and discussed ways for Carlos to relax, reduce his stress, and make the best use of his social support network during this potentially difficult time.

Carlos decided to spend some time in these latter sessions talking about his image of his future. He wanted to do more than simply muse about "what he wanted to be when he grew up"; he wanted to begin to lay the groundwork for making his life better and to get on a trajectory toward greater meaning, purpose, and fulfillment. Dr. N. agreed to discuss this broad issue but also asked whether Carlos would be willing to balance the session agendas by taking a more fine-grained analysis of what he would need to do to keep his life stabilized.

As a result of this arrangement, approximately half the time in session was spent on topics such as Carlos's ideas for continuing his education, enhancing his career, working on his marriage, adding new types of recreational activities to his life, exploring the possibility of achieving closer relationships with his siblings, and being a good father someday. The other half of the session time was spent in reviewing the full range of Carlos's cognitive therapy self-help skills, including DTRs, scheduling productive activities (but not too many), problem-solving (e.g., examining pros and cons), getting feedback from others, delaying the urge to act impulsively, and other techniques.

Notably, Carlos and Dr. N. did a comprehensive review of early-warning signs of depression and mania. Carlos understood that by recognizing his prodromal symptoms, he would be able to buy himself some time to use his cognitive therapy strategies, seek support from his social network, and consult with his psychiatrist in case changes in medications were warranted. Carlos was adept at noting (and writing down) that his early-warning signs for depression included (a) getting up late in the morning, (b) being uncommunicative with Sabine, (c) not caring to play music, and (d) having streams of pessimistic and cynical thoughts about himself and his future. Similarly, he knew the signs of impending hypomania and mania: (a) becoming argumentative too easily, (b) staying awake until the wee hours of the morning, (c) having the urge to telephone people at odd hours on the spur of the moment, (d) having an "I don't care" attitude about things that should worry him (e.g., money concerns), and (e) going out of his way to learn personal things about women other than his wife.

Carlos expressed a sense of readiness to face the rest of his life with hope and ambition. At the same time, he commented that he was just now starting to realize how much he appreciated the way that his therapist took an active part in helping him. He said, "I hope I can direct myself as well as you directed me." Dr. N. replied, "Gee, I hope I didn't come across as bossing you around—but for the record, yes, I think you are ready to become your own cognitive therapist."

Sessions 47–48: Saying Farewell

During the final two sessions, Carlos continued to speak about his hopes for the future, including fatherhood. His mood seemed level, and his thoughts seemed reasonably optimistic. These sessions had much more of a "social" feel about them. Carlos and Dr. N. spent a significant part of the time reminiscing about the course of therapy and the memorable moments. They joked (in David Letterman style) about the Top 10 Reasons to be in cognitive therapy and playfully reenacted some of their earlier clinical squabbles in caricature form.

Carlos was very gracious. He thanked Dr. N. profusely, saying things such as, "If it were not for you, I wouldn't be in the great emotional shape I'm in today," as well as other genuine but overstated compliments. The therapist responded by telling Carlos that he should take most of the credit himself and that his willingness to continue being his own cognitive therapist in the future supported this accolade. However, Dr. N. added, "I'll take my 10% cut of the credit, like any good agent."

Although they knew that the study allowed for some potential follow-up sessions within the coming year, both parties were aware that this was the end of therapy as they knew it, at least in terms of their work together as a team. The farewell was heartfelt on both sides.

Follow-up Assessment

Carlos came in for "blind" assessments by independent clinicians at 6 months and 12 months posttherapy. He had shown no recurrences of mania, although he reported a brief depressive period and two hypomanic phases that did not escalate. This represented a substantial period of time in which his functioning was relatively within normal limits. It was also a good time to assess his Axis II characteristics. The raters did not give him a full-fledged personality disorder diagnosis, but they listed him as having "dependent and histrionic features." Carlos reported that he was still faithfully taking his medications and that this had become second nature, with "just a few slip-ups now and then."

Carlos came in to see Dr. N. for a "check-up" session, not because he was symptomatic but "just to say hello again." They talked about the changes in his life, including his new job in advertising. The biggest change, however, was that he and Sabine would be expecting their first child in 5 months. He expressed great pride, and just a slightly detectable trace of anxiety. He spoke of the wonders of the couples counseling (which had since been discontinued) and how he and Sabine were communicating better than ever before.

Dr. N. inquired about Carlos's active use of the coping skills he had learned in cognitive therapy. Carlos recounted that in the year since cognitive therapy ended he had had to "pick himself up" and become more active, and a number of times he had had to "rein himself in" and calm down. He asserted that he had been "entirely monogamous" and that he was keeping to a fairly regular work cycle. Above all, he did not feel badly about his bipolar disorder, having read accounts of famous, talented, and successful people who had the disorder. At the same time, Carlos did not deny the existence of his illness, and so he continued to take his medication and practice his cognitive therapy strategies in everyday life. Carlos was very hopeful about his future and felt confident that he could cope with stressors and symptom recurrences.

CONCLUSION

As the case of Carlos illustrates, symptom recurrences, crisis situations, medication difficulties, marital and family distress, general life disruptions, and the pernicious effects of stigma on self-esteem are just some of the obstacles facing manic–depressive individuals, their family members, and their mental health treatment providers. Although Carlos was euthymic and functioning well at termination and at 1-year follow-up, *outcome* is difficult to define clearly when the disorder has a lifetime impact. Patients such as Carlos should continue to take medications and to have them monitored regularly, and should take precautions to avoid high-risk stressors that could trigger unnecessary symptom recurrences. It is also imperative that bipolar patients "work their program" of cognitive therapy self-monitoring and coping skills for the rest of their lives.

Working with patients such as Carlos requires that therapists be active, energetic, caring, hopeful, armed with strategies and techniques that fit the case conceptualization, and willing to conduct couples or family sessions. As is the case in doing psychotherapy with most patients, going through the ups and downs, the fears and the hopes, and the rifts and reconciliations with bipolar patients is part of what creates the strong therapeutic bond and the meaningfulness of the relationship.

EPILOGUE: FUTURE DIRECTIONS

The clinical methods presented in this volume represent a compilation and extension of the knowledge base of cognitive factors in the nature and treatment of bipolar disorder. Cognitive therapists have borrowed from the empirically supported methods used in the treatment of unipolar depression and anxiety disorders; taken into account the strong biological component of hypomania and mania; incorporated the literature on stress and its subjective perception; and derived a promising, psychosocial approach to the treatment of bipolar disorder.

A 20-site study funded by the National Institute of Mental Health (NIMH), the Systematic Treatment Enhancement Program for Bipolar Disorder (STEP–BD; Principal Investigators, Gary S. Sachs, MD, and Michael E. Thase, MD), is currently under way, one in a series of NIMH initiatives to support treatment effectiveness studies for severe mental illness. The STEP–BD is a longitudinal study (5 to 8 years) that examines the outcome associated with psychosocial interventions as they occur in combination with pharmacotherapy treatment algorithms. The psychosocial interventions under study include a manualized, individual cognitive–behavioral therapy (Otto et al., 1999), family focused treatment (Miklowitz & Goldstein, 1997), and interpersonal and social rhythm therapy (Frank et al., 1994). A fourth intervention, collaborative care plus, provides patients with a psychoeducational videotape on bipolar disorder, a self-help workbook, and three sessions with a therapist to facilitate the learning of these materials. The psychosocial treatments are hypothesized to have direct effects on helping patients recover from acute depression and maintain treatment gains following recovery. It is also hypothesized that each of the psychosocial treatments may aid outcome by increasing adherence to pharmacotherapy. We view the Otto et al. (1999) approach (although distinct and independently designed from our own) as one that is fundamentally compatible with the approach described in this volume. The data that emerge from STEP–BD on the cognitive–behavioral treatment undoubtedly will inform the ongoing development of our cognitive therapy programs for bipolar disorder.

The STEP–BD research also will help clarify the dismaying finding that the treatment of bipolar disorder has been found to have less favorable outcome in naturalistic settings than controlled and (for pharmacotherapy) double-blind trials (e.g., Dickson & Kendall, 1986; Prien & Gelenberg, 1989). The model reflects common clinical practices, and no patient receives a placebo treatment. Patients always take at least one active medication. Notably, this project examines not only the traditional outcome variables of mood episodes and thought processes, but also broader, socially relevant variables such as economic status and quality of life. This stems from previous findings that some bipolar patients may appear to be "treatment successes" from the standpoint of mood moderation but may have significantly limited lives that the patients themselves would not consider optimally desirable (Dion et al., 1988; Harrow, Goldberg, Grossman, & Meltzer, 1990). The breadth of the STEP–BD program enables researchers to evaluate the outcome of treatment models such as cognitive–behavioral therapy across many treatment centers, representing a diversity of ethnic and geographic subgroups. Each patient's clinical records provide detailed, longitudinal assessments that are maintained in the trial database. This enables researchers to estimate overall morbidity (and unfortunately, mortality) of all of the patients participating in the project, controlling for important variables such as initial severity of the illness and course of the illness, among other important factors.

Thus, the study provides valuable data on the outcome of cognitive–behavioral therapy for the various subtypes of bipolar disorder, as well as the benefits of additional interventions for a variety of comorbid conditions, such as substance abuse, attention deficit hyperactivity disorder, anxiety disorders, and eating disorders. Finally, the coordinated network of treatment centers, including Massachusetts General Hospital and the University of Pennsylvania (where the majority of the authors of this text are based), may provide a national resource for future, independent researchers of bipolar disorder.

We are looking forward to training a new generation of therapists in the methods described in this book. Although our approach seems simple on the surface, its use in session—with real patients with substantive problems—is deceptively challenging. As with any manualized treatment, a great deal of commitment and diligence is required to master the conceptual and technical skills of a full program of treatment such as cognitive therapy. This involves seeing many patients for at least a year, and probably longer, to go along with intensive supervision that involves the reviewing of audio and videotapes of therapy sessions. Formal outcome studies often include such arrangements in their structure, but we would advocate the use of this rigorous approach whenever possible during the course of clinical training, whether at the level of graduate studies or postgraduate continuing education (such as at the Beck Institute for Cognitive Therapy and Research in suburban Philadelphia; for information, see the web site at www.beckinstitute.org).

In summary, we have attempted to provide not only a clear explication of the most up-to-date methods of cognitive therapy in its application to bipolar disorder, but also a flavor of the "art and the heart" involved in treating patients who have either lost so much or fear they might. We also want to emphasize that, like any psychotherapeutic approach that is empirically grounded, our treatment constitutes a work in progress. Although we have made it a point to explain the devastating impact of bipolar disorder and to describe the difficulties involved in treating it, we are optimistic that clinical and research developments in psychosocial approaches such as cognitive therapy parallel pharmacological advances, toward the goal of making the quality of the lives of patients with bipolar disorder better and considerably more hopeful.

Finally, we reiterate that it is imperative for therapists to be caring and respectful to each of their patients, to acknowledge their individual differences, to strive to conceptualize their world views in light of their developmental histories, and to be responsive to the immediacy of the clinical moment in session. This requires abilities that cannot be easily spelled out in therapy manuals. Years of experience help in this cause, as well as an open-minded approach, an ability to work flexibly within the outline of the treatment protocol, and a life-long striving to understand oneself better as a person and as a therapist. Although we have not explicated these qualities in their own right, we hope that we have implicitly communicated—through our descriptions of techniques, our clinical vignettes, and our case chapter of Carlos—some ways in which the reader can "put it all together," thus delivering state-of-the-art cognitive therapy, with heart, imagination, and humanity.

REFERENCES

Abramson, L. Y., Alloy, L. B., & Metalsky, G. I. (1995). Hopelessness depression. In G. M. Buchanan & M. E. P. Seligman (Eds.), *Explanatory style* (pp. 113–134). Hillsdale, NJ: Lawrence Erlbaum Assoc. Inc.

Abramson, L. Y., Metalsky, G. I., & Alloy, L. B. (1989). Hopelessness depression: A theory-based subtype of depression. *Psychological Review, 96,* 358–372.

Albanese, M., Bartel, R., & Bruno, R. (1994). Comparison of measures used to determine substance abuse in an inpatient psychiatric population. *American Journal of Psychiatry, 151,* 1077–1078.

Alloy, L. B., Reilly-Harrington, N. A., Fresco, D. M., Whitehouse, W. G., & Zechmeister, J. S. (1999). Cognitive styles and life events in subsyndromal unipolar and bipolar disorders: Stability and prospective prediction of depressive and hypomanic mood swings. *Journal of Cognitive Psychotherapy: An International Quarterly, 13,* 21–40.

American Psychiatric Association. (1994). *Diagnostic and statistical manual of mental disorders* (4th ed.). Washington, DC: Author.

Amsterdam, J. D., Winokur, A., Lucki, I., Caroff, S., Snyder, P., & Rickels, K. (1983). A neuroendocrine test battery in bipolar patients and healthy subjects. *Archives of General Psychiatry, 40,* 515–521.

Andreasen, N. C. (1987). Creativity and mental illness: Prevalence rates in writers and their first-degree relatives. *American Journal of Psychiatry, 144,* 1288–1292.

Arana, G. W., Pearlman, C., & Sahder, R. L. (1985). Alprazolam–induced mania: Two clinical cases. *American Journal of Psychiatry, 142,* 368–369.

Basco, M. (2000). Cognitive–behavioral therapy for bipolar I disorder. *Journal of Cognitive Psychotherapy, 14,* 287–304.

Basco, M., & Rush, A. J. (1996). *Cognitive–behavioral therapy for bipolar disorder.* New York: Guilford Press.

Bassuk, E. L., Schoonover, S. C., & Gelenberg, A. J. (Eds.). (1983). *The practitioner's guide to psychiatric drugs* (2nd ed.). New York: Plenum.

Baucom, D. H., & Epstein, N. (1990). *Cognitive behavioral marital therapy.* New York: Brunner/Mazel.

Bauer, M. S., Callahan, A. M., Jampala, C., Petty, F., Sajatovic, M., Schaefer, V., Wittlin, B., & Powell, B. J. (1999). Clinical practice guidelines for bipolar disorder from the Department of Veterans Affairs. *Journal of Clinical Psychiatry, 60,* 9–21.

Bauer, M. S., Crits-Christoph, P., Ball, W., Dewees, E., McAllister, T., Alahi, P., Cacciola, J., & Whybrow, P. (1991). Independent assessment of manic and depressive symptoms by self-rating scale. Characteristics and implications for the study of mania. *Archives of General Psychiatry, 48,* 807–812.

Bauer, M. S., Gyulai, L., Yeh, H.-S., Gonnel, J., & Whybrow, P. C. (1994). Testing definitions of dysphoric mania and hypomania: Prevalence, clinical characteristics, and inter-episode stability. *Journal of Affective Disorder, 32,* 201–211.

Bauer, M., & McBride, L. (1996). *Structured group psychotherapy for bipolar disorder: The life goals program.* New York: Springer.

Bauer, M. S., & Whybrow, P. C. (1990). Rapid cycling bipolar affective disorder. II: Adjuvant treatment of refractory rapid cycling with high dose thyroxin. *Archives of General Psychiatry, 47,* 435–440.

Bech, P., Bolwig, T. G., Kramp, P., & Rafaelsen, O. J. (1979). The Bech–Rafaelsen Mania Scale and the Hamilton Depression Scale: Evaluation of homogeneity and inter-observer reliability. *Acta Psychiatrica Scandinavica, 30,* 330–351.

Beck, A. T. (1976). *Cognitive therapy and the emotional disorders.* New York: International Universities Press.

Beck, A. T. (1996). Beyond belief: A theory of modes, personality, and psychopathology. In P. M. Salkovskis (Ed.), *Frontiers of cognitive therapy* (pp. 1–25). New York: Guilford Press.

Beck, A. T., Brown, G., Berchick, R. J., Stewart, B. L., & Steer, R. A. (1990). Relationship between hopelessness and ultimate suicide: A replication with psychiatric outpatients. *American Journal of Psychiatry, 147,* 190–195.

Beck, A. T., Brown, G., & Steer, R. A. (1989). Prediction of eventual suicide in psychiatric inpatients by clinical ratings of hopelessness. *Journal of Consulting and Clinical Psychology, 57*(2), 309–310.

Beck, A. T., Brown, G. K., Steer, R. A., Dahlsgaard, K. K., & Grisham, J. R. (1999). Suicide ideation at its worst point: A predictor of eventual suicide in psychiatric outpatients. *Suicide and Life Threatening Behavior, 29*(1), 1–9.

Beck, A. T., Butler, A. C., Brown, G. K., Dahlsgaard, K. K., Newman, C. F., & Beck, J. S. (in press). Dysfunctional beliefs discriminate personality disorders. *Behavior Therapy and Research.*

Beck, A. T., Epstein, N., Harrison, R., & Emery, G. (1983). *Development of the Sociotropy–Autonomy Scale: A measure of personality factors in depression.* University of Pennsylvania, Philadelphia.

Beck, A. T., Freeman, A., & Associates. (1990). *Cognitive therapy of personality disorders.* New York: Guilford Press.

Beck, A. T., Rush, A. J., Shaw, B., & Emery, G. (1979). *Cognitive therapy of depression.* New York: Guilford Press.

Beck, A. T., Steer, R. A., Beck, J. S., & Newman, C. F. (1993). Hopelessness, depression, suicidal ideation, and clinical diagnosis of depression. *Suicide and Life Threatening Behavior, 23,* 139–145.

Beck, A. T., Steer, R. A., Kovacs, M., & Garrison, B. (1985). Hopelessness and eventual suicide: A 10-year prospective study of patients hospitalized with suicidal ideation. *American Journal of Psychiatry, 142,* 559–563.

Beck, A. T., Steer, R. A., & Ranieri, W. F. (1988). Scale for suicide ideation: Psychometric properties of a self-report version. *Journal of Clinical Psychology, 44,* 499–505.

Beck, A. T., Ward, C., Mendelson, M., Mock, J., & Erbaugh, J. (1961). An inventory for measuring depression. *Archives of General Psychiatry, 4,* 53–63.

Beck, A. T., Weissman, A., Lester, D., & Trexler, L. (1974). The measurement of pessimism: The Hopelessness Scale. *Journal of Consulting and Clinical Psychology, 42,* 861–865.

Beck, A. T., Wright, F. D., Newman, C. F., & Liese, B. S. (1993). *Cognitive therapy of substance abuse.* New York: Guilford Press.

Beck, J. S. (1995). *Cognitive therapy: Basics and beyond.* New York: Guilford Press.

Bertelsen, A. (1979). A Danish twin study of manic-depressive disorders. In M. Schou & E. Stromgen (Eds.), *Origin, prevention, and treatment of affective disorders* (pp. 227–239). London: Academic Press.

Bertelsen, A., Harvald, B., & Hauge, M. (1977). A Danish twin study of manic–depressive disorders. *British Journal of Psychiatry, 130,* 330–351.

Blatt, S. J. (1995). The destructiveness of perfectionism: Implications for the treatment of depression. *American Psychologist, 50,* 1003–1020.

Bodie, Z., Kane, A., & Marcus, A. J. (1996). *Investments.* Chicago: Irwin.

Bohn, J., & Jefferson, J. (1992). *Lithium and manic depression.* Madison: University of Wisconsin, Lithium Information Center.

Boland, R. J., & Keller, M. B. (1999). Mixed-state bipolar disorders: Outcome data from the NIMH Collaborative Program on the psychobiology of depression. In J. F. Goldberg & M. Harrow (Eds.), *Bipolar disorders: Clinical course and outcome* (pp. 115–128). Washington, DC: American Psychiatric Association.

Bongar, B. (1991). *The suicidal patient: Clinical and legal standards of care.* Washington, DC: American Psychological Association.

Bowden, C. L. (1998). New concepts in mood stabilization: Evidence for the effectiveness of valproate and lamotrigine. *Neuropsychopharmacology, 19,* 194–199.

Bowden, C. L. (1999). Comparison of open versus blinded studies in bipolar disorder. In J. F. Goldberg & M. Harrow (Eds.), *Bipolar disorders: Clinical course and outcome* (pp.149–170). Washington, DC: American Psychiatric Press.

Bowden, C. L., & Rhodes, L. J. (1996). Mania in children and adolescents: Recognition and treatment. *Psychiatric Annals, 26*(7, Suppl.), S430–S434.

Bower, G. H. (1981). Mood and memory. *American Psychologist, 36,* 129–148.

Bower, G. H. (1987). Commentary on mood and memory. *Behavior Research and Therapy, 25,* 443–455.

Brady, K. T., & Lydiard, B. (1992). Bipolar affective disorder and substance abuse. *Journal of Clinical Psychopharmacology, 12,* 17S–22S.

Brady, K. T., & Sonne, S. C. (1995). The relationship between substance abuse and bipolar disorder. *Journal of Clinical Psychiatry, 56,* 19–24.

Brent, D. A., Bridge, J., Johnson, B. A., & Connolly, J. (1996). Suicidal behavior runs in families. A controlled family study of adolescent suicide victims. *Archives of General Psychiatry, 53,* 1145–1152.

Brent, D. A., Moritz, G., Bridge, J., Perper, J. A., & Canobbio, R. (1996). The impact of adolescent suicide on siblings and parents: A longitudinal follow-up. *Suicidal and Life-Threatening Behavior, 26,* 253–259.

Brodie, H. K. H., & Leff, M. J. (1971). Bipolar depression: A comparative study of patient characteristics. *American Journal of Psychiatry, 127,* 1086–1090.

Burns, D. (1989). *The feeling good handbook.* New York: Plume.

Burns, D. D., & Auerbach, A. H. (1992). Does homework compliance enhance recovery from depression? *Psychiatric Annals, 22,* 464–469.

Burns, D. D., & Nolen-Hoeksema, S. (1991). Coping styles, homework compliance, and the effectiveness of cognitive–behavioral therapy. *Journal of Consulting and Clinical Psychology, 59,* 305–311.

Calabrese, J. R., Bowden, C. L., McElroy, S. L., Cookson, J., Andersen, J., Keck, P. E., Rhodes, L., Bolden-Watson, C., Zhou, J., & Ascher, J. A. (1999). Spectrum of activity of lamotrigine in treatment-refractory bipolar disorder. *American Journal of Psychiatry, 156,* 1019–1023.

Calabrese, J. R., Rapport, D. J., Shelton, M. D., & Kimmel, S. E. (1998). Clinical studies on the use of lamotrigine in bipolar disorder. *Neuropsychobiology, 38,* 185–191.

Chadwick, P., & Lowe, C. (1994). A cognitive approach to modifying delusions. *Behaviour Research and Therapy, 32,* 355–367.

Chakrabati, S., Kulhara, P., & Verma, S. K. (1992). Extent and determinants of burden among families of patients with affective disorders. *Acta Psychiatrica Scandinavica, 86,* 247–252.

Chen, Y.-W., & Dilsaver, S. C. (1995). Comorbidity of panic disorder in bipolar illness: Evidence from the Epidemiologic Catchment Area survey. *American Journal of Psychiatry, 152,* 280–282.

Chor, P., Mercier, M., & Halper, I. (1988). Use of cognitive therapy for treatment of a patient suffering from a bipolar affective disorder. *Journal of Cognitive Psychotherapy: An International Quarterly, 2,* 51–58.

Chouinard, G., Annable, L., Tumier, L., Holobow, N., & Szkrumelak, N. (1993). A double-blind randomized clinical trial of rapid tranquilization with I.M. clonazepam and I.M. haloperidol in agitated psychotic patients with manic symptoms. *Canadian Journal of Psychiatry, 38,* S114–S121.

Cochran, S. D. (1984). Preventing medical non-compliance in the outpatient treatment of bipolar affective disorder. *Journal of Consulting and Clinical Psychology, 52,* 873–878.

Copeland, M. E. (1992). *The depression workbook: A guide for living with depression and manic depression.* Oakland, CA: New Harbinger.

Copeland, M. E. (1994). *Living without depression and manic depression: A workbook for maintaining mood stability.* Oakland, CA: New Harbinger.

Corrigan, P. W. (1998). The impact of stigma on severe mental illness. *Cognitive and Behavioral Practice, 5,* 201–222.

Coryell, W. (1999). Bipolar II disorder: The importance of hypomania. In J. F. Goldberg & M. Harrow (Eds.), *Bipolar disorders: Clinical course and outcome* (pp. 219–236). Washington, DC: American Psychiatric Press.

Coryell, W., Andreasen, N., Endicott, J., & Keller, M. (1987). The significance of past mania or hypomania in the course and outcome of major depression. *American Journal of Psychiatry, 144*, 309–315.

Coryell, W., Endicott, J., Andreasen, N., & Keller, M. (1985). Bipolar I, bipolar II, and nonbipolar major depression among the relatives of affectively ill probands. *American Journal of Psychiatry, 142*, 817–821.

Coryell, W., Endicott, J., Keller, M., Andreasen, N., Groove, W., Hirschfeld, R. M. A., & Scheftner, W. (1989). Bipolar affective disorder and high achievement: A familiar association. *American Journal of Psychiatry, 146*, 983–988.

Coryell, W., Keller, M., Endicott, J., Andreasen, N., Clayton, P., & Hirschfeld, R. (1989). Bipolar II illness: Course and outcome over a five-year period. *Psychological Medicine, 19*, 129–141.

Coryell, W., Scheftner, W., Keller, M., Endicott, J., Maser, J., & Klerman, G. L. (1993). The enduring psychosocial consequences of mania and depression. *American Journal of Psychiatry, 150*, 720–727.

Court, B. L., & Nelson, G. E. (1996). *Bipolar puzzle solution: A mental health client's perspective.* Washington, DC: Accelerated Development.

Curry, S., Marlatt, G. A., & Gordon, J. R. (1987). Abstinence violation effect: Validation of an attributional construct with smoking cessation. *Journal of Consulting and Clinical Psychology, 55*, 145–149.

Cutler, N. R., & Post, R. M. (1982). Life course of illness in untreated manic–depressive patients. *Comprehensive Psychiatry, 23*, 101–115.

Dattilio, F. M., & Freeman, A. (Eds.). (1994). *Cognitive–behavioral strategies in crisis intervention.* New York: Guilford Press.

Dattilio, F. M., & Freeman, A. (Eds.). (2000). *Cognitive–behavioral approaches to crisis intervention* (2nd ed.). New York: Guilford Press.

Dattilio, F. M., & Padesky, C. (1990). *Cognitive therapy with couples.* Sarasota, FL: Professional Resource Exchange.

Denicoff, K. D., Blake, K. D., Smith-Jackson, E. E., Jacob, P. A., Leverich, G., & Post, R. M. (1994). Morbidity in treated bipolar disorder: A one-year prospective study using daily life chart ratings. *Depression, 2*, 95–104.

DePaolo, J. R., Simpson, S. G., Folstein, S., & Folstein, M. (1989). The new genetics of bipolar affective disorder: Clinical implications. *Clinical Chemistry, 35*(7), B28–B32.

Depue, R. A., & Collins, P. F. (1998). Neurobiology of the structure of personality: Dopamine, facilitation of incentive motivation, and extraversion. *Behavioral and Brain Sciences, 22*, 491–569.

Depue, R. A., Collins, P. F., & Luciana, M. (1996). A model of neurobiology: Environment interaction in developmental psychopathology. In M. F. Lenzenweger (Ed.), *Frontiers of developmental psychopathology* (pp. 44–77). New York: Oxford University Press.

Depue, R. A., & Iacono, W. G. (1989). Neurobehavioral aspects of affective disorders. *Annual Review of Psychology, 40*, 457–492.

Depue, R. A., Luciana, M., Arbisi, P., Collins, P., & Leon, A. (1994). Dopamine and the structure of personality: Relation of agonist-induced dopamine activity to positive emotionality. *Journal of Personality and Social Psychology, 67,* 485–498.

Dickson, W. E., & Kendell, R. E. (1986). Does maintenance lithium therapy prevent recurrences of mania under ordinary clinical conditions? *Psychological Medicine, 16,* 521–530.

Dion, G. L., Tohen, M., Anthony, W. A., & Waternaux, C. (1988). Symptoms and functioning of patients with bipolar disorder six months after hospitalization. *Hospital and Community Psychiatry, 39,* 652–657.

Dobson, K. S. (1989). A meta-analysis of the efficacy of cognitive therapy for depression. *Journal of Consulting and Clinical Psychology, 57,* 414–419.

Dries, D. C., & Barklage, N. E. (1989). *Electro-convulsive therapy: A guide.* Madison: University of Wisconsin, Lithium Information Center.

Dunner, D. L. (1999). Rapid-cycling bipolar affective disorder. In J. F. Goldberg & M. Harrow (Eds.), *Bipolar disorders: Clinical course and outcome* (pp. 199–217). Washington, DC: American Psychiatric Press.

Dunner, D. L., & Fieve, R. R. (1974). Clinical factors in lithium prophylactic failure. *Archives of General Psychiatry, 30,* 229–233.

Edwards, R., Stephenson, U., & Flewett, T. (1991). Clonazepam in acute mania: A double-blind trial. *Australia and New Zealand Journal of Psychiatry, 2,* 238–242.

Ehlers, C. L., Frank, E., & Kupfer, D. J. (1988). Social zeitgebers and biological rhythms: A unified approach to understanding the etiology of depression. *Archives of General Psychiatry, 45,* 948–952.

Ehlers, C. L., Kupfer, D. J., Frank, E., & Monk, T. H. (1993). Biological rhythms and depression: The role of zeitgebers and zeitstorers. *Depression, 1,* 285–293.

Ellicott, A., Hammen, C., Gitlin, M., Brown, G., & Jamison, K. (1990). Life events and the course of bipolar disorder. *American Journal of Psychiatry, 147,* 1194–1198.

Ellis, T. E., & Newman, C. F. (1996). *Choosing to live: How to defeat suicide through cognitive therapy.* Oakland, CA: New Harbinger.

Ellis, T. E., & Ratliff, K. G. (1986). Cognitive characteristics of suicidal and nonsuicidal psychiatric inpatients. *Cognitive Therapy and Research, 10,* 625–634.

Endicott, J., Nee, J., Andreasen, N., Clayton, P., Keller, M., & Coryell, W. (1985). Bipolar II: Combine or keep separate? *Journal of Affective Disorders, 8,* 17–28.

Epstein, N., Schlesinger, S., & Dryden, W. (1988). *Cognitive–behavioral therapy with families.* New York: Brunner/Mazel.

Evans, J. M. G., Hollon, S. D., DeRubeis, R. J., Piasecki, J. M., Grove, W. M., Garvey, M. J., & Tuason, V. B. (1992). Differential relapse following cognitive therapy and pharmacology for depression. *Archives of General Psychiatry, 49,* 802–808.

Evans, J., Williams, J., O'Loughlin, S., & Howells, K. (1992). Autobiographical memory and problem-solving strategies of parasuicide patients. *Psychological Medicine, 22,* 399–405.

Faedda, G. L., Tondo, L., Baldessarini, R. J., Suppes, T., & Tohen, M. (1993). Outcome after rapid versus gradual discontinuation of lithium treatment in bipolar disorders. *Archives of General Psychiatry, 50,* 448–455.

Fatemi, S. H., Rapport, D. J., Calabrese, J. R., & Thuras, P. (1997). Lamotrigine in rapid-cycling bipolar disorder. *Journal of Clinical Psychiatry, 58,* 522–527.

Fawcett, J., Scheftner, W., Clark, D., Hedeker, D., Gibbons, R., & Corell, W. (1987). Clinical predictors of suicide in patients with major affective disorders: A controlled prospective study. *American Journal of Psychiatry, 144*(1), 35–40.

Fieve, R. R. (1989). *Moodswing.* New York: Bantam Books.

Fingerhut, R. (1999). *The impact of interpersonal life events and sociotropy on the course of bipolar disorder.* Unpublished doctoral dissertation, University of Miami.

Frances, A., Docherty, J. P., & Kahn, D. A. (1996). The expert consensus guideline series: Treatment of bipolar disorder. *Journal of Clinical Psychiatry, 57*(Suppl. 12A), 1–88.

Frank, E., Kupfer, D. J., Ehlers, C. L., Monk, T. H., Comes, C., Carter, S., & Frankel, D. (1994). Interpersonal and social rhythm therapy for bipolar disorder: Integrating interpersonal and behavioural approaches. *Behaviour Therapy, 17,* 143–149.

Frankl, V. (1960). Existential analysis and logotherapy. *Acta Psychotherapeutica et Psychosomatica, 8,* 171–187.

Freeman, M. P., & Stoll, A. L. (1999). Mood stabilizer combinations for bipolar disorder: Reply. *American Journal of Psychiatry, 156,* 980–981.

Geller, B., & Luby, J. (1997). Child and adolescent bipolar disorder: Review of the past ten years. *Journal of the American Academy of Child and Adolescent Psychiatry, 36,* 1168–1176.

Gershon, E. S., Hamovit, J. H., Guroff, J. J., & Nurnberger, J. I. (1987). Birth-cohort changes in manic and depressive disorders in relatives of bipolar and schizoaffective patients. *Archives of General Psychiatry, 44,* 314–319.

Ghaemi, S. N., Sachs, G. S., Baldassano, C. F., & Truman, C. J. (1997). Acute treatment of bipolar disorder with adjunctive risperidone in outpatients. *Canadian Journal of Psychiatry, 42,* 196–199.

Gillberg, I. C., Hellgren, L., & Gillberg, C. (1993). Psychotic disorders diagnosed in adolescence: Outcome at 30 years. *Journal of Child Psychology and Psychiatry and Allied Disciplines, 34,* 1173–1185.

Gitlin, M. J., & Hammen, C. (1999). Syndromal and psychosocial outcome in bipolar disorder: A complex and circular relationship. In J. F. Goldberg & M. Harrow (Eds.), *Bipolar disorders: Clinical course and outcome* (pp. 39–55). Washington, DC: American Psychiatric Press.

Gitlin, M. J., Swendsen, J., Heller, T. L., & Hammen, C. (1995). Relapse and impairment in bipolar disorder. *American Journal of Psychiatry, 152,* 1635–1640.

Goldberg, J. F., & Harrow, M. (Eds.). (1999a). *Bipolar disorders: Clinical course and outcome*. Washington, DC: American Psychiatric Press.

Goldberg, J. F., & Harrow, M. (1999b). Poor-outcome bipolar disorders. In J. F. Goldberg & M. Harrow (Eds.), *Bipolar disorders: Clinical course and outcome* (pp. 1–19). Washington, DC: American Psychiatric Press.

Goldberg, J. F., Harrow, M., & Grossman, L. S. (1995). Course and outcome in bipolar affective disorder: A longitudinal follow-up study. *American Journal of Psychiatry, 152,* 379–384.

Goldberg, J. F., & Kocsis, J. H. (1999). Depression in the course of bipolar disorder. In J. F. Goldberg & M. Harrow (Eds.), *Bipolar disorders: Clinical course and outcome* (pp. 129–147). Washington, DC: American Psychiatric Association.

Goldfried, M. R., & Davison, G. C. (1994). *Clinical behavior therapy* (4th ed.). New York: Wiley.

Goleman, D. (1995). *Emotional intelligence: Why it can matter more than IQ.* New York: Bantam Books.

Goodwin, F. K. (1999). Foreword. In J. F. Goldberg & M. Harrow (Eds.), *Bipolar disorder: Clinical course and outcome* (pp. xii–xvii). Washington, DC: American Psychiatric Press.

Goodwin, F. K., & Jamison, K. R. (1990). *Manic-depressive illness.* New York: Oxford University Press.

Goodwin, F. K., & Sack, R. L. (1974). Behavioral effects of a new dopamine-beta-hydroxylase inhibitor (dusaric acid) in man. *Journal of Psychiatric Research, 11,* 211–217.

Gorman, J. M. (1990). *The essential guide to psychiatric drugs.* New York: St. Martin's Press.

Gorman, J. M. (1995). *The essential guide to psychiatric drugs* (2nd ed.). New York: St. Martin's Press.

Gray, J. A. (1990). Brain systems that mediate both emotion and cognition. *Cognition and Emotion, 4,* 269–288.

Gray, J. A. (1991). Neural systems, emotions, and personality. In J. Madden IV (Ed.), *Neurobiology of learning, emotion, and affect* (pp. 273–306). New York: Hillsdale Press.

Greenberger, D., & Padesky, C. A. (1995). *Mind over mood: A cognitive therapy treatment manual for clients.* New York: Guilford Press.

Greil, W., Kleindienst, N., Erazo, N., & Muller-Oerlinghausen, B. (1998). Differential response to lithium and carbamazepine in the prophylaxis of bipolar disorder. *Journal of Clinical Psychopharmacology, 18,* 455–460.

Haaga, D. A. F., Dyck, M. J., & Ernst, D. (1991). Empirical status of cognitive therapy of depression. *Psychological Bulletin, 110,* 215–236.

Hackman, A. L., Ram, R. N., & Dixon, L. B. (1999). Psychosocial treatment of bipolar disorder in the public sector: Program for assertive community treatment model. In J. F. Goldberg & M. Harrow (Eds.), *Bipolar disorders: Clinical course and outcome* (pp. 259–274). Washington, DC: American Psychiatric Press.

Halberstadt, L. J., & Abramson, L. Y. (1998). *The Halberstadt Mania Inventory (HMI): A self-report measure of manic/hypomanic symptomatology*. Department of Psychology, University of Wisconsin, Madison.

Hamilton, M. (1960). A rating scale for depression. *Journal of Neurology, Neurosurgery, and Psychiatry, 23*, 56–62.

Hammen, C., Ellicott, A., & Gitlin, M. (1992). Stressors and sociotropy/autonomy: A longitudinal study of their relationship to course of bipolar disorder. *Cognitive Therapy and Research, 16*, 409–418.

Hammen, C., Ellicott, A., Gitlin, M., & Jamison, K. R. (1989). Sociotropy/autonomy and vulnerability to specific life events in patients with unipolar depression and bipolar disorders. *Journal of Abnormal Psychology, 98*, 154–160.

Hammen, C., & Gitlin, M. J. (1997). Stress reactivity in bipolar patients and its relation to prior history of disorder. *American Journal of Psychiatry, 154*, 856–857.

Hansen-Grant, S., & Riba, M. B. (1995). Contact between psychotherapists and psychiatric residents who provide medication back-up. *Psychiatric Services, 46*, 774–777.

Harrow, M., Goldberg, J., Grossman, L., & Meltzer, H. (1990). Outcome in manic disorders. *Archives of General Psychiatry, 47*, 665–671.

Hayward, P., & Bright, J. A. (1997). Stigma and mental illness: A review and critique. *Journal of Mental Health, 6*, 345–354.

Hewitt, P. L., Flett, G. L., & Weber, C. (1994). Dimensions of perfectionism and suicide ideation. *Cognitive Therapy and Research, 18*, 439–460.

Himmelhoch, J. M. (1986). Sources of lithium resistance in mixed mania. *Psychopharmacological Bulletin, 22*, 613–620.

Himmelhoch, J. M. (1994). On the failure to recognize lithium failure. *Psychiatric Annals, 24*, 241–250.

Himmelhoch, J. M. (1999). The paradox of anxiety syndromes comorbid with the bipolar illnesses. In J. F. Goldberg & M. Harrow (Eds.), *Bipolar disorders: Clinical course and outcome* (pp. 237–258). Washington, DC: American Psychiatric Press.

Himmelhoch, J. M., Thase, M. E., Mallinger, A. G., & Houck, P. (1991). Tranylcypromine versus imipramine in anergic bipolar depression. *American Journal of Psychiatry, 148*(7), 910–916.

Hirshfeld, D. R., Gould, R. A., Reilly-Harrington, N. A., Morabito, C., Cosgrove, V., Guille, C., Friedman, S., & Sachs, G. S. (1998, November). *Short-term adjunctive cognitive–behavioral group therapy for bipolar disorder: Preliminary results from a controlled trial*. Paper presented at the annual meeting of the Association for the Advancement of Behavior Therapy conference, Washington, DC.

Hollon, S. D., DeRubeis, R. J., & Seligman, M. E. P. (1992). Cognitive therapy and the prevention of depression. *Applied and Preventive Psychiatry, 1*, 89–95.

Hollon, S. D., Kendall, P. C., & Lumry, A. (1986). Specificity of depressogenic cognitions in clinical depression. *Journal of Abnormal Psychology, 95*, 52–59.

Holmes, E. P., & River, L. P. (1998). Individual strategies for coping with the stigma of severe mental illness. *Cognitive and Behavioral Practice, 5*, 231–239.

Hunt, N., Bruce-Jones, W., & Silverstone, T. (1992). Life events and bipolar affective disorder. *Journal of Affective Disorders, 25*, 13–20.

Isometsä, E. T. (1993). Course, outcome, and suicide risk in bipolar disorder: A review. *Psychiatria Fennica, 24*, 113–124.

Isometsä, E. T., & Lonnqvist, J. K. (1998). Suicide attempts preceding completed suicide. *British Journal of Psychiatry, 173*, 531–535.

Jacobs, L. (1982). Cognitive therapy of post-manic and post-depressive dysphoria in bipolar illness. *American Journal of Psychotherapy, 36*, 450–458.

Jamison, K. R. (1993). *Touched with fire: Manic–depressive illness and the artistic temperament.* New York: Free Press.

Jamison, K. R. (1995). *An unquiet mind: A memoir of moods and madness.* New York: Knopf.

Jamison, K. R. (1999). *Night falls fast: Understanding suicide.* New York: Knopf.

Jamison, K. R., & Akiskal, H. (1983). Medication compliance in patients with bipolar disorder. *Psychiatric Clinics of North America, 6*, 175–192.

Jamison, K. R., Gerner, R., & Goodwin, F. (1979). Patient and physician attitudes towards lithium: Relationship to compliance. *Archives of General Psychiatry, 36*, 866–869.

Jefferson, J. W., & Griest, J. H. (1996). *Divalproex and manic depression: A guide.* Madison: University of Wisconsin, Lithium Information Center.

Joffe, R. T., Kutcher, S., & MacDonald, C. (1988). Thyroid function and bipolar affective disorder. *Psychiatry Research, 25*, 117–121.

Johnson, S. L., Meyer, B., Winett, C., & Small, J. (2000). Social support and self-esteem predict changes in bipolar depression but not mania. *Journal of Affective Disorders, 58*, 79–86.

Johnson, S. L., & Miller, I. (1997). Negative life events and time to recovery from episodes of bipolar disorder. *Journal of Abnormal Psychology, 106*, 449–457.

Johnson, S. L., & Roberts, J. (1995). Life events and bipolar disorder: Implications from biological theories. *Psychological Bulletin, 117*, 434–439.

Johnson, S. L., Sandrow, D., Meyer, B., Winters, R., Miller, I., Solomon, D., & Keitner, G. (November, 1999). *Life events involving goal-attainment and increases in manic symptoms.* Paper presented at the annual conference of the Association for the Advancement of Behavior Therapy, Toronto, Canada.

Johnson, S. L., Winett, C., Meyer, B., Greenhouse, W., & Miller, I. (1999). Social support and the course of bipolar disorder. *Journal of Abnormal Psychology, 108*, 558–566.

Joiner, T. E., & Rudd, M. D. (2000). Intensity and duration of suicidal crises vary as a function of previous suicide attempts and negative life events. *Journal of Consulting and Clinical Psychology, 68*, 909–916.

Joyce, P. R. (1984). Age of onset in bipolar affective disorder and misdiagnosis as schizophrenia. *Psychological Medicine, 15*, 145–149.

Kahn, D. A., Ross, R., Printz, D. J., & Sachs, G. S. (2000). Treatment of bipolar disorder: A guide for patients and families. In G. S. Sachs, D. J. Printz, D. A. Kahn, D. Carpenter, & J. P. Docherty (Eds.), *Medication treatment of bipolar disorder. The Expert Consensus Guidelines Series* (pp. 97–104). New York: McGraw-Hill.

Kavanagh, D. J. (1992). Recent developments in expressed emotion in schizophrenia. *British Journal of Psychiatry, 160,* 601–620.

Keller, M. B., Lavori, P. W., Kane, J. M., Gelenberg, A. J., Rosenbaum, J. F., Walzer, E. A., & Baher, L. A. (1992). Subsyndromal symptoms in bipolar disorder: A comparison of standard and low serum levels of lithium. *Archives of General Psychiatry, 49,* 371–376.

Kennedy, S., Thompson, R., Stancer, H. C., Roy, A., & Persad, E. (1983). Life events precipitating mania. *British Journal of Psychiatry, 142,* 398–403.

Kessler, R. C., McGonagle, K. A., Zhao, S., Nelson, C. B., Hughes, M., Eshleman, S., Wittchen, H. U., & Kendler, K. S. (1994). Lifetime and 12-month prevalence of DSM–III–R psychiatric disorders in the United States: Results from the National Comorbidity Survey. *Archives of General Psychiatry, 51,* 8–19.

Kiesler, D. J. (1966). Some myths of psychotherapy research and the search for a paradigm. *Psychological Bulletin, 65,* 110–136.

Kingdon, D. G., & Turkington, D. (1994). *Cognitive–behavioral therapy of schizophrenia.* New York: Guilford Press.

Kleepsies, P. M., & Dettmer, E. L. (2000). An evidence-based approach to evaluating and managing suicidal emergencies. *Journal of Clinical Psychology, 56,* 1109–1130.

Krauthammer, C., & Klerman, G. L. (1978). Secondary mania: Manic syndromes associated with antecedent physical illness or drugs. *Archives of General Psychiatry, 35,* 1333–1339.

Kupfer, D. J., Carpenter, L. L., & Frank, E. (1988a). Is bipolar II a unique disorder? *Comparative Psychiatry, 29,* 228–236.

Kupfer, D. J., Carpenter, L. L., & Frank, E. (1988b). Possible role of antidepressants in precipitating mania and hypomania in recurrent depression. *American Journal of Psychiatry, 145,* 804–808.

Kusumakar, V., & Yatham, L. N. (1997). Lamotrigine treatment of rapid cycling bipolar disorder. *American Journal of Psychiatry, 154,* 1171–1172.

Labbate, L. A., & Rubey, R. N. (1997). Lamotrigine for treatment-refractory bipolar disorder (letter). *American Journal of Psychiatry, 154,* 1317.

Lam, D. H., Bright, J., Jones, S., Hayward, P., Schuck, N., Chisholm, D., & Sham, P. (2000). Cognitive therapy for bipolar disorder—A pilot study of relapse prevention. *Cognitive Therapy and Research, 24,* 503–520.

Lam, D. H., Jones, S. H., Hayward, P., & Bright, J. A. (1999). *Cognitive therapy for bipolar disorder: A therapist's guide to concepts, methods, and practice.* Chichester, UK: Wiley.

Lam, D. H., & Wong, G. (1997). Prodromes, coping strategies, insight and social functioning in bipolar affective disorders. *Psychological Medicine, 27,* 1091–1100.

Layden, M. A., Newman, C. F., Freeman, A., & Morse, S. B. (1993). *Cognitive therapy of borderline personality disorder.* Boston: Allyn & Bacon.

Leahy, R. L. (1997). An investment model of depressive resistance. *Journal of Cognitive Psychotherapy: An International Quarterly, 11,* 3–19.

Leahy, R. L. (1999). Decision making and mania. *Journal of Cognitive Psychotherapy: An International Quarterly, 13,* 83–105.

Leahy, R. L. (2000). Mood and decision-making: Implications for bipolar disorder. *The Behavior Therapist, 23*(3), 62–63.

Leahy, R. L., & Beck, A. T. (1988). Cognitive therapy of depression and mania. In R. Cancro & R. Georgotas (Eds.), *Depression and mania.* (pp. 517–537). New York: Elsevier.

Linehan, M. M. (1993). *Cognitive–behavioral treatment of borderline personality disorder.* New York: Guilford Press.

Linehan, M. M., Camper, P., Chiles, J., Strosahl, K., & Shearin, E. (1987). Interpersonal problem-solving and parasuicide. *Cognitive Therapy and Research, 11,* 1–12.

Link, B. G., Mirotznik, J., & Cullen, F. T. (1991). The effectiveness of stigma coping orientations: Can negative consequences of mental illness labeling be avoided? *Journal of Health and Social Behavior, 32,* 302–320.

Lithium Information Center. (1993). *Carbamazepine and manic depression: A guide.* Madison: University of Wisconsin, Author.

Lovell, R. W. (1999). Mood stabilizer combinations for bipolar disorder. *American Journal of Psychiatry, 156,* 980.

Lozano, B. E., & Johnson, S. L. (1999, November). *Personality traits as predictors of mania and depression.* Paper presented at the annual conference of the Association for the Advancement of Behavior Therapy, Toronto, Canada.

Ludwig, A. M. (1995). *The price of greatness: Resolving the creativity and madness controversy.* New York: Guilford Press.

Lundin, R. K. (1998). Living with mental illness: A personal experience. *Cognitive & Behavioral Practice, 5,* 223–230.

Mahoney, M. J. (Ed.). (1995). *Cognitive and constructive psychotherapies: Theory, research, and practice.* New York: Springer.

Maj, M. (1999). Lithium prophylaxis of bipolar disorder in ordinary clinical conditions: Patterns of long-term outcome. In J. F. Goldberg & M. Harrow (Eds.), *Bipolar disorders: Clinical course and outcome* (pp. 21–37). Washington, DC: American Psychiatric Association.

Malkoff-Schwartz, S. F., Frank, E., Anderson, B., Sherrill, J. T., Siegel, L., Patterson, D., & Kupfer, D. J. (1998). Stressful life events and social rhythm disruption in the onset of manic and depressive bipolar episodes: A preliminary investigation. *Archives of General Psychiatry, 55,* 702–707.

Marlatt, G. A., & Gordon, J. R. (1985). *Relapse prevention: Maintenance strategies in the treatment of addictive behaviors.* New York: Guilford Press.

Martin, R. C., Kuzniecky, R., Ho, S., Hetherington, H., Pan, J., Sinclair, K., Gilliam, F., & Faught, E. (1999). Cognitive effects of topiramate, gabapentin, and lamotrigine. *Neurology, 52,* 321–327.

McGuffin, P. W. (1998). Stigma: Compounding the problem. Response paper. *Cognitive and Behavioral Practice, 5,* 285–295.

Meloy, J. R. (1988). *The psychopathic mind: Origins, dynamics, and treatment.* Northvale, NJ: Jason Aronson.

Mendelwicz, J., & Rainer, J. D. (1977). Adoption study supporting genetic transmission in manic-depressive illness. *Nature, 268,* 327–329.

Meyer, B., Johnson, S. L., & Winters, R. (1999, November). *Responsiveness to threat and incentive in bipolar disorder: Relations of the BIS/BAS Scales with symptoms.* Paper presented at the annual conference of the Association for the Advancement of Behavior Therapy, Toronto, Canada.

Miklowitz, D. J. (1992). Longitudinal outcome and medication noncompliance among manic patients with and without mood-incongruent psychotic features. *Journal of Nervous & Mental Disease, 180,* 703–711.

Miklowitz, D. J. (1994). Family risk indicators in schizophrenia. *Schizophrenia Bulletin, 20,* 137–149.

Miklowitz, D., & Frank, E. (1999). New psychotherapies for bipolar disorder. In J. F. Goldberg & M. Harrow (Eds.), *Bipolar disorders: Clinical course and outcome* (pp. 57–84). Washington, DC: American Psychiatric Press.

Miklowitz, D., & Goldstein, M. J. (1997). *Bipolar disorder: A family-focused treatment approach.* New York: Guilford Press.

Miklowitz, D. J., Goldstein, M., Nuechterlein, K., Snyder, M., & Mintz, J. (1988). Family factors and the course of bipolar affective disorder. *Archives of General Psychiatry, 45,* 225–230.

Miklowitz, D. J., Simoneau, T. L., Sachs-Ericsson, N., Warner, R., & Suddath, R. (1996). Family risk indicators in the course of bipolar affective disorder. In C. H. Mundt, M. J. Goldstein, K. Halweg, & P. Fiedler (Eds.), *Interpersonal factors in the origin and course of affective disorders* (pp. 204–217). London: Gaskell Books.

Miklowitz, D. J., Wendel, J. S., & Simoneau, T. L. (1998). Targeting dysfunctional family interactions and high expressed emotion in the psychosocial treatment of bipolar disorder. *In–Session: Psychotherapy in Practice, 4*(3), 25–38.

Mintz, J., Mintz, L. I., Arruda, M. J., & Hwang, S. S. (1992). Treatment of depression and the functional capacity to work. *Archives of General Psychiatry, 49,* 761–768.

Molnar, G., Feeney, M., & Fava, G. (1988). The duration and symptoms of bipolar prodromes. *American Journal of Psychiatry, 145,* 1575–1578.

Moras, K., & DeMartinis, N. (1999). *Provider's manual: Consultation for combined treatment (CCM-P) with treatment resistant, depressed psychiatric outpatients* [Unpublished manual for National Institute of Mental Health Grant R21

MH52737. Karla Moras, Principal Investigator]. University of Pennsylvania, Philadelphia.

Moras, K., Newman, C. F., & Schweizer, E. (2000). Depression Beliefs Questionnaire—Version I (DBQ-I). In A. M. Nezu, G. F. Ronan, E. A. Meadows, & K. S. McClure (Eds.), AABT clinical assessment series: Vol. 1. Practitioner's guide to empirically based measures of depression (pp. 199–202). Norwell, MA: Kluwer Academic/Plenum Press.

Needleman, L. D. (1999). Cognitive case conceptualization: A guide for practitioners. Mahwah, NJ: Erlbaum.

Neimeyer, R. A., & Feixas, G. (1990). The role of homework and skill acquisition in the outcome of group cognitive therapy for depression. Behavior Therapy, 21, 281–292.

Newman, C. F. (1994). Understanding client resistance: Methods for enhancing motivation to change. Cognitive and Behavioral Practice, 1, 47–69.

Newman, C. F. (1997). Maintaining professionalism in the face of emotional abuse from clients. Cognitive and Behavioral Practice, 4, 1–29.

Newman, C. F., & Beck, A. T. (1992). Cognitive therapy of rapid-cycling bipolar affective disorder. Unpublished treatment manual, University of Pennsylvania, Center for Cognitive Therapy, Philadelphia.

Newman, C. F., & Haaga, D. A. F. (1995). Cognitive skills training. In W. O'Donohue & L. Krasner (Eds.), Psychological skills training (pp. 119–143). Boston: Allyn & Bacon.

Nezu, A. M., Nezu, C. M., & Perri, M. G. (1989). Problem-solving therapy for depression: Theory, research, and clinical guidelines. New York: Wiley.

Nilsson, A. (1999). Lithium therapy and suicide risk. Journal of Clinical Psychiatry, 60(Suppl. 2), 85–88.

Normann, C., Langosch, J., Schaerer, L. O., Grunze, H., & Walden, J. (1999). Treatment of acute mania with topiramate. American Journal of Psychiatry, 156, 2014.

O'Connell, R. A., Mayo, J. A., Flatow, L., Cuthbertson, B., & O'Brien, B. E. (1991). Outcome of bipolar disorder on long-term treatment with lithium. British Journal of Psychiatry, 159, 123–129.

Otto, M. W., Reilly-Harrington, N. A., Kogan, J. N., Henin, A., & Knauz, R. O. (1999). Cognitive–behavior therapy for bipolar disorder: Treatment manual. Unpublished manuscript, Massachusetts General Hospital and Harvard Medical School.

Palmer, A. G., & Williams, H. (1997). Early warning signs. Unpublished rating scale, Norwich, England.

Palmer, A. G., Williams, H., & Adams, M. (1995). CBT in a group format for bipolar affective disorder. Behavioural and Cognitive Psychotherapy, 23, 153–168.

Perry, A., Tarrier, N., Morriss, R., McCarthy, E., & Limb, K. (1999). Randomised controlled trial of efficacy of teaching patients with bipolar disorder to identify early symptoms of relapse and obtain treatment. *British Medical Journal, 318,* 139–153.

Persons, J. B., Burns, D. D., & Perloff, J. M. (1988). Predictors of drop-out and outcome in cognitive therapy for depression in a private practice setting. *Cognitive Therapy and Research, 12,* 557–575.

Peselow, E., Sanfilipo, M., & Fieve, R. (1995). Relationship between hypomania and personality disorders before and after successful treatment. *American Journal of Psychiatry, 152,* 232–238.

Physician's Desk Reference. (2000). Edition 54. Montvale, NJ: Medical Economics, Co., Inc.

Post, R. M. (1993). Issues in the long-term management of bipolar affective illness. *Psychiatric Annals, 23,* 86–93.

Post, R. M., Denicoff, K. D., Frye, M. A., Leverich, G. S., Cora-Locatelli, G., & Kimbrell, T. A. (1999). Long-term outcome of anticonvulsants in affective disorders. In J. F. Goldberg & M. Harrow (Eds.), *Bipolar disorders: Clinical course and outcome* (pp. 85–114). Washington, DC: American Psychiatric Press.

Post, R. M., Frye, M. A., Denicoff, K. D., Leverich, G. S., Kimbrell, T. A., & Dunn, R. T. (1998). Beyond lithium in the treatment of bipolar illness. *Neuropsychopharmacology, 19,* 206–219.

Post, R. M., Ketter, T. A., Denicoff, K., & Pazzaglia, P. J. (1996). The place of anticonvulsant therapy in bipolar illness. *Psychopharmacology, 128,* 115–129.

Post, R. M., Rubinow, D., & Ballenger, J. (1985). Conditioning, sensitization, and kindling: Implication for the course of affective illness. In R. Post & J. Ballenger (Eds.), *Neurobiology of mood disorders* (pp. 432–466). Baltimore: Williams & Wilkins.

Post, R. M., Rubinow, D. R., & Ballenger, J. C. (1986). Conditioning and sensitization in the longitudinal course of affective illness. *British Journal of Psychiatry, 149,* 191–201.

Post, R. M., & Weiss, S. R. (1989). Sensitization, kindling, and anticonvulsants in mania. *Journal of Clinical Psychiatry, 50*(Suppl.), 23–30.

Preda, A., Fazeli, A., McKay, B. G., Bowers, M. B. Jr., & Mazure, C. M. (1999). Lamotrigine as prophylaxis against steroid-induced mania. *Journal of Clinical Psychiatry, 60,* 708–709.

Priebe, S., Wildgrube, C., & Muller-Oerlinghausen, B. (1989). Lithium prophylaxis and expressed emotion. *British Journal of Psychiatry, 154,* 396–399.

Prien, R. F., Caffey, E. M., Jr., & Klett, C. J. (1974). Factors associated with treatment success in lithium carbonate prophylaxis: Report of the Veterans Administration and National Institute of Mental Health Collaborative Study Group. *Archives of General Psychiatry, 31,* 189–192.

Prien, R. F., & Gelenberg, A. (1989). Alternatives to lithium for the preventive treatment of bipolar disorder. *American Journal of Psychiatry, 146,* 840–848.

Primakoff, L., Epstein, N., & Covi, L. (1989). Homework compliance: An uncontrolled variable in cognitive therapy outcome research. In W. Dryden &

P. Trower (Eds.), *Cognitive psychotherapy: Stasis and change* (pp. 175–187). New York: Springer.

Ramsay, J. R. (1998). Postmodern cognitive therapy: Cognitions, narratives, and personal meaning-making. *Journal of Cognitive Psychotherapy, 12,* 39–56.

Regier, D. A., Farmer, M. E., Rae, D. S., Locke, B. Z., Keith, S. J., Ludd, L. L., & Goodwin, F. K. (1990). Comorbidity of mental disorders with alcohol and other drug abuse: Results from the Epidemiologic Catchment Area (ECA) study. *Journal of the American Medical Association, 264,* 2511–2518.

Reilly-Harrington, N. A., Alloy, L. B., Fresco, D. M., & Whitehouse, W. G. (1999). Cognitive styles and life events interact to predict bipolar and unipolar symptomatology. *Journal of Abnormal Psychology, 108,* 567–578.

Robins, L. N., Helzer, J. E., Weissman, M. M., Orraschel, H., Gruenberg, E., Burke, J. D., Jr., & Reiger, D. A. (1984). Lifetime prevalence of specific psychiatric disorders in three sites. *Archives of General Psychiatry, 41,* 949–958.

Rosen, H. (1988). The constructivist-development paradigm. In R. A. Dorfman (Ed.), *Paradigms of clinical social work* (pp. 317–355). New York: Brunner/Mazel.

Roy-Byrne, P., Post, R. M., Uhde, T. W., Porcu, T., & Davis, D. (1985). The longitudinal course of recurrent affective illness: Life chart data from research patients at the NIMH. *Acta Psychiatrica Scandinavica, 71*(Suppl. 317), 1–34.

Rush, A. J. (1988). Cognitive approaches to adherence. In A. J. Francis & R. J. Hales (Eds.), *American psychiatric press review of psychiatry* (Vol. 8, pp. 627–642). Washington, DC: American Psychiatric Association.

Sachs, G. S. (1996). [Mood chart]. Unpublished assessment measure, The Harvard Bipolar Research Program, Massachusetts General Hospital, Boston, MA.

Sachs, G. S., Printz, D. J., Kahn, D. A., Carpenter, D., & Docherty, J. P. (2000). *Medication treatment of bipolar disorder. The Expert Consensus Guidelines Series.* New York: McGraw-Hill.

Salkovskis, P. M., & Clark, D. M. (1989). Affective response to hyperventilation: A test of the cognitive model of panic. *Behaviour Research and Therapy, 28,* 51–61.

Salzman, C. (1998). Integrating pharmacotherapy and psychotherapy in the treatment of a bipolar patient. *American Journal of Psychiatry, 155,* 686–689.

Schildkraut, J. J., Hirschfeld, A. J., & Murphy, J. M. (1994). Mind and mood in modern art: II. Depressive disorders, spirituality, and early deaths in the abstract expressionistic artists of the New York School. *American Journal of Psychiatry, 151,* 482–488.

Schotte, D., & Clum, G. (1987). Problem-solving skills in suicidal psychiatric patients. *Journal of Consulting and Clinical Psychology, 55,* 49–54.

Schou, M. (1989). *Lithium treatment of manic-depressive illness: A practical guide.* Basel, Switzerland: Karger.

Schou, M. (1990). Lithium treatment during pregnancy, delivery, and lactation: An update. *Journal of Clinical Psychiatry, 51,* 410–413.

Scott, J. (1996a). Cognitive therapy for clients with bipolar disorder. *Cognitive and Behavioral Practice, 3*, 29–51.

Scott, J. (1996b). The role of cognitive behavior therapy in bipolar disorders. *Behavioural and Cognitive Psychotherapy, 24*, 195–208.

Scott, J. (in press). Cognitive therapy as an adjunct to medication in bipolar disorder. *British Journal of Psychiatry* (Supplement on Bipolar Disorders).

Scott, J., Garland, A., & Moorhead, S. (in press). A randomized controlled trial of cognitive therapy for bipolar disorders. *Psychological Medicine.*

Scott, J., Stanton, B., Garland, A., & Ferrier, N. (2000). Cognitive vulnerability to bipolar disorder. *Psychological Medicine, 30*, 467–472.

Seligman, M. E. P. (1991). *Learned optimism.* New York: Knopf.

Silverman, M., Berman, A., Bongar, B., Litman, R., & Maris, R. (1998). Inpatient standards of care and the suicidal patient: Part II. An investigation with clinical risk management. In B. Bongar, A. Berman, R. Maris, M. Silverman, E. Harris, & W. Packman (Eds.), *Risk management with suicidal patients* (pp. 34–64). New York: Guilford Press.

Silverstone, T., & Romans-Clarkson, S. (1989). Bipolar affective disorder: Causes and prevention of relapse. *British Journal of Psychiatry, 154*, 321–335.

Simoneau, T. L., Miklowitz, D. J., & Saleem, R. (1998). Expressed emotion and interactional patterns in the families of bipolar patients. *Journal of Abnormal Psychology, 107*, 497–507.

Simpson, S. G., & Jamison, K. R. (1999). The risk of suicide in patients with bipolar disorders. *Journal of Clinical Psychiatry, 60*(Suppl. 2), 53–56.

Small, J. G., Kellams, J. J., Milstein, V., & Small, I. F. (1980). Complications with electroconvulsive treatment combined with lithium. *Biological Psychiatry, 15*, 103–112.

Smith, J., & Tarrier, N. (1992). Prodromal symptoms in manic depressive psychosis. *Social Psychiatry and Psychiatric Epidemiology, 27*, 245–248.

Solomon, D. A., Keitner, G. I., Miller, I. W., Shea, M. T., & Keller, M. B. (1995). Course of illness and maintenance treatments for patients with bipolar disorder. *Journal of Clinical Psychiatry, 56*, 5–13.

Solomon, D. A., Keitner, G. I., Ryan, C. E., & Miller, I. W. (1996). Polypharmacy in bipolar I disorder. *Psychopharmacology Bulletin, 32*, 579–587.

Solomon, D. A., Keitner, G. I., Ryan, C. E., & Miller, I. W. (1998). Lithium plus valproate as maintenance polypharmacy for patients with bipolar I disorder: A review. *Journal of Clinical Psychopharmacology, 18*, 38–49.

Sonne, S. C., Brady, K. T., & Morton, W. A. (1994). Substance abuse and bipolar affective disorder. *Journal of Nervous and Mental Disease, 182*, 349–352.

Spitzer, R. L., Williams, J. B., Gibbon, M., & First, M. B. (1992). The Structured Clinical Interview for DSM–III–R (SCID): I. History, rationale, and description. *Archives of General Psychiatry, 49*, 624–629.

Staab, J. (September, 2000). *Difficulties in diagnosis of bipolar disorder.* Paper presented at the conference Spectrum of Mood Disorders in the Millenium: A Two-Day Mini-Fellowship, Philadelphia, PA. Sponsored by Abcomm, Inc.

Stanford, E., Goetz, R., & Bloom, J. (1994). The no harm contract in the emergency assessment of suicidal risk. *Journal of Clinical Psychiatry, 55,* 344–348.

Strakowski, S. M., McElroy, S. L., Keck, P. E., Jr., & West, S. A. (1996). The effects of antecedent substance abuse on the development of first episode psychotic mania. *Journal of Psychiatric Research, 30,* 59–68.

Strober, M., Morrell, W., Lampert, C., & Burroughs, J. (1990). Relapse following discontinuation of lithium maintenance therapy in adolescents with bipolar I illness: A naturalistic study. *American Journal of Psychiatry, 147,* 457–461.

Swann, A. C., Bowden, C. L., Calabrese, J. R., Dilsaver, S. C., & Morris, D. D. (1999). Differential effect of number of previous episodes of affective disorder on response to lithium or divalproex in acute mania. *American Journal of Psychiatry, 156,* 1264–1266.

Targum, S. D., Dibble, E. D., Davenport, Y. B., & Gershon, E. S. (1981). The Family Attitudes Questionnaire: Patients' and spouses' views of bipolar illness. *Archives of General Psychiatry, 38,* 562–568.

Tkachuk, G. A., & Martin, G. L. (1999). Exercise therapy for patients with psychiatric disorders: Research and clinical implications. *Professional Psychology: Research and Practice, 30,* 275–282.

Tohen, M., Waternaux, C. M., & Tsuang, M. T. (1990). Outcome in mania: A 4-year prospective follow-up of 75 patients using survival analysis. *Archives of General Psychiatry, 47,* 1106–1111.

Tohen, M., & Zarate, C. A. (1999). Bipolar disorder and comorbid substance abuse disorder. In J. F. Goldberg & M. Harrow (Eds.), *Bipolar disorders: Clinical course and outcome* (pp. 171–184). Washington, DC: American Psychiatric Press.

Tondo, L., Jamison, K. R., & Baldessarini, R. J. (1997). Effect of lithium maintenance on suicidal behavior in major mood disorders. *Annals of the Academy of Sciences, 836,* 339–351.

Trout, D. L. (1980). The role of social isolation in suicide. *Suicide and Life Threatening Behavior, 10,* 10–23.

Van Dongen, C. J. (1991). Experiences of family members after a suicide. *Journal of Family Practice, 33,* 375–380.

Vehmanen, L., Kaprio, J., & Loennqvist, J. (1995). Twin studies of bipolar disorder. *Psychiatria Fennica, 26,* 107–116.

Viguera, A. C., Nonacs, R., Cohen, L. S., Tondo, L., Murray, A., & Baldessarini, R. J. (2000). Risk of recurrence of bipolar disorder in pregnant and nonpregnant women after discontinuing lithium maintenance. *American Journal of Psychiatry, 157,* 179–184.

Walden, J., Normann, C., Langosch, J., Berger, M., & Grunze, H. (1998). Differential treatment of bipolar disorder with old and new antiepileptic drugs. *Neuropsychobiology, 38,* 181–184.

Wehr, T. A., Sack, D. A., & Rosenthal, N. E. (1987). Seasonal affective disorder with summer depression and winter hypomania. *American Journal of Psychiatry, 144*(12), 1602–1603.

Wehr, T. A., Sack, D. A., Rosenthal, N. E., & Cowdry, R. W. (1988). Rapid cycling affective disorder: Contributing factors and treatment responses in 51 patients. *American Journal of Psychiatry, 145,* 179–184.

Wehr, T. A., Turner, E. H., Shimada, J. M., Lowe, C. H., Barker, C., & Leibenluft, E. (1998). Treatment of a rapidly cycling bipolar patient by using extended bed rest and darkness to stabilize the timing and duration of sleep. *Biological Psychiatry, 43,* 822–828.

Weishaar, M. E. (1996). Cognitive risk factors in suicide. In P. M. Salkovskis (Ed.), *Frontiers of cognitive therapy* (pp. 226–249). New York: Guilford Press.

Weiss, R. D., & Mirin, S. M. (1987). Substance abuse as an attempt at self-medication. *Psychiatric Medicine, 3,* 357–367.

Weissman, A., & Beck, A. T. (1978, November). *Development and validation of the Dysfunctional Attitudes Scale.* Paper presented at the annual meeting of the Association for the Advancement of Behavior Therapy, Chicago, IL.

Wendel, J. S., & Miklowitz, D. J. (1997, November). *Attributions and expressed emotion in the relatives of patients with bipolar disorder.* Poster presented at the 31st annual conference of the Association for the Advancement of Behavior Therapy, Miami Beach, FL.

West, S. A., McElroy, S. L., Strakowski, S. M., Keck, P. E., Jr., & McConville, B. J. (1995). Attention-deficit hyperactivity disorder in adolescent mania. *American Journal of Psychiatry, 152,* 271–273.

Whybrow, P. C. (1997). *A mood apart: Depression, mania, and other afflictions of the self.* New York: Basic Books.

Whybrow, P. C., & Bauer, M. S. (1991). *The chronorecord booklet.* Unpublished measure, University of Pennsylvania, Philadelphia.

Williams, J. M. G., & Broadbent, K. (1986). Autobiographical memory in suicide attempters. *Journal of Abnormal Psychology, 95,* 144–149.

Williams, J. M. G., & Scott, J. (1988). Autobiographical memory in depression. *Psychological Medicine, 18,* 689–695.

Winokur, G., Clayton, P. J., & Reich, T. (1969). *Manic depressive illness.* St. Louis, MO: Mosby.

Winters, K. C., & Neale, J. M. (1985). Mania and low self-esteem. *Journal of Abnormal Psychology, 94,* 282–290.

Woodruff, R. A., Robins, L. N., Winokur, G., & Reich, T. (1971). Manic–depressive illness and social achievement. *Acta Psychiatrica Scandinavica, 47,* 237–249.

Wright, J., & Schrodt, R. (1989). Combined cognitive therapy and pharmaco-therapy. In A. Freeman, K. Simon, L. Beutler, & H. Arkowitz (Eds.), *Handbook of cognitive therapy* (pp. 267–282). New York: Plenum Press.

Wright, J., & Thase, M. (1992). Cognitive and biological therapies: A synthesis. *Psychiatric Annals, 22,* 451–458.

Young, J. E. (1994). *Cognitive therapy for personality disorders: A schema-focused approach* (Rev. ed.). Sarasota, FL: Professional Resource Exchange.

Young, J. E. (1999). *Cognitive therapy for personality disorders: A schema-focused approach* (3rd ed.). Sarasota, FL: Professional Resource Exchange.

Young, M. A., Fogg, L. F., Scheftner, W., Fawcett, J., Akiskal, H., & Maser, J. (1996). Stable trait components of hopelessness: Baseline and sensitivity to depression. *Journal of Abnormal Psychology, 105,* 155–165.

Young, R. C. (1997). Bipolar mood disorders in the elderly. *Psychiatric Clinics of North America, 20,* 121–136.

Young, R. C., Biggs, J. T., Ziegler, V. E., & Meyer, D. A. (1978). A rating scale for mania: Reliability, validity, and sensitivity. *British Journal of Psychiatry, 133,* 429–435.

Zemeckis, Robert (Producer/Director). (1997). *Contact.* [Film].

Zuroff, D. C., Blatt, S. J., Sotsky, S. M., Krupnick, J. L., Martin, D. J., Sanislow, C. A. III, & Simmens, S. (2000). Relation of therapeutic alliance and perfectionism to outcome in brief outpatient treatment of depression. *Journal of Consulting and Clinical Psychology, 68,* 114–124.

AUTHOR INDEX

Rainer, J. D., 12
Ram, R. N., 5
Ramsay, J. R., 53
Ranieri, W. F., 81
Rapport, D. J., 106
Ratliff, K. G., 95
Regier, D. A., 8
Reich, T., 11, 175
Reiger, D. A., 18
Reilly-Harrington, N. A., x, 15, 34, 41,
    42, 223
Rhodes, L. J., 11
Riba, M. B., 133
River, L. P., 175
Roberts, J., 15, 34, 41, 67, 103
Robins, L. N., 10, 175
Romans-Clarkson, S., 112
Rosen, H., 36
Rosenthal, N. E., 13, 14, 51
Ross, R., 27
Roy, A., 15
Roy-Byrne, P., 104
Rubey, R. N., 106
Rubinow, D. R., 14
Rudd, M. D., 82
Rush, A. J., ix, 26, 29, 80, 112, 113, 122,
    134
Ryan, C. E., 103, 104

Sachs, G. S., 27, 29, 105, 106n1, 108n,
    111n, 117, 223
Sachs-Ericsson, N., 141
Sack, D. A., 13, 14, 51
Sack, R. L., 13
Sagan, C., 172
Sahder, R. L., 107
Saleem, R., 141
Salkovskis, P. M., 71
Salzman, C., 178
Sandrow, D., 13, 15, 34, 45, 50, 65
Sanfilipo, M., 9
Schaerer, L. O., 106
Scheftner, W., 21
Schildkraut, J. J., 175
Schlesinger, S., 147
Schoonover, S. C., 120
Schotte, D., 95
Schou, M., 109, 119
Schrodt, R., 117, 119
Schweizer, E., 134

Scott, J., x, 25, 26, 29, 33, 34, 38, 43,
    95, 97, 113, 133, 192
Seligman, M. E. P., 39, 92
Shaw, B., ix, 80, 122
Shea, M. T., 102
Shearin, E., 89
Shelton, M. D., 106
Silverman, M., 86
Silverstone, T., 15, 112
Simoneau, T. L., 141
Simpson, S. G., 6, 11, 12, 21, 80
Small, I. F., 109
Small, J., 15
Small, J. G., 109
Smith, J., 30, 47
Snyder, M., 19
Solomon, D. A., 102–104, 109
Sonne, S. C., 4, 9, 18, 49
Spitzer, R. L., 193
Staab, J., 108
Stancer, H. C., 15
Stanford, E., 86
Stanton, B., 38, 95, 97
Steer, R. A., 20, 79, 81, 83, 85, 116
Stephenson, U., 107
Stewart, B. L., 79
Stoll, A. L., 106
Strakowski, S. M., 11, 18
Strober, M., 112
Strosahl, K., 89
Suddath, R., 141
Suppes, T., 22
Swann, A. C., 108
Swendsen, J., 4
Szkrumelak, N., 107

Targum, S. D., 142
Tarrier, N., 30, 33, 47
Thase, M. E., 104, 133, 223
Thompson, R., 149
Thuras, P., 106
Tkachuk, G. A., 94
Tohen, M., 4, 8, 9, 11, 17, 22, 110
Tondo, L., 22, 102, 118
Trexler, L., 82
Trout, D. L., 98
Truman, C. J., 105
Tsuang, M. T., 11
Tumier, L., 107
Turkington, D., 18

Uhde, T. W., 104

Van Dongen, C. J., 91
Vehmanen, L., 12
Verma, S. K., 142
Viguera, A. C., 111

Walden, J., 103, 106
Ward, C., 82
Warner, R., 141
Waternaux, C. M., 4, 11
Weber, C., 95
Wehr, T. A., 13, 14, 51
Weishaar, M. E., 95
Weiss, R. D., 8
Weiss, S. R., 3
Weissman, A., 40, 82, 178
Weissman, M. M., 10
Wendel, J. S., 141
West, S. A., 11, 18, 75
Whitehouse, W. G., 15, 34
Whybrow, P. C., 13, 14, 29, 107, 148, 199
Wildgrube, C., 19
Williams, H., x, 30, 32

Williams, J. B., 193
Williams, J. M. G., 95, 97
Winett, C., 15, 19, 97
Winokur, G., 11, 175
Winters, K. C., 16, 61
Winters, R., 45
Wong, G., 22, 23, 47, 67, 203
Woodruff, R. A., 175
Wright, F. D., 18, 73, 128
Wright, J., 117, 119, 133

Yatham, L. N., 106
Yeh, H.-S., 14
Young, J. E., 20, 25, 36, 39, 40, 59
Young, M. A., 84
Young, R. C., 50, 140

Zarate, C. A., 8, 9
Zechmeister, J. S., 15, 34
Zemeckis, R., 172
Zhao, S., 10
Ziegler, V. E., 50
Zuroff, D. C., 96

SUBJECT INDEX

Imagery technique, 63–65
Impulsivity, reduction of, 62–70
Incompetency schema, 36
Insomnia, 5, 6
Internal State Scale, 49
Interpersonal and social rhythm therapy (IP/SRT), 14
Interpersonal psychotherapy (IPT), 14
"I" statements, 154–155

Jamison, Kay, 11, 74, 187

"Kindling effect," 3–4, 14
Klonopin. See Clonazepam

Lack of individuation schema, 37
Lamotrigine (Lamictal), 106
Lethal weapons, use of, 69
Life events, stressful, 14–15, 40–44
Listening skills, 66–67
Lithium, 9, 10, 102–103, 107–109, 123
Lithium Information Center, 119
Lorazepam (Ativan), 106–107
Low energy, 5

Major depressive episodes (MDEs), 5–8
Maladaptive schemas, early. See Early maladaptive schemas
Mania. See Hypomania and mania
Manic–depression (term), xi, 3
Manic episodes, 5–6
MAOIs. See Monoamine oxidase inhibitors
Massachusetts General Hospital, 32, 224
MDEs. See Major depressive episodes
Mistrust schema, 36
Mixed episodes, 6
Modes, 38
Monoamine oxidase inhibitors (MAOIs), 104–105

NAMI. See National Alliance for the Mentally Ill
Narcissistic Personality Disorder (NPD), 193
National Alliance for the Mentally Ill (NAMI), 98, 99, 182

National Depressive and Manic Depressive Association (NDMDA), 98, 99, 182
National Institute of Mental Health (NIMH), 223
NDMDA. See National Depressive and Manic Depressive Association
Neurological dysfunction, 6
Night Falls Fast (Kay Jamison), 11–12
NIMH. See National Institute of Mental Health
Norepinephrine, 13
NPD (Narcissistic Personality Disorder), 193

Olanzapine (Zyprexa), 105
Onset
    of bipolar disorder, 10–11, 17
    of hypomania and mania, 48–51
Other professionals, collaboration of therapist with, 133–135

Paxil (paroxetine), 109
PDR (Physician's Desk Reference), 117
Perfectionism, 96
Personal Beliefs Questionnaire, 40, 46
Personality disorders, 9–10, 19–20
Pharmacotherapeutic alliance, 119–121, 146
Pharmacotherapy, ix, 101–136
    with anticonvulsant/antianxiety medications, 106–107
    with antidepressants, 104–105
    with antipsychotic medications, 105
    basic principles for, with bipolar disorder, 107, 108
    and beliefs encouraging discontinuation of medication, 113–116
    with carbamazepine, 103–104
    cognitive–behavioral strategies for use with, 121–132
    cognitive therapy vs., 38
    and collaboration with other professionals, 133–135
    current therapies, 102–105
    with divalproex, 103
    and interepisode symptoms, 109–110
    with lamotrigine, 106
    with lithium, 102–103

ABOUT THE AUTHORS

Cory F. Newman, PhD, ABPP, is director of the Center for Cognitive Therapy in the School of Medicine at the University of Pennsylvania, where he is an associate professor of psychology in the Department of Psychiatry. Dr. Newman is a founding Fellow of the Academy of Cognitive Therapy and a Diplomate of the American Board of Professional Psychology, specializing in Behavioral Psychology. Dr. Newman is author of dozens of articles and chapters and coauthor of four books, as well as an international lecturer on topics relating to cognitive therapy. Dr. Newman is the moderator of the cognitive–behavioral panel of the Psychological Broadcasting Corporation, providing APA-approved continuing education symposia over the Internet.

Robert L. Leahy, PhD, earned his doctorate at Yale University. He is the editor of the *Journal of Cognitive Psychotherapy: An International Quarterly* and president-elect of the International Association for Cognitive Psychotherapy. Dr. Leahy is on the Executive Committee of the Academy of Cognitive Therapy. His recent books include *Cognitive Therapy: Basic Principles and Applications*; *Practicing Cognitive Therapy: A Guide to Interventions*; *Treatment Plans and Interventions for Depression and Anxiety Disorders* (with Stephen Holland); and *Overcoming Resistance in Cognitive Therapy*. Dr. Leahy is the director of the American Institute for Cognitive Therapy in New York (www.cognitivetherapynyc.com) and clinical associate professor in the Department of Psychiatry of Weill-Cornell University Medical College, Ithaca, NY.

Aaron T. Beck, MD, University Professor of Psychiatry, University of Pennsylvania, is a graduate of Brown University (1942) and Yale Medical School (1946). The recipient of numerous awards and honorary degrees, he is the only psychiatrist to receive research awards from the American

Psychological Association and the American Psychiatric Association. The author or coauthor of over 400 articles, he has recently published a new book, *Prisoners of Hate: The Cognitive Basis of Anger, Hostility and Violence.* He is president of the Beck Institute of Cognitive Therapy.

Noreen A. Reilly-Harrington, PhD, is an instructor in psychology at Harvard Medical School and is on the staff of the Harvard Bipolar Research Program at Massachusetts General Hospital. She is a graduate of the University of Pennsylvania and Temple University. Dr. Reilly-Harrington is a founding Fellow of the Academy of Cognitive Therapy and has received research awards from the Society for Research in Psychopathology, the Association for the Advancement of Behavior Therapy, and Massachusetts General Hospital for her work examining the role of life stress and cognition on the course of bipolar mood disorders. She has lectured both nationally and internationally on the topic of cognitive therapy for bipolar disorder and is a Pathway Leader for the National Institute of Mental Health's Systematic Treatment Enhancement Program for Bipolar Disorder.

Laszlo Gyulai, MD, is associate professor of psychiatry and director of the Bipolar Disorders Program at the University of Pennsylvania Medical Center. He graduated summa cum laude from Semmelweis Medical University in Budapest, Hungary, and joined the University of Pennsylvania Department of Biochemistry and Biophysics in 1980, where he conducted research and published on brain neurochemistry using magnetic resonance spectroscopy. He joined the faculty at the University of Pennsylvania Medical Center in 1989. He has published on novel treatments of and on brain imaging and lithium magnetic resonance spectroscopy for bipolar disorder. He has conducted clinical trials with new medications for the treatment of bipolar disorder.